Book *of* Value

the fine art of investing wisely

Book *of* Value

the fine art of investing wisely

First Edition

Anurag Sharma, Ph.D.

 Invest Wisely

This publication is designed to provide accurate and authoritative information in regard to the subject matter covered. It is sold with the understanding that the publisher is not engaged in rendering legal, accounting or other professional service. If legal advice or other expert assistance is required, the services of a competent professional person should be sought.

—Declaration of Principles jointly adopted by
a Committee of the American Bar Association and
a Committee of Publishers and Associations

Library of Congress Cataloging-in-Publication Data

Sharma, Anurag

Book of Value: *the fine art of investing wisely* / Anurag Sharma

ISBN: 0988446219
ISBN-13: 9780988446212

Investment philosophy—value investing. 2. History of investing. 3. Investor psychology. 4. Philosophy of science. 5. Decision-making. 6. Valuation and stock selection. 7. Company analysis. 8. Investment policy. 1. Title

Library of Congress Control Number: 2012924100

Mukti Press, Amherst, Massachusetts

www.bookofvalue.org

For

Mary, Helen, and Monika

In memory of my father

Mahendra Bhushan

Contents

_____

Preface . . . .*ix*

Prologue: A Short History of Investing. . . . . *xvii*

Introduction: Method Investing . . . . *xxix*

BOOK I   **Illusion**

1. Opinions and Beliefs. 1

2. Correlation of Errors. 11

3. The Dark Arts. 25

4. Purveyors of the Dark Arts 33

5. Victims of the Dark Arts. 49

BOOK II   **Verity**

6. Defense Against the Dark Arts 65

7. Logic–Data–Doubt. 73

8. Investing as a Negative Art 89

9. How to be a Wise Investor 95

10. The Art of Looking. 101

BOOK III   **Foundations**

11. Price and Value. 111

12. How to Value a Business. 119

13. Risk and Uncertainty 127

14. The Simple Math of Valuation 143

15. Yield–Stability–Strength 163

BOOK IV **Diligence**

16. Depth Analysis 187
17. Dive for Strength 191
18. Define Good Business. 207
19. Meet the Managers 225
20. Watch the Game. 247

BOOK V **Policy**

21. Diversification. 261
22. Another Way to Portfolio 269
23. Core Holdings 277
24. Growth 285
25. The Buffett Portfolio. 297

Conclusion: Noise Control *307*
Acknowledgements. *315*

Notes *317*
Bibliography *327*
Index *333*

Preface

_____

By the time I started teaching value investing more than a dozen years ago, I had already been reading Warren Buffett's letters to shareholders. Just a few years earlier, I had turned to Graham and Dodd's _Security Analysis_ because of repeated references to it in association with Buffett's style of investing. Phil Fisher's _Common Stocks and Uncommon Profits_ had also been on my reading list.

I soon realized that, to these and many other successful investors, investing was largely about analyzing businesses and understanding people. As a professor of strategy, I had long studied how businesses were organized, how they were led, how they functioned, and how they created wealth. Now, here were some of the most successful investors essentially making the point that business analysis and judgments about people were at the heart of investing.

It was also clear that the successful investors I had come to admire did not pay much heed to theoretical finance that was (and is) widely taught in business schools. In fact, they mostly ignored it. Buffett once boldly stated something to the effect that academic finance was wrong-headed.[1] Many in academia retorted that Buffett and those like him were statistical anomalies, three-sigma events in a random game of chance.[2] There was, in fact, great skepticism in academic finance that analysis of business fundamentals was even useful when investing. There was just too much randomness in the markets, academics argued, for business analysis to have much of any effect on investment performance.

To me, all this raised an obvious question. Why is there such a large disconnect between academic finance and finance as practiced by so many successful investors?

As a dyed-in-the-wool academic and an active investor, I decided that I had to understand both sides. I was already peripherally aware of the academic literature but began reading more of it. I also needed to understand in more detail the logic of why and how the star performers did what they did. I wondered whether the stellar investment performance of successful investors was a long streak of good luck, or whether their success was grounded in some teachable set of skills. In a way, I wanted a peek into their inner lives, see what the world of investing looked like to them, and understand how they made the choices they did.

Unfortunately, I had no personal contact with the people whose thought processes I sought to understand. So, I took an alternate route: I hit the book stacks in the library and began combing through the vast body of writings about the inner life of our species. I reasoned that if I understood what we know about how people think and reason, and what psychological and emotional obstacles we have to overcome to live rationally in a rather perplexing world around us, perhaps I would understand the mental machinery of the people I wanted to decode. I had my work cut out for me.

I learned that academic finance was devoid of deep insights about investors as real people. Instead, finance theory makes naïve assumptions about economic actors (people), mostly to enable conceptual arguments and ease mathematical modeling of investment behavior. There are few, if any, penetrating insights about the inner life of people; much of theory essentially casts investors as simple calculating machines maximizing their self-interest. Modern investment theory mostly ignores the fact that businesses are complex human systems, that investors are severely constrained in their ability to comprehend the complexities inherent in the endeavor, and that the financial markets are fundamentally human constructions that defy purely mathematical explanations.

I learned that the dominant analytical frameworks for teaching investments in the business schools are rooted in work started in the early 1950s, by a graduate student named Harry Markowitz. Spurred by those at-first obscure beginnings, academic finance has taken a strong turn towards statistical analysis of prices, and increasingly, towards the advanced mathematical techniques common in the hard sciences such as physics and astronomy.

It soon became apparent to me that there were three significant consequences of the sharp turn towards the complex mathematics of prices and returns. First, as I will discuss in this book, mathematicians have shaped investing in the image of their own long-standing fascination with the problem of gamble. As such, increasingly, investing is no longer conceived as being about carefully deploying capital in sound businesses that are also well-run. Instead, investment analysis has come to be mostly about finding the best gamble with the quickest payoff;[3] the key analytical device for solving this problem is the seemingly objective but deeply flawed measure of risk as standard deviation of returns. Furthermore, the portfolio logic of diversification has been taken to the extreme to justify owning a very large number of poorly understood securities. Over time, as this view has taken root, investing is seen not as making judgments about economic worth but more so as gambling with a very short time horizon. The mathematicians have cast the financial markets as giant casinos and followed through with trying to teach people how to become better gamblers.

The second consequence of the strong turn to mathematics is that the study of investments has become increasingly insulated from advances in other spheres of intellectual activity. Breakthrough thinking of behavioral economists about, for instance, how we humans reason and make judgments under uncertainty is grudgingly accepted, but still relegated to a small corner outside mainstream finance. Advances in Bayesian statistics too have for the most part remained in the shadows, even as the old ways of frequentist statistics continue to dominate the methods of analysis. Perhaps most importantly, revolutionary insights about personality and identity, perception and attention, imitation and influence—factors that play immensely crucial roles in the framing of investment decisions—all go largely missing from investment research and analysis.

Finally, overemphasis on mathematics has had the effect of fixing the attention of investors on the statistical characteristics of historical returns; it has decontextualized investment analysis from important particulars of the people and the assets being analyzed. That is, abstract mathematics has removed the act of investing from direct experiences and meaning-making of those doing the investing; it encourages action based on numbers alone, devoid of understanding about the real economic activity that may be producing those numbers. As such, the search for mathematical laws and regularities virtually removes from consideration the many important business-related factors that differentiate the few good investment opportunities from many bad ones. Subjective judgments and intuitions about qualitative factors, such as leadership, are cast aside as unscientific, leaving the hapless investors with dry, lifeless statistics with which to make meaningful decisions. Unmistakable in all this is the encouragement to ignore important information and deep, company-specific analysis. Lost, as a result, is the ability of the investor to be a discerning consumer of financial information.

The financial markets have spawned a variety of responses to such limitations of modern investment theory. Outside the equity markets, for instance, in such arenas as private equity and new venture financing, the pretense of objective risk gives way to deep subjective evaluation of operating and product-market uncertainties. Specifics of the business matter a great deal in such evaluations, as does the quality of the people who are charged with building the business. Private equity and new venture financing are finite-horizon investment endeavors, however; as investment vehicles, they are for the most part outside the reach of ordinary investors. Yet, they hold important lessons for equity investors, the least of which is that investment analysis is inseparable from business analysis. As we will see in this book, equity investors too can shed their dependence on the modern investment theory and develop an outlook that relies instead on deep analysis of businesses and the people who lead them.

Certainly, mathematization of finance has brought some benefits to the study of investments in equity markets. We now know a great deal more about mathematical risk than we did sixty years ago. From normal distributions with fat tails to ubiquitous power laws, an increasingly better understanding of quantitative risk informs investment models in applications such as insurance and indexing. More importantly, the normative goal of efficient markets has encouraged an unrelenting demand for policies that make the financial markets deeper, more transparent and liquid and, therefore, fairer.

The modern portfolio theory and the underlying efficient market hypothesis are powerful frameworks precisely because of their seductive, if misguided, simplicity—and the normative implications of fairness. The strength of the theory also lies in the fact that the elegance of the mathematical models is impossible to defeat with vague protests that they are built on unrealistic assumptions about human rationality and market efficiency. Even so, for all the reasons stated above, limiting investments to the mathematical modeling and statistical analysis of prices is just the wrong thing to do. We need a better approach.

Clearly, the search for an alternative is not about replacing one simple and elegant model with another. Rather, it is about a deep understanding of our humanity that requires broadly integrating psychological insights with robust analytical approaches. In this alternative, we have to concede a high degree of complexity but one that is more helpful because it is grounded in the real world of real people. I believe we can start building such an approach to investing by incorporating into investment theory a greater degree of realism and, for that, by reaching into disciplines other than mathematics.

In this book, I set about to do just that. I submit that investing must be cast *not* simply as a problem of gamble, as mathematicians would like to have us do, but foremost as a problem of choice. I argue that, while chance does influence investment performance, analytical and emotional skills exert a much greater influence on the experiences that investors have when investing. Such a shift in emphasis from luck to skill puts the focus, and the onus, back on understanding how to use reason correctly and how to incorporate rich quantitative *and* qualitative data into well-rounded analysis. Sound analysis, in turn, helps manage and leverage the powerful emotions that surround and cloud the judgments people make when doing anything that is related with money. Wise investing, I submit, flows from making good choices; investors *must* learn to make good choices.

Developing this way of thinking, of casting investing as a problem of choice and then drawing upon a broad range of disciplines to improve the quality of choice is, in essence, what I would like to accomplish in this book.

Amherst, MA
January 8, 2013

———

Capital follows knowledge.

Get knowledge.

———

Prologue

A Short History of Investing

—

Those who have taken it upon themselves to lay down the theories about investing, whether they have done so from the bully pulpit of the Ivory Tower or from the editorials of widely watched media, have left the average investor confused between the conflicting urges of caution and aggression. Through a vast edifice of knowledge built over the last sixty or so years, in fact, the high priests of modern finance appear to have established that investing is more mathematics than business, that Greek symbols are more important than common business sense and that, in essence, investing is no different from speculation or gambling.

Increasingly, as a result, when people think about investing, they think not about carefully and defensively deploying their precious capital in sound businesses; instead, they appear to be mostly preoccupied with buying ticker symbols on the screen, hoping to sell out as soon as prices go up a little. The businesses underlying the ticker figure very little, or in many cases nowhere, in much of the buying and selling that goes on. Far too often, it seems, market transactions are conducted with neither party fully comprehending the rights and risks being exchanged. Such, unfortunately, is the unintended legacy of the many brilliant minds that built the foundations of modern portfolio theory.

In this book, I'd like to follow and further develop the ideas of a different breed of people, those who subscribe to a common sense view that investing must be approached with caution and be firmly grounded in the principles of business analysis. In order to understand why doing so is important, let's briefly review below what the state of investment theory was before it got mathematized to the extreme, as it is today.

The Classics

Our story begins about a decade or more before Harry Markowitz developed the tools of modern portfolio theory in the early 1950s.[4] At that time, two investment masterpieces had instructed investors on how to avoid getting caught up in the casino-like atmosphere that had led into the stock market crash of 1929. The first was *Security Analysis* (1934, 1940, & 1951) by Benjamin Graham and David Dodd, and the second was *The Theory of Investment Value* (1938) by John Burr Williams. Both these books were upended by Markowitz and quickly became obscure, overshadowed by the subsequent rapid rise of investment theory as we know it today.

Security Analysis encapsulated a systematic approach to analyzing bonds and stocks, instructing investors in the art of evaluating securities for reasonableness of the prices at which they traded. Among the key lessons of the book was that price and value are distinct concepts and, as such, investors need to learn to recognize when the two become detached from each other. Graham and Dodd offered several criteria for evaluating first bonds and then stocks, developing along the way not just an analytical approach but also an outline of the psychological apparatus necessary for investing rationally.

The Theory of Investment Value picked up on the idea of intrinsic value; Williams agreed with Graham and Dodd that the *real worth* of a business was distinct from its market price. He argued that market prices of a stock were driven not just by expectations and counter-expectations of capital appreciation but by the fundamental economic worth of that stock. He went a step further, moreover, by formalizing the idea that the worth, or *investment value*, of a stock was the present value of future dividends and the eventual selling price. In doing so, Williams put the emphasis on future earnings and dividends and, therefore, on the ability of the underlying business to continue delivering profits and growth. This forward-looking approach was in sharp contrast to Graham and Dodd, who were suspicious of projections and advised investors to scrutinize the present in terms of past performance. Williams is fairly credited with the dividend discount model, the dividends in the model later changed by some to earnings and cash flows. To this day, the discount model remains a helpful way to think about business worth.

The Graduate Student

To the above two classics was drawn a graduate student, Harry Markowitz, in search of a dissertation topic for his doctorate in economics. Intrigued by Williams' formulation of value, Markowitz noted that given the uncertainties about the future, the rate at which the expected dividends were to be discounted depended on the degree to which they were deemed risky, or the chance that the company may cut or stop paying the dividends. Following conventional wisdom that investors should spread their bets, the usual practice at the time was to control risk through broad diversification.[5] Markowitz thought that was sensible. He argued that risk is a portfolio level issue and the problem to solve was one of mitigating the risk not of a single purchased security but that of the entire portfolio.

As he pondered the problem, Markowitz realized that no quantifiable measures of portfolio risk had yet been developed. So, being mathematically oriented, he made the fateful decision to seek out basic statistics texts,[6] largely because therein lay the potentially useful tools with which to quantify portfolio-level risk and compute objective measures of it.

Now, since Markowitz was a graduate student in the economics department, he was perhaps not fully versed in the debates that had been raging among the objectivist and subjectivist statisticians ever since Thomas Bayes' paper was published posthumously in 1763.[7] The dominant view prevailing in the discipline was that probability of any event was based on frequency count, that it was an objective measure of odds derived from previously recorded observations.

Yet, a vocal minority of statisticians resisted this dominant view. They held that probability was a mode of judgment, that probability did not inhere in the object or event but in the expectations of the person making judgments. Even so, statistics departments around the country shunned this alternate view of probability as subjective assessment.

Ironically, in his dissertation, *Portfolio Selection* (1955), Markowitz acknowledges Leonard (Jimmy) Savage, who was perhaps the strongest and most vocal proponent of subjective probability at the time. Savage had been at the University of Chicago since 1947, had founded the new statistics department in 1949, and was the department head from 1956 to 1960. In fact, in 1954, he had published an influential text[8] in which he had challenged the frequentist approach to probability and had argued that the whole of statistics ought to be validly seen and profitably recast in personal and subjective terms. He rejected objective probability.

Had Markowitz followed Savage, he probably would have continued in the tradition of Graham and Williams and, who knows, could have even extended them by formalizing the role of subjectivity and judgment in invest-ment decisions.[9] But, perhaps urged on by his other teachers, such as Milton Friedman,[10] and not wanting to get mired in the debates of another disci-pline,[11] Markowitz chose to bow to the prevailing dogma and pursued the objective probability angle instead.[12]

Intent on bringing mathematics and statistics to investing, Markowitz applied the standard tools of objectivist probability to come upon the idea that the effect of diversification on risk ought to be reflected in the variability of portfolio returns. As such, risk could be computed using the variance of the returns of each individual stock and the co-variances between each pair of the stocks in the portfolio.

Since variances and co-variances of past returns were easy to calculate as long as historical data were available, Markowitz defined the problem of investing as the problem of managing portfolio risk—by properly allocating stocks to build a portfolio that had the highest expected return for a given level of risk, or lowest risk for a desired expected return. He defined risk as the standard deviation of expected portfolio returns and operationalized it simply as a mathematical number that was computed using the historical returns of individual stocks in the portfolio.

It turns out that group variance is smaller than the variance of any of its components. For two uncorrelated stocks,[13] each with 0.2 as the variance and, therefore, 0.45 as the standard deviation of past returns, the joint variance is 0.04 and joint standard deviation (risk) is 0.20.

By using standard deviation as a proxy for risk, Markowitz showed the benefits of grouping uncorrelated stocks. Even more importantly, he showed that the benefits of systematic grouping were substantial even when the stocks were partially correlated. Complete independence of returns was not necessary for diversification to reduce risk.

A corollary to Markowitz's insight was the claim that, in portfolios with large number of stocks, the risk of an individual stock did not matter as much as the average pairwise co-variance among stocks in the portfolio. That is, using standard statistical concepts, he shifted the attention away from the risk of each stock to the weighted effect of any one stock on the overall portfolio risk. This insight was about all he needed. Statistics took it from there. There was no longer the need to analyze each individual stock in detail; it was enough to simply assemble lightly-correlated stocks with desired means and variances of returns, and mix them up to *engineer* portfolios with the best expected risk-reward ratios. Thus, in the 1950s, was born the modern portfolio theory.

In essence, then, Markowitz created the modern portfolio theory by quantifying risk using a simple, albeit computationally intense, mathematical formulation. His notion of portfolio risk was an advance over the state of knowledge at the time, and it was embellished later by others such as William Sharpe and John Lintner,[14] but the definition of risk as incorporating variance and standard deviations of past returns has remained at the heart of finance ever since. Measuring risk in the way that Markowitz defined it meant that, as the size of the portfolio increased, the computational power needed to calculate portfolio risk increased exponentially. But that problem was soon to be solved with computers and it is even less of a limitation today.

Defining risk mathematically in a world where computational power was rapidly increasing solved an emerging problem, as it allowed investment theory to be delivered at an industrial scale. Billions of dollars were already coming into the capital markets from the savings and retirement accounts of a growing middle class after World War II; investing these funds successfully would be difficult picking one company at a time based on subjective or personal assessments of risk.

Investing at a large scale was deemed especially difficult, as there were no sure-shot formulae to solve the problem of selecting stocks and bonds from a fast expanding list. Mathematically computing the risk-return trade-off and dishing out advice backed by seemingly infallible mathematical formulae was an attractive alternative. The financial services industry eagerly adopted the formulaic approach made possible by the math and the computers.

At the same time, a strong theoretical framework (efficient markets) along with the availability of massive amounts of historical data allowed researchers to publish papers and teach computational techniques to the large numbers of students pouring into the universities. Soon, multitudes of students were learning the new financial math in universities across the country and going on to apply them in the practical world of finance.

As a result of all these developments, the revolution started by Markowitz was soon to become deeply institutionalized both on Wall Street and in the Ivory Tower, with institutions in one sphere feeding on those in the other to build a crescendo of approval for mathematization of finance. What had started as a simple insight of a graduate student toiling in a university library had, in a few short decades, become a dominant conception about how the world of investments worked.

Over time, the computational tools have become increasingly more sophisticated,[15] with world-class universities offering graduate degrees in financial mathematics or financial engineering. Ph.D. programs in business schools now routinely hire students with math and other quant-oriented training almost exclusively; articles in academic journals have become virtually inaccessible to anyone not steeped in high order mathematics; financial institutions are populated with doctorates in physics and other quant-heavy disciplines. Both the teaching and practice of investments are now inseparable from the maddeningly complex math for analyzing risk and the probabilistic movement of prices.

Amazingly, Markowitz[16] and his followers had used the mathematical logic of portfolio theory to reduce stocks to two simple quantities: mean and variance. The focus on portfolio and risk defined simply as standard deviation of past returns meant, in effect, that the details of the underlying business were no longer worthy of analysis. Risk was reduced to a measurable quantity and investing to a problem of optimization. *Poof!* In came portfolio engineering and out went business analysis and judgment. Investing became an exercise in mathematics.

The Dissent

Yet, there were dissenting voices. Even as modern portfolio theory was gathering steam, some remained skeptical about what they thought was an elaborate ruse. These were small voices at first, protesting the foundational assumptions that made the math possible. They were concerned that the models required the investor to be hyper-rational, somebody who could do immensely complicated math and remain steadfastly objective in the evaluation of utility and risk. Rejected and ignored at first, these small voices slowly gained traction and, ultimately, a hearing about their objections to the modern portfolio theory.[17]

The first cracks began to appear in the early 1970s, barely twenty years after the first Markowitz paper, through the works of two psychologists, Amos Tversky and Daniel Kahneman. Starting with a paper in 1971 and carrying on for more than two decades after that, the pair began compiling impressive evidence about the systematic biases that plague people as they make choices. They argued, for example, that both lay people and professionals have markedly erroneous intuitions about the laws of chance. Over time, their experiments shredded the assumption that people maximize utility in all situations or that decision makers were even rational. In particular, they are credited with developing *prospect theory*, which highlights the difficulty people have in handling risk. Irrationality, they declared, was endemic in economic choices.

Prospect theory was picked up by economists, and soon became a basis for what has come to be called behavioral economics. Over time, this line of thinking has highlighted not only cognitive biases but also social and emotional factors that influence how people make economic and investment decisions.

Much of what we now know about how people actually make decisions is at odds with the caricature of hyper-rational decision makers that the modern portfolio theory assumes. Of particular help have been the insights about how people handle and incorporate risk in decision-making.

It turns out that risk is a much more complex issue than its simple conception as the standard deviation of past returns, as Markowitz had assumed. Risk is subjective to the person, in fact, not simply an objective fact about a stock. Most investors have trouble grasping the essence of risk and make common errors when making judgments about where and when to invest.

Even mathematically, the idea of standard deviation as risk is indefensible, as it incorrectly assumes that the underlying distributions are known in advance. Historical returns typically are assumed to be normally distributed, even though they may be skewed and have much larger spreads than those assumed by the usual models of risk;[18] unanticipated events happen a lot more frequently than assumed.[19] As such, even after decades of thinking on the subject, investment risk is still misunderstood and poorly captured by the mathematical models.

So, a key contribution of prospect theory and behavioral finance has been an honest appraisal of how we humans make decisions. Such an appraisal is missing from modern portfolio theory, which is underpinned instead by the caricature of people as all-knowing decision makers. Behavioral researchers have made great strides in highlighting the systematic errors in judgment and they have painstakingly formalized the intuition that it is not easy to be rational.

Yet, in spite of all the insights about systematic biases and the ineptitude of an average decision maker, there is no mention in behavioral finance of business as a wealth creating enterprise; analyzing businesses for their investment potential is nowhere on the agenda. Focusing on human frailties, theorists in behavioral finance are concerned with analyzing the investors but not the investment. They are as far removed as portfolio theory is from actually analyzing the businesses that issue the securities. Business analysis gets lost in the mix; it is neither a concern nor a focus.

Graham and Dodd had, in fact, intuited the common sense findings of behavioral finance. Having observed the mania of the late 1920s, the collapse of 1929, and the subsequent Depression, Graham understood quite well that people get carried away and make foolish decisions in the financial markets. In fact, as indicated in the first part of their book, one of their motivations for writing *Security Analysis* was to offer the mental apparatus that would help investors be rational when investing.

Interestingly, the intellectual and empirical debates between behavioral and portfolio theorists revolve around investor behavior and the consequences that has for how the markets function. To the former, it is puzzling why the latter do not see how irrational people can really be, especially when it comes to money and investing. To the latter, investor behavior is beside the point, as the invisible hand of the markets somehow solves that problem of individual irrationality. Yet, to the befuddled investor watching these debates, neither of those two traditions is interested in digging into the specifics of companies to understand what makes them tick and how they create value.

Back to Investing

Markowitz is so important to our story because he opened the doors for many brilliant mathematicians to come pouring into the world of investing. The age-old problems of chance, with which mathematicians had been fascinated for many centuries, now suddenly became incredibly interesting—Markowitz had led them to a rich bounty of data that seemed to suggest that prices moved randomly and, therefore, that chance played a mighty role in the stock market. This was a unique stage on which to apply and sharpen the long tradition of thinking about the games of chance. In recasting the problem of stock selection as a problem of portfolio optimization, in other words, Markowitz put in motion a movement that made investing less about business judgment and almost entirely about mathematical rules for gambling.

Risk was no longer a subjective judgment about odds; it was an objective, quantifiable measure based on frequencies in the past data. From a broad consideration of factors that influence future outcomes, risk became a narrowly defined technical term measured solely from the price data—so as to enable the mathematics of portfolio optimization. Accused of vagueness, business judgment became a poor cousin to the sharp and elegant models of mathematically trained financial economists.

It is important to understand that mathematical thinking is indispensable to investing. The mental discipline inspired by simple mathematical concepts is necessary for correctly framing investment problems and for synthesizing the influences of the different forces that may be bearing down on an investment thesis. Such structured thinking is powerful because it helps the mind grasp slippery concepts and helps organize the data so that any patterns as may exist become visible.

Clearly, Graham was a strong proponent of seeking and organizing information and, as is evident in *Security Analysis*, he was among the first to insist on mathematical logic in investment analysis. To him, collating financial statistics and evaluating relationships between key variables was very much a part of making judgments when investing.

But the mathematics we see in modern finance is often overly abstract and far removed from the real world of organizations, the people who inhabit them, and even the outsiders who seek to evaluate their potential as investments. The abstract mathematical models of investment theory seek, in fact, to remove judgment by removing from view such inconvenient facts as organization, leadership, strategy, products, relationships, and, above all, the many frailties of human decision-makers.

The dominance of complex mathematics in modern finance has had real consequences for how we learn, teach, and practice investing. Not only has the heavy use of mathematical abstractions encouraged framing of investing solely as a *problem of gamble*, it has also for the most part shut out further development of alternative approaches to investment analysis. Over time, such affinity for abstractions has drawn substantial resources away from the potentially far more productive lines of inquiry that would put realism back into investing and business judgment squarely at the center of investment decisions.

Increasingly, as a result, investment theory has fallen far behind other disciplines that more realistically assess our cognitive limitations and the many constraints on our ability to comprehend the world around us. Consequently, even as mathematically-oriented investment professionals search for ever more abstract models of risk, we continue to be starved of the conceptual aids that would help us understand risk holistically and subjectively, and that would help us make sound judgments about the many hazards that we face when investing.

Behavioral economists do much to correct the gallant—and glaringly wrong—assumptions about how people think about risk and make judgments under uncertainty. But they do little to help investors evaluate the merits of the companies in which they may choose to invest. That is, behavioral insights are very helpful in making us aware about common and systematic biases we all have, and I will draw on many such insights in the chapters that follow. Yet, behavioral theorists have little to say about how to evaluate investment opportunities for their economic worth.

Understandably, both portfolio theory and behavioral finance have attracted many smart people who are mathematicians and psychologists but do not necessarily have the affinity for or interest in making business judgments. High math and psychological theories of investor behavior are now the indispensable means with which to publish in intensely competitive academic journals; subjectivity and judgment are deemed too vague to qualify as honest scholarly work. Graham and Williams are long forgotten in academia, their lines of inquiry a distant memory carried on by the few stragglers who remain skeptical about the benefits that, some claim, accrue from the mathematization of finance.

In this book, therefore, I bring investors back to old-fashioned investing, hoping to reconnect with and revive the study of investments in the spirit of Graham and Dodd, and with a bow to Williams. I go beyond their two classics, however, by drawing in the many insights about human reasoning and about business analysis that researchers have uncovered during the past several decades.

Staying with the spirit of Graham to understand investing as an application of business judgment, I build a decision framework for investment analysis that fully acknowledges our many human frailties. I incorporate Savage's ideas about subjective probabilities and the Bayesian approach to updating expectations, but to the extent possible do so in commonsense and non-technical terms. Finally, as a check on the strong biases that potentially corrupt subjective assessments and distort decision-making, I follow a long line of thinkers in order to color the entire endeavor of investing with the *principle of negation,* which is to discover economic worth through a systematic process of refutation and disconfirmation.

All in all, in this book, I show how to understand investing the old-fashioned way—building portfolios one stock at a time—but with the aid of thinking that is grounded in current state-of-the-art understanding about how we really think and reason, and how companies create wealth and value. Aside from theory, however, I also show how investors can apply the investment decision (negation) framework—so that they may re-learn the art of investing intelligently and wisely.

It is time to invest.

Introduction

Method Investing

———

There are well more than $15 trillion sloshing around in the U.S. stock market alone, not to mention the tens of trillions more in stock exchanges around the world. And then there are countless more dollars whiplashing the system in bonds, commodities, options, futures and what not. Yet, research shows that rather than make money, individual investors typically lose money in the stock market.[20]

Successful investing is elusive because it requires putting up current real dollars for an uncertain future gain. Doing so entails making connections between actions now and consequences later, in venues (the markets) that are incredibly complex and volatile. It is easy to make mistakes in investing, therefore, and those mistakes can be costly.

Some mistakes in investing are self-inflicted, others induced from the outside. They arise from the secret workings of enemies internal and external, each more formidable than the other. Internal enemies are our own emotions, needs and desires, those deep-rooted primal urgings that tug at the psyche and cloud the mind. Fear, hope, greed, and more are as much part of the human psyche as anything else; these are always present, always lurking beneath the surface, easily activated by any number of things and, when intensified, strongly encourage behavior that is as foolish as it is harmful to our own economic interests.

As investors, we also have to contend with the push and pull of external influences, those that insist in whispers and shouts, from screen, print, and radio, to buy this and sell that. Tricks, cons, and outright lies get inextricably mixed with hints, allusions, and possible truths. The noise out there is deafening, an information din, as an unending array of thoughts, opinions, and hallucinations make it to the airwaves and invade the consciousness. They fray the nerves, fragment the imagination, and dissipate the most important resource that any investor has: his attention span. It is hard to distinguish signal from noise, as a result, and good advice from deceit; the hapless investor is often buried in all this, prone to premature action or paralyzing confusion or worse.

Contrary to daily hype and urgings dished out in the media, in other words, investing is a bewilderingly difficult game. Yet, so many believe or are seduced into believing that they can make an easy buck with a quick buy here and a hasty sell there. Gripped by dreams of riches but unprepared for what awaits them, there they go, by the millions, to the market, like cannon-fodder to the front lines, to an endeavor where the odds are heavy against them.

The challenge for most lay investors and some professionals, too, is that they may not fully appreciate the complexity of the endeavor, at least until a few costly setbacks.

As such, forays into the financial markets are often blinded by the hopes of easy money rather than by skilled efforts to solve a fundamental *problem of choice* that investing presents. That is, investors face the problem of picking from among a very large number of targets that are partly visible and in constant motion on an incredibly noisy stage, and they do so under the unrelenting pull of internal urges and external inducements.

Clearly, if investing seems simple, it is only deceptively so. Successful investing is more involved than meets the eye; more than anything, it requires adequate defenses against some very powerful internal and external obstacles to making good choices. Yet, such defenses do not come naturally to us. They must be carefully built, concept-by-concept, to help overcome deep flaws in how we think and to help ward-off the external influences that induce us into doing foolish things with our money. Without such defenses, investors remain extremely vulnerable.

Method to the Rescue

Given the deep hazards inherent in investing, a systematic approach is essential for investors to be able to avoid steep losses and hold their own amidst the churn of the markets. Perhaps more than anything else, investing wisely requires learning how to be careful and to avoid mistakes to which so many so routinely fall easy prey. As the football aphorism goes, offense wins games but defense wins championships.[21] As in football, so it is in investing.

Through trial and error and by careful study, investors need over time to develop their own system of thinking, a *method* that helps sort through the jumble of information, stabilizes emotions, focuses attention, and provides consistency to decisions. If internal psyche and external enticements are formidable enemies, then the method, a systematic but guarded approach to investing, is the armor with which investors can join the battle and prevail.

There are more ways than one to approach the markets, however, and no single method can work equally well for all who do so. Those who have the need for speed and quick gratification may gravitate towards high-speed trading systems, whereas those that are inclined to be cautious may be partial to slower analytical approaches. What is best for one may not be so for another, as each method is a particular way of looking at the world and, to be effective, it must suit you and the specific problems you may be trying to solve. The method-personality fit is particularly important because the last thing you want to do is fight yourself and your own natural inclinations when in the thick of battle.

Examples are many, but consider just a few of the most famous names in investing from the last years. Jesse Livermore,[22] for instance, developed notoriety for shorting stocks from years of direct experiences in the stock market. Benjamin Graham[23] developed an intellectual approach and numerical benchmarks to uncover undervalued stocks and bonds. Philip Fisher[24] used a systematic qualitative approach to evaluate future prospects of technology companies. George Soros[25] relied mostly on insights into mass psychology and developed what he called the *Theory of Reflexivity*. Still countless others, such as Warren Buffett,[26] tactfully combined elements of more than one basic approach to form their own particular ways of seeking and evaluating investment options.

The markets are so large and complex that they offer many kinds of problems for investors to solve. Success in the financial markets is essentially a reward for properly defining the problems that interest you and developing the methods that help focus on and systematically address those particular problems as defined by you.

The Investment Problem

Not all problems are created equal, however. Some are highly complex and defy any solution, whereas others are more solvable with modicum of effort. Knowing where the prices are going to go next, for instance, is perhaps the most difficult of all problems. Considerable research and thinking suggests that market prices move randomly and are essentially unpredictable.[27] Still, unwittingly perhaps, many in the market try to solve just this problem, and predicting whether prices will go up or down is a big preoccupation in the financial media. From thence come all varieties of chart readers, pattern seekers, market timers, and momentum traders—all speculating, swinging wildly and hoping that something hits.

At least part of the reason for such price-driven behaviors is that, ever since the early 1950s when modern portfolio theory came into being, investing has been cast as gambling. Naturally interested in the age-old problem of gamble, or chance, mathematically-trained investment researchers have, over time, cast investing in their own image. Understandably, they look at the financial markets as a goldmine of data and problems that could be defined with the concepts of probability that mathematicians have been developing for several centuries. Defined in this way, investing attracts those who are inclined to speculate and gamble and, in so doing, focus on prices and their probabilistic movements.

Although sensible speculation is sometimes a worthwhile endeavor, in this book I sidestep altogether the problem of trying to predict prices and focus instead on a relatively simpler, although not simple, problem of comparing prevailing prices with careful estimates of economic worth. That is, instead of focusing on the *problem of chance*, I recast investing as a *problem of choice* and, therefore, as requiring judgments about the key uncertainties that may surround an investment prospect.

Learning to make judgments about economic worth keeps the spotlight on behaviors and actions that create economic value. Instead of locking on and chasing prices, the gaze shifts to the fundamental drivers of economic worth. Instead of passive indexing or frenzied buying and selling, such a shift in orientation expands the investment horizon and encourages well-thought-out commitments of capital to economically attractive opportunities.

Make no mistake. Both gambling and investing are about making decisions now for outcomes in the unknown future. As such, they both require making assessments about the odds; understanding the underlying math is essential in either case.[28] The difference is that whereas gamblers usually seek low odds with high payoff (say, 1–9 odds for doubling their money or more), investors are inclined to stay on the sidelines until they can get much more favorable odds for reasonably good returns (say, 90–1 odds for 15 percent return with much upside potential). Marginally favorable odds (say, 51–49) would induce eager action from gamblers but none from investors.

The unfavorable or marginally favorable odds make gamblers depend a great deal on luck, however, as the outcomes depend largely on what hands they draw. Moreover, the math of marginal odds is such that they require a very large volume of transactions for the endeavor to be profitable. As a result, gamblers are prone to trade a great deal and are not inclined to hold positions for long. The short time horizon, in turn, necessitates an unending search for new opportunities with marginally favorable odds. The math for such endeavors quickly becomes complex, and that is perhaps why mathematical finance has been so ascendant ever since the mathematicians, fascinated by the *problem of chance,* turned their attention to the financial markets.

In contrast, investors do not need high transaction volumes because the high odds of success that they prefer can deliver performance with just a few thoughtful and well-researched positions. As such, they seek near-certainty by thinking strategically about the underlying factors that may be shaping the odds—so that they may be able to play long for position and build durable strengths in their investment program.[29] To the extent possible, investors work diligently to try to reduce reliance on luck and focus instead on the skills necessary for understanding the fundamental drivers of economic performance. It is this affinity for highly favorable odds that makes investors fundamentally different from gamblers. They focus on a different problem. Gamblers want to take chances; investors want to make good choices. Gamblers want to trade; investors want to invest.

Clearly, analytical ability and technique are necessary for investing well. Knowing how to compute weighted probabilities or assess mathematical expectations is an important skill for investing wisely. But what is even more important is the ability to regulate emotions, think independently, and see clearly when making investment choices. Yet, controlling emotions and seeing clearly is not easy, as the financial markets are incredibly noisy and ripe with half-baked opinions, innuendos, and cons; they overwhelm the senses, confuse and disorient, and invite all varieties of deceptions and self-deceptions.

So, although the key to investing wisely, making good choices is not easy. The moment we define investing as being about choice, it also becomes a good deal about emotion; the noise and confusion that we face as investors intensify the emotions and the biases that are lodged inextricably in our very being, create internal turmoil, and suppress deliberative reasoning. Our biases so mix things up in our minds that they corrupt our perceptions and have the potential to make analysis meaningless if not outright misleading. Moreover, our emotions tend to move with those of others around us, making it very difficult for us to think independently.

No lesson on investing is complete, therefore, without showing how our perceptions are easily distorted and how to correct those distortions. The *problem of choice*, or the problem of being able to see the true potential of investment opportunities, is harder than it may seem at first glance: seeing clearly requires that we not only learn moderately complex analytical techniques but also that we know how to correct perceptions that are liable to be severely distorted.

Overview of the Book

As such, unlike most other books on investing, I discuss at length why our perceptions are so prone to be distorted and how we may try to correct them when making investment choices. To such an end, I take you through an intellectual journey, a short detour away from finance and into the world of philosophers who have long wrestled with the problem of how we humans think. Although this material may seem strange at first, I hope you will realize that the key lessons from the works of many great philosophers have a direct bearing on how well you invest. They give us a peek into our inner lives so that we may be able to live—and invest—more thoughtfully.

I devote the first ten chapters of the book, therefore, to discussing the problems of perceptions and then outlining a decision framework to help correct the inevitable distortions in our perceptions—so that we may be able to make good investment choices. Only after I have developed and fleshed out the framework do I go into the particulars of analytical techniques that are directly applicable to evaluating stocks and building stock portfolios.

In essence, I submit that a healthy dose of skepticism, when grounded in good data and logic, is essential for investing wisely. To that end, I develop and present a formal *process of refutation and disconfirmation*, and show how to apply good methods so as to make good investment plays and build robust stock portfolios. In doing so, I show that good business judgment and prudence are at the center of being a successful investor.

So, on with the show!

Book I

Illusion

Chapters

———

1. Opinions and Beliefs
2. Correlation of Errors
3. The Dark Arts
4. Purveyors of the Dark Arts
5. Victims of the Dark Arts

———

1

Opinions and Beliefs

———

Consider this simple experiment. There are four cards on a table, each having a letter on one side and a number on the other, but you can only see what is on the side facing up. What you see are two letters and two numbers.

Suppose you are told that the rule governing these cards is that if a card has a vowel on one side, then it has an even number on the other side. Now, which two cards do you need to turn over to find out whether the rule is true or false?

If you are like most people, you will turn the cards A and 4; in doing so, also like most people, you will have made the incorrect choice. And the error you made is one of the most common as revealed from hundreds of years of thinking about human reasoning, now known as *confirmation bias*.[30]

What you did was to try to *confirm* the rule that the cards that have a vowel will also have an even number. Turning A is obvious, as being a vowel it can clearly falsify the rule if an odd number turns up on the other side. An even number on the other side of A would validate the rule but you would not know whether it holds in all cases. But what is behind 4 is not relevant to the issue at hand. If you find a vowel behind 4, then you will have confirmed the rule but would still not be able to say for sure that the rule is true; but if there is a consonant behind 4, then you have not violated the rule (the rule doesn't say that a consonant can't have an even number on the other side). So, turning 4 gives you no useful information.

The correct response to the task is to turn over card A and card 7, both of which can clearly falsify the rule. The difference between cards 4 and 7 is that only the latter can provide *disconfirming* evidence. The subtle but powerful inclination to confirm the rule induces most people to turn over the card with 4 on it.

The above was an experiment first devised by psychologist Peter Cathcart Wason in 1966, and over the years it has been repeated innumerable times by experimental psychologists trying to understand how people reason. Although the many variations of the experiment have yielded a range of results, one of the key insights gained from all such effort is that confirmation bias is pervasive in human reasoning. People have a tenacious inclination to confirm *seemingly* correct rules and whatever they already believe, no matter why they hold those beliefs or where their beliefs come from.

Beliefs and Their Persistence

There is a whole spectrum of theories about what a belief is, but where beliefs come from is utterly puzzling. Why people believe in some things versus others and how people come to hold those beliefs remains shrouded in mystery. Modern philosophers continue to wonder whether beliefs are brain states, although many doubt that any such thing as a belief even exists.[31]

Still, beliefs are considered to be propositional attitudes in the sense that people appear to be always tending toward some ideas or views on how the world works or ought to work, on what is or is not or ought to be or ought not to be. Whether it is a medley of past experiences or some dominant event or trauma in a person's life, education or indoctrination, suggestion or coercion, there are perhaps more instigators of beliefs than there are stars in the sky.

So, there is no knowing what people will believe. History books are filled with examples of highly intelligent people holding beliefs that in hindsight appear to be patently ridiculous. Isaac Newton, the supremely intelligent Englishman immortalized for discovering the physical laws of motion, believed that the earth was no more than 6,000 years old. Galileo, even when presented the evidence to the contrary, believed that tides were created not by the pull of the moon but by the "irregular" motion of the earth.[32] Belief in witchcraft was perfectly natural for eons, and sorcery was considered for a very long time the root cause of a variety of ills, individual and social.

The modern world, of course, is not immune from beliefs in all and sundry things. Mythical creatures such as fairies, gnomes, and elves continue to feed the imagination of people around the world. Many rural fairs in the United States continue to present the opportunity for people to get a psychic to read into their past and the future, the paranormal powers put into service for anyone willing to pay a fee, of course. Testimonials abound about the existence of unidentified flying objects, alien abductions, and crop circles. Carlos Castaneda, the superbly successful novelist of the 1970s, sold millions of copies of his books full of stories about out-of-body experiences and other-world realities. Then, the more recent bestsellers by J. K. Rowling are based on witches and wizards, ghosts and goblins and black cats, fascinating the imaginations of untold millions.

Whatever may be their source and content, a particularly interesting feature of beliefs is that they can begin to form fairly quickly and often on the most tenuous grounds. Modern psychological studies have shown that when having to acquire information in order to make decisions, people generally give much weight to the information that is obtained first, and they often rely on information that already exists in their minds, is easily recalled, or is readily obtained from sources nearby. Called *primacy effect*, this is the tendency to form opinions early in the process, often based on what is available, and then to selectively seek and creatively use subsequent information in ways that support the initial opinions. Nothing new, this observation was made long ago by Francis Bacon, the English polymath of late 16th and early 17th centuries, who once remarked that the first conclusion colors everything and pulls all later information towards it. We see what we believe.

Beliefs also have a tenacious hold on people. Turning into ideologies in the extreme, beliefs stubbornly resist even the most compelling counter-evidence. In the 1950s, for instance, a social psychologist by the name of Leon Festinger did a fascinating study of a doomsday cult that had prophesized the end of the world before dawn on December 21, 1954. When no such calamity came, members of the cult declared that God had called off the destruction of the world. Festinger explained that evidence counter to a strongly held belief is extremely painful for people. In order to avoid the pain, true believers strengthen their social bonds with others who validate their beliefs, insist upon the correctness of their thinking, deny any evidence to the contrary, and when the evidence is undeniable, they turn around and distort it so as to maintain the integrity of their prior beliefs.

Festinger's insights on the psychological effects of disconfirming evidence informed much subsequent research and they remain relevant today. It is now well understood that people with well-formed beliefs easily distort the selection, evaluation, and interpretation of data so as to justify their views. Especially when information is ambiguous, people with strong beliefs selectively co-opt the evidence for support. Such co-optation is not necessarily irrational, however, as people have been shown to use facile logic and sophistic reasoning to contort evidence to reinforce their preferential positions. Repeatedly, studies have shown that even when they are shown the evidence that contradicts the information on which the original belief was formed, people continue to hold onto unfounded beliefs. Evidence that contradicts the position is ignored or explained away in the interest of preserving the pre-existing belief.

Once again, *belief persistence* afflicts everyone and spares no one, not even those normally considered highly intelligent. For a millennium, those practicing medicine persisted in bleeding and purging patients even though the curative effects were usually quite unclear and painful death a more likely outcome. Of course, sometimes patients recovered from their illness and that was taken as validating the brutal methods. Those instances in which the patients recovered without administration of torture in the guise of medicine or, instances in which the illness became worse, were conveniently ignored.

The history of science is replete with instances in which whole fields of scientists, presumably some of the most educated in society, clung to a theory despite rapidly developing evidence to the contrary. For example, in spite of numerous observations that contradicted it, Ptolemy's earth-centric view of the cosmos persisted among the keenest minds for considerably more than a thousand years. The heliocentric model that sought to replace it was strongly opposed by the scientists of the day, who were apt to question and discard any evidence that was not consistent with the idea that the earth was the center of the universe.

When the mounting evidence could not be ignored, it was force-fit into the system of belief. When that failed, the belief structure itself was tweaked so as to accommodate the anomaly, but while still preserving the larger system of thought. It was only when a new constellation of ideas, formalized by Copernicus in 1543, could not be ignored that the old system finally bowed to the notion of earth moving around the sun.

Needless to say, belief persistence is not simply a malady of a bygone era. The modern world offers plenty of examples of how simple ideas take hold of the mind. The notion that gravity ought to pull the universe into a single point troubled Newton so much that, in seeking consistency in his theories, he assumed a static and infinite space which had no center on which to collapse. This assumption became received wisdom, and for 200 years most everybody "knew" that the universe was static. Along with others in the scientific community, Einstein too strongly subscribed to this theory and dismissed out of hand both Alexander Friedman and Georges Lemaître when, using Einstein's own theory of general relativity, they independently proposed that the universe was expanding. It was only later that Einstein saw his error and publicly acknowledged that Lemaître was correct,[33] and the assumption of a static universe finally gave way to what we now think of as the Big Bang theory.

Persistence of beliefs is common in other arenas as well. In studies about how doctors make diagnoses, researchers have noted that the thesis about a patient's illness is often made early in the process. This initial thesis then guides the acquisition and interpretation of subsequent information and often constrains the range of options or alternative hypotheses considered. Faulty diagnoses, in other words, are usually the result of persistence of belief that is formed early in the process of evaluation.[34]

The same phenomenon has been observed in studies of jurors.[35] Researchers have found that jurors can form initial impressions based on superficial cues such as the defendant's demeanor; these impressions can then persist as jurors, admonitions to the contrary notwithstanding, selectively look for evidence to support a particular verdict that they may have tentatively formed early in the trial or even before the trial.

Psychologists have also tried to differentiate between strongly held beliefs that people are motivated to defend or not, as the case may be. It is in a way understandable to defend a belief because of material or psychological interest in it. If you are a small business owner who stands to lose if Wal-Mart moves nearby, for instance, it would surprise no one when you oppose that move.

Yet, people are known to defend beliefs even when they do not have a clear material stake. For someone living far removed from the history or the particulars of conflict in the Middle East, a specific violent but localized clash should not have material bearing. Even so, it is common to find people in faraway places around the world expressing strong opinions about who is right and who is wrong, about what Palestinians ought to be doing and Israel not. For some inexplicable reason, people have a strong inclination to believe any proposition that they find pleasing or would like to be true.

Belief Persistence Among Investors

Primacy effect, belief persistence, and confirmation bias, in short, strongly influence what choices people make and how they make them. These deeply psychological dispositions interfere with both the acquisition and interpretation of information, and they do so below conscious awareness, subtly but powerfully shaping thought and choice.

For investors whose success depends on making good choices about where to invest their money and where not to do so, such psychological hindrances can be costly. Taken to the extreme, mistakes induced by poor thinking can be disastrous. Getting drawn into an investment can create a belief-enhancing cycle in which wrong ideas attract an increasing commitment of resources until the day of reckoning when all is lost.

The problem for investors and decision makers in general is, in fact, even more intractable because these interferences occur irrespective of whether the beliefs are true or false. Even though the examples above emphasize errors in judgment, confirmation bias operates equally strongly when beliefs are in fact correct or consistent with some well-conceived standards or objective criteria. And this creates yet another problem.

When caught in a confirmation cycle, lightly held beliefs and opinions that are legitimately grounded in some verifiable facts may become much stronger than warranted by evidence. This latter problem, of strong beliefs built on hints of truth, is as common as beliefs that have absolutely no basis in fact. A little truth, in other words, can be stretched to absurd levels, out of all proportion to available evidence and eventually divorced from it.

During the tech bubbles of the 1990s, for example, the emergence of the world-wide web created legitimate opportunities for new business models and profit possibilities. The data traffic on the web started growing rapidly and at one point it grew at the rate of 100 percent in ninety days. This basic fact became a mantra, of course, and was repeated for the next several years, even though such a high level of growth was an anomaly discernible only for a short period of time. As is now widely known, the little truth about the web was extrapolated to extremes, contributing to one of the most rapid rises in asset prices ever seen.

Researchers have argued, in fact, that self-deception is all too common among investors and makes them vulnerable to predatory exploitation by shrewd firms and institutions.[36] Researchers have shown, moreover, that investors with strong confirmation bias are also more overconfident, trade more, and have poorer investment performance.[37]

The formation and persistence of beliefs occur not only at the level of the individual, but also on the larger scale where entire populations get consumed by it. How the errors in belief can gain mass appeal, sometimes quickly and sometimes persistently, is an exciting area of inquiry which I will review briefly in the next chapter. Suffice it to say at this juncture that mass delusions have been with us for a very long time. As far back as 1841, for instance, Charles Mackay wrote:[38]

In the reading of history of nations, we find that, like individuals, they have their whims and their peculiarities; their seasons of excitement and recklessness, when they care not what they do. We find that whole communities suddenly fix their minds upon one object, and go mad in its pursuit; that millions of people become simultaneously impressed with one delusion, and run after it, till their attention is caught by some new folly more captivating than the first. We see one nation suddenly seized, from its highest to its lowest members, with a fierce desire for military glory; another as suddenly becoming crazed upon a religious scruple; and neither of them recovering its senses until it has shed rivers of blood and sowed a harvest of groans and tears, to be reaped by its posterity.

Students of financial history are, of course, familiar with financial manias that have periodically wrought havoc in the lives of millions.[39] From the tulip craze in the seventeenth century Netherlands to the Mississippi scheme in eighteenth century France and the South Sea Bubble in eighteenth century England; from the railway mania in nineteenth century Britain to the Florida land boom of the 1920s; from the periodic stock market booms and busts of the last century to the housing market crisis in our own times; we are well acquainted with what confirmation bias, combined with other human frailties, can do to us.

Many Other Pitfalls

Of course, confirmation bias is not the only source of errors in judgment that people make both in investing and other activities. Modern psychology has uncovered a plethora of systematic errors or biases that appear to be as much part of the human heritage as anything else. Among the other well-known biases are the tendencies for people to be overconfident about their own abilities, and to be optimistic about the outcomes of their actions. Similarly noted is the inclination of people, on the one hand, to overreact to chance events and, on the other, to think that they could have predicted that which has already occurred.

Perhaps the most exciting recent developments in the understanding of human reasoning have been insights into visceral factors that constantly influence us as we go about our daily routines. Of course, entire treatises have been written about the biases and visceral drivers that influence our choices; I will touch upon some such insights in due course in the pages that follow.

My purpose here is to simply highlight that the rational decision or the rational investor is a caricature of theory; perfect rationality holds only for a normative model that does not exist naturally in real life. The sooner we clearly acknowledge that we are biologically and psychologically predisposed to make poor choices, the better we are likely to be able to accommodate our vulnerabilities when making high-stakes investing decisions.

The various biases that come into play are subtle and powerful, and they confound decision-making in many different ways. It is, therefore, common for us to hold all varieties of faulty opinions and then, quite likely through the operation of confirmation bias, come to believe in those opinions-turned-beliefs as if they were the Gospel Truth. The human mind is, in fact, a confused medley of opinions, thoughts, and ideas, some fleeting, others half-formed, and still others firmly held, for reasons that are only partially clear, sometimes.

Errors in judgment resulting from our human heritage are not benign, however. Certainly, those who know how their decision-making can be severely distorted by our very human frailties can try to mitigate those distortions by taking precautionary measures. But those who understand how those distortions operate can also use that knowledge, as many have used it throughout history, for ends both good and bad.

In the following chapter, therefore, I show how individual errors aggregate into mass delusions and discuss in subsequent chapters the techniques of manipulation, the *Dark Arts* I call them, that are practiced upon us while we go about our daily lives as consumers, voters, and investors—even as or, ironically, because we continue to hold the illusion that we are independent thinkers free of all and sundry influences.

2

Correlation of Errors

———

On Friday October 24, 2008, panic gripped the financial markets. The Chicago Board Options Exchange (CBOE) volatility index (VIX),[40] also known as the Fear Index, reached an all-time high during trading that day. Having traded under thirty for most of the preceding year, and since its inception in 1990 having tended to hover between ten and twenty, the Index suddenly began climbing in early September, quickly crossed the previous historical high of forty-four and, on October 24 exploded to eighty-nine. The fear as reflected in VIX was clearly evident in the panic selling in the stock market.

In just one month, the market as a whole, as measured by the S&P 500 Index, dropped 26 percent and wiped out more than $2 trillion of equity investment in large publicly traded firms.

The economic news had been growing increasingly worse since the summer, but the speed of the market crash caught even the professionals by surprise. The newspapers were replete with stories about savvy institutions and big brokerage houses losing tens of billions of dollars and more. Many companies saw their market value plummet like a rock dropped from on high, and scores of people saw their life savings disappear in what seemed like a blink of an eye.

The remarkable thing about the sudden panic in the financial markets was that just a few years earlier the sentiment had been quite the opposite. The S&P 500 Index had reached an historical high of 1,552 in October of the previous year and the housing market had been booming for several years. The

Aggregate Case-Shiller Index of housing prices had risen from 125 in January 2002 to a peak of 251 in May 2006, at a rate two-and-a-half times faster than the rate of growth for the preceding four years. The euphoria that had been building for the previous half-dozen years was, in the fall of 2008, quickly and suddenly replaced by panic. Along with the decline in the stock market, housing prices plummeted too; the Case-Shiller Index plunged more than 15 percent in one year.

Clearly, the euphoria and panic of the first decade of the century were not without precedence. Yet, unlike many others that are usually confined to a region, this particular upheaval was global. Instant news and rapid globalization had so connected the markets globally that what previously would have been somewhat contained now quickly spread throughout the world.

For the month of October through day 24, as the stock market indexes dropped precipitously in the United States, stock indexes around the world saw similar losses or worse. Brazil was down 48 percent, Peru 42 percent, Britain 31 percent, Germany 35 percent, Japan 23 percent, South Korea 46 percent, and India 36 percent.[41]

All the stock markets globally had been riding high just about one year earlier; now, it seemed as if people the world over were experiencing a collective panic attack and stampeding out of the stock markets.

Booms and busts have been with us as long as there have been markets, and in some ways even longer. In spite of the best efforts to contain them, such cycles have persisted in their unpredictability and will most likely continue to do so well into the future.

It is understandable, therefore, that many interesting theories seek to explain why economies and markets undergo periods of excess in both directions. These theories are mostly technical in nature and thrive in such explanations as aggregate demand, money supply, interest rates, debt, and inventory. For the most part, they imagine the economy to be a machine, as if the fix is in pushing this button or pulling that lever.

The technical explanations beg the questions, however, as to why the aggregate demand explodes or crashes, why the money supply goes astray or debt gets to be excessive or inventories get bloated. Why do such mishaps happen with such speed and surprise even the savvy investors?

To these questions there are few answers, at least partly because the technical reasons are abstracted from real, ground-level human feelings and emotion; they miss the larger human story at play in the periodic but unpredictable swings. Technical explanations miss the crucial point that economic activity is not an island unto itself; that what happens in the markets is closely connected with life *outside* the realm of dry economics.

Participants in the markets are, after all, human; we are the same species that has for eons produced flash riots and convulsive revolutions, street disturbances and long-enduring movements; we are the same psycho-biological beings whose collective follies are duly noted by many authors and, as noted in the last chapter, more than 150 years ago so entertainingly catalogued by Charles Mackay.

Although the world of finance provides a fascinating and highly visible example of collective mood swings, virtually the whole of human experience is in fact composed of emotions of multitudes moving in unison. Both in finance and beyond, the combined fears and hopes and more of millions take on a life of their own, answerable to no one, relentlessly moving to extremes in any given direction until their eventual, and often abrupt and forceful, dissolution.

In order to understand what happens in the financial markets it is, therefore, instructive to look to the larger human experiences. In order to comprehend how the financial markets function and how we as people indulge in them, it is important to identify how we, the people, participate in mass actions generally. I discuss below, in brief, two recent examples of mass follies so that we may be able to understand the emotional propellants that drive considerable action in the financial markets.

The Atkins Diet

Consider, as a very different kind of example, the Atkins Diet craze that swept across the United States a few years before the market crash of late 2008. As is well known, obesity and related ills have long concerned Americans, prompting a never-ending search for cures and quick fixes that would magically help people lose weight. As a result, different approaches to dieting have been in the American lexicon for more than a hundred years. Today, there is a well-developed cottage industry, including several thriving corporations, with many products and much advice about how to shed weight without the pain of regular exercise or the disappointment of small portions at mealtime.

The first recorded modern diet therapy came in the late 1890s, when a man named Horace Fletcher claimed that for healthy eating it was necessary to chew thirty-two times before swallowing. He made a bundle preaching his own package of ideas, convincing scores of people to masticate diligently. Mastication became quite a craze for a while, in fact, until it yielded to the calorie-counting approaches to dieting that began to emerge around the end of World War I.

All through the twentieth century, a wide variety of diet plans followed one another in rapid succession, each claiming to solve the weight problem, and each doing its part to modify the eating habits of many. The medical profession weighed in with warnings of the dangers of obesity; the insurance companies got into the game, linking premiums to weight; the drug companies joined in with pills that would do the trick; corporations tapped into a growing market for diet products by developing sugar substitutes and selling consumables that they claimed did not add to body weight. Interest in the problem grew, begetting its own momentum.

Virtually everybody seemed to be persuaded that the problem of obesity had to be confronted, and there was a general consensus, varying over time, as to what was the most appropriate solution to that problem. For the most part, by around mid-century, the default thinking was to lower the intake of fat and to cut down on sugar.

Then, in 1972, a cardiologist named Robert Atkins published a controversial book, challenging the prevailing wisdom that a low-fat diet was necessary for shedding excess weight. Instead, he claimed that the real culprits were high-carbohydrate foods because of the stress they placed on the insulin-producing mechanisms in the body.

Contrary to what most of the medical community had been recommending, Dr. Atkins lifted almost all restrictions on high-fat foods and encouraged people to eat as much protein as they wanted. But he counseled people to severely restrict their intake of carbohydrates to a daily dosage much lower than what most other experts insisted was the necessary minimum for good health.

The controversy persisted for years after the publication of the book, as most nutrition experts remained skeptical of the low-carbohydrate, high-fat, and high-protein diets Atkins was recommending. The American Heart Association warned repeatedly that high-fat diets increased the risk of heart disease, stroke, and several types of cancer. High-protein diets, they warned, could trigger kidney and liver disorders and osteoporosis.

Still, Atkins stuck to his claims, publishing in the early 1990s a highly successful revised edition of his book. Millions of people read it and were relieved to learn that they could eat all the fat and protein they wanted and still lose weight. Even so, the conventional wisdom remained unshaken and the Atkins Diet remained on the periphery of mainstream nutritional advice.

Around 2001, almost thirty years after the publication of Dr. Atkins' first book, interest in low-carbohydrate diets began to grow for no apparent reason. Within the next three years, interest surged to such a degree that the Atkins Diet became a virtual craze.

Suddenly, people were avoiding carbohydrates as if they were poison. Office talk was filled with comparisons between low-carbohydrate and low-fat diets. People talked knowingly of this diet and that. Everybody seemed to have a story about their own dietary choices or those of others they had heard about. People were glad to be eating steak without guilt. They were ordering hamburgers without buns. Pasta was out, meat was in. Fruit had to be consumed sparingly, but cheddar cheese omelets were alright. Eggs and bacon were back on the breakfast menu; toast and bagels were off it. Rich creamy foods were once again a pleasure without worries, but wheat and cereal gave people pause. *Dr. Atkins' New Diet Revolution*, published back in 1992, now became a phenomenal bestseller.

By 2004, the low-carb revolution was in full swing. Millions changed their habits, revising their meal plans even as they ignored decades of expert advice to the contrary.

The new patterns of food consumption had real consequences, of course. Restaurants had to change their menus to accommodate the movement now afoot. Those that resisted putting low-carb items on the menu saw their sales plummet. Large food companies got into the act with new product lines to meet the new demand.

As donuts and pastries lost their appeal, thousands of small bakeries went out of business or came on the verge of doing so. In just one year, the market value of Krispy Kreme, the famous donut maker, dropped 75 percent from $2.2 billion to $542 million.

Two of the largest makers of pasta, the New World Pasta Company and the American Italian Pasta Company, declared bankruptcy and wiped out their investors. Other businesses barely held on as people by the millions removed bread and pasta from their pantries and took them off their weekly grocery shopping lists. All carbohydrate foods were suspect, and the infrastructure that had over time developed around delivering such foods seemed to be suddenly under enormous stress.

Prospering in this environment was, of course, Atkins Nutritionals, the company that Dr. Atkins had founded in 1989 to promote his theories. The company had grown rapidly and by 2004 it had more than 350 products sold through a variety of outlets. It was developing a continuous stream of new diet plans and working with restaurants and food companies to implement low-carbohydrate items in their menus and product lines. The burgeoning demand for low-carbohydrate foods presented good opportunities and Atkins Nutritionals was well positioned to capitalize on those.

Then, almost as quickly as it had come, the Atkins Diet craze was over. Dr. Atkins had died in 2003 from a slip and a fall, and a rumor began to circulate that cardiac arrest had played a role in his death. The rumor was vigorously contested, it could not be verified, and it likely did not play much of a role in people's sudden move away from the Atkins Diet.

Yet, the following year, for no apparent reason, interest in low-carb diets waned significantly and it did so quickly. People now suddenly repudiated the beliefs that had propelled the craze, switching back to the more traditional ways of weight loss; they slowed down on the rich creams, butter, and meats. Pasta was back in business, and bread and bagels again appeared in the kitchen.

Unable to withstand the reversal of tide, Atkins Nutritionals declared bankruptcy in 2005. Within a few years, the storm had come and gone. By 2008, only quiet residues of Atkins remained in diets across America; nowhere anymore did fats and proteins blatantly dictate the meal plans as they had done briefly only a few years earlier.

Genocide in Bosnia

Stock market and diet crazes aside, we can learn about collective emotions by peeking into other spheres as well. The case of genocide in Bosnia provides another illustration of how emotions build up at a large scale to influence the thoughts and actions of individuals, creating the context in which ordinary people make decisions and justify deeds that would be unacceptable under normal circumstances.

Bosnia-Herzegovina was one of the six republics within the Socialist Federal Republic of Yugoslavia (SFRY). Its large Muslim population had a long history of co-existing with the other religious ethnicities, mainly Slavic Christians and Roman Catholics. Josip Broz Tito's authoritarian rule had held the different religious groups in the federation since the end of World War II, but the strains had begun to appear very soon after his death 1980. Rising nationalism among the various groups had created political turmoil, as the desire of Serbian nationalists to centralize power met resistance from the others, such as the Albanian nationalists, who wanted greater autonomy. It was in this context of nationalism and power struggle that a mass of emotion began to form, with drastic consequences for all involved.

We pick up the story in 1989 when, by some estimates, about one million people had gathered around the Gazimestan monument in central Kosovo.[42] They had come from all over Serbia and other parts of the world to commemorate a battle long ago, one in which the medieval Serbs had fought the invading Ottoman Turks, one in which their legendary hero, Prince Lazar, had fallen. The battle had marked the end of a once-prosperous Serbian kingdom and the beginning of five centuries of subjugation by foreigners of a different religion.

June 28, 1989 was the 600th anniversary of the Battle of Kosovo, fought on the site now considered the holiest of places for all Serbs. The monument, made of stones the color of blood and shaped like a medieval tower 100 feet tall, sat on a hill about four miles north-northeast of the Kosovo Polje (field) on which the two sides had fought the bloody battle. For the nationalists, it was a symbol of Serb identity and evoked emotions that resided deep in the psyche of a whole nation. It was a reminder of the heroes who had laid down their lives, and of the great power that Serbia could have been were it not for the Ottomans.

Of all the legends out of which the Serbian nationalist narrative was constructed,[43] the heroism of Prince Lazar in particular had attained an aura of mythic proportions. He was the hero who had pulled together a force to oppose the more powerful enemy; he was the martyr who had sacrificed himself in defense of his people, choosing to die in battle rather than to live as a vassal of a foreign power.

The anniversary celebrations had started two years earlier, when a coffin said to contain Prince Lazar's mummified remains started making its way from the patriarchate of Belgrade towards mostly Albanian province of Kosovo.[44] The procession went through monasteries in areas that the Serbs claimed to be their new state, at each stop drawing large mourning crowds dressed in black. Repeatedly during the journey, Prince Lazar was symbolically buried at night and reincarnated in the morning, until he was finally reburied at Kosovo Polje.[45]

By the time of the million-strong rally around the Gazimestan monument, the emotions were at fever pitch. This was the day to remember and to be proud, Serb leaders told the crowds before them. Representatives of the Orthodox Church were up there on the podium along with anybody who was somebody, including Slobodan Milosevic, the president of Serbia. This was the day for reiterating the conviction that the Serbs were a wronged but great people, whose day was yet to come.

It seemed as if those gathered imagined themselves as direct descendants of Prince Lazar's people, who had made the ultimate sacrifice defending against the Muslims and who, according to a nationalist narrative, had defended the rest of Christian Europe. The emotions of one were as if the emotions of the whole; the million were as if a single being, with unity of feeling and unity of purpose. The commemoration appeared to have succeeded in prompting solidarity among millions of Serbs everywhere—those present this day on the holy site and those tied into it from elsewhere—convincing them that they shared not only a common history but also a common destiny. On this day, 600 years after the battle that had triggered their decline, the Serbs were one proud people.

Unfortunately, accompanying the shared pride was a shared sense of victimization. For 600 years, the nationalist narrative seemed to suggest that the rest of Europe had remained ungrateful for the ultimate sacrifice. Were it not for the resistance put up by the Serbs of long ago, who knows how far deep into the continent the invaders from the east would have gone? Yet, there had been no acknowledgement of the bravery and sacrifice of so many of their forebears who had perished fighting for and defending Christianity.

For the Serb nationalists, the lost battle of long ago was the start of an endless series of events in which Serbia figured as the martyr. It provided the basis for a powerful narrative of heroic victimization and formed an interpretive framework in which the demands for autonomy by the Albanians came to be seen as acts of aggression against the Serbian nation—a perception that may have been justified, no doubt, by the demands and actions of the Albanian nationalists.

Increasingly, it seems, the Serbian nationalists conflated all the Muslims living in Kosovo with the invading Turks of long ago, and accused them of plotting to take over the lands that "rightfully" belonged to the Serbs. Slowly but surely, collective memory turned collective pride into collective paranoia, and demonization of the "other" took hold. Collective emotions intensified quickly and, encouraged by the political elite, resisting the "enemy" became a dominant preoccupation of a whole nation.

Of course, not all Serbians bought into the narrative that was shaping the collective opinion against non-Serbs. Sure, there was dissent against this rising tide of emotion, and anti-war groups openly opposed what seemed like an unstoppable march towards war. But the narrative of heroic victimization was so powerful and the mass of emotion so immense that the dissent was easily marginalized.

Within a few years, a series of brutal ethnic wars broke out in the region. Just two years after the million-strong gathering on Kosovo Polje, bitter ethnic wars broke out and the Serbs were accused of committing ethnic cleansing across the then Yugoslavia; some years later, in 1995, they were accused of having committed genocide against the Muslim population of a Bosnian town less than one hundred miles north.

The twin tragedies of ethnic cleansing and genocide were neither solo acts nor the responsibility of any one person; they were the result of the direct action of thousands and indirect support of millions. They were, in fact, collective actions inspired by intense collective feelings, subsuming millions of people in a mass of emotion and inciting them to behave as if they were one body carrying out a single act.

Obviously different from each other in any number of ways, millions nonetheless joined the growing chorus of feelings and emotions about themselves as Serbs, about their history and their destiny, and about others who were different. Basic distinctions between individuals, differences of thoughts and feelings, differences of personality, differences of social class, all appeared to have been overwhelmed by the surging emotion and smothered into sameness. Even organized opposition by the anti-war groups and dissent from those Serbs who opposed the nationalistic fervor could not contain the emotional mass that had built up to support the aspirations of a Greater Serbia.

Such was the context in which scores of normal people committed incredibly brutal deeds. Good citizens and patriots, kind in many other ways, seemed to have been drawn-in by the mass of emotion into killing thousands of their compatriots, including women and children, not for what they may have done but simply for being who they were.

Large-Scale Swings

The story of the Atkins Diet craze is vastly different from the one of violence in the former Yugoslavia. One is about butter, the other about guns. Despite the job losses and broken dreams, those affected by the economic consequences of the Atkins wave lived for another day; those on the wrong side of live ammunition are dead or live a life of trauma.

The diet craze appears to have been propelled by concerns about personal health, while the genocide and ethnic violence appear to have been motivated by anxieties about collective identity, anxieties that seemed to have been intensified by collective recollections of events long ago.

Yet, these differences are largely superficial. Underlying the surface appearances, the two episodes reveal several deep similarities. For instance, it is clear that the behavior of people in either case could not have been based on unalterable objective truths, simply because there were no such truths to be had.

Most dieters could not have quite grasped the science of dieting and the complexities of how different foods interact with the chemistry of the body. Those are nuanced scientific issues that remain mired in debates among specialists. Lay people have neither the training nor the time to make fully educated decisions about the food they consume, let alone resolve long-standing and technical debates about food science.

Similarly, the Battle of Kosovo had taken place six centuries earlier and the myth of Prince Lazar had been subject to numerous subsequent embellishments. By 1989, a hitherto disputed version had taken hold, one that was convenient for the anti-Muslim political sentiments then prevailing in the lands.

Both episodes were, in fact, based not on thorough analytical evaluation of incontrovertible evidence, not on rational calculus of the data at hand, but on stories that had been in circulation for years before they suddenly generated intense interest. Although the Atkins Diet had generated interest periodically after it first surfaced in 1972, the peak did not come until about thirty years later in 2004; the story of Serb sacrifice had evolved for six centuries before the Gazimestan gathering.

Both episodes also were characterized by rapid dissipation following a gradual buildup to the peak. The collective fascination with the Atkins Diet faded soon after the sudden death of Mr. Atkins; the Serbian emotion was violently discharged, for a time, through the wars that followed the commemoration at Gazimestan.

Both episodes followed a rough cycle of rapid buildup after a long period of gestation, and then a relatively quick dissolution following a peak of intensity. They were storms of sorts that for a period ensnared the attention of millions and then quickly passed through, leaving behind a swath of destruction and unsavory consequences.

Though extreme, the Atkins craze and the Balkan brutality are examples of behavior that is all too common in human affairs. The story of humanity is in fact a manifold story of behavioral storms. Large numbers of people on occasion become highly energized about a narrow set of issues, feeling and acting as if in unison, creating a mass of emotion that erupts seemingly unannounced. Having done its work, the mass then dissolves, leaving only dispersed individuals and residues of their collective action deposited as fresh layers on the scale of time, only to be followed by yet another surge of a different variety in another place.

Granted, aggregate patterns of human behavior are many and varied; their forms and their consequences vary greatly by situation. But perhaps there is something common, something fundamentally human that impels people to think alike and act alike, to produce similar behaviors that quickly aggregate into patterns that are real as life and clear as daylight.

Not only wars and insurgencies, but also consumer fads and fashion, public opinion and political sensibilities, religious beliefs and ethnic identities, these are only some of the large variety of intermingling collectivities from which we derive our own experiences of life.

What all this conveys is that our hopes and anxieties are often shaped strongly by the powerful undercurrents of social memories and narratives that run deep. Individual choice is not simply a matter of doing rational calculus with facts in the moment but more so it is a product of how facts are framed given the normative scripts or stories that run in the background, in our minds. These scripts shape what we pay attention to and what we do with the information to which we do pay attention.

Such scripts are particularly potent when they are or come to be shared by large numbers of people. Such sharing is inevitable, moreover, because of the simple fact that we are social beings, unavoidably immersed in a social milieu. Aware of it or not, the sources of our sameness with others around us are many and they act on us constantly, propping us up and hammering us into shape, exerting intense uniformity pressures, the squeeze of which we feel from the cradle to the grave.

What is the Investor to do?

We make investment choices in the context of deeply human experiences. It is easy to think that we are making choices based on objective criteria when, in fact, personal experiences and the social environment profoundly shape our thoughts and actions. Like the choices we make in other spheres, our investment choices too are shaped by the social memories that lurk beneath conscious awareness and by the potent social forces that shape us into who we are.

It should be no surprise that larger narratives strongly influence our investment decisions. That mortgage bonds were safe because homeowners would not default on by far their most significant investment was a script that fueled the housing bubble, the effects of which we are still feeling four years after it burst. That stocks always go up in the long-run is another script that often informs investors as they formulate their investment portfolios. That broad diversification across asset classes is the best way to reduce risk is yet another widely shared script that shapes investment choices among both professional and lay investors alike.

The world of investments is, in other words, full of scripts that enable us to take things for granted and pay selective attention to data that are agreeable with those scripts. The way we make investment decisions is, in essence, not very different from the way choices were made by those who were caught up in the Atkins diet craze or the rhetoric of the Serbian nationalists.

Investing, in essence, is subject to pressures of which we may be only dimly aware. It can be, as it often is, a struggle to make good choices. Examining those struggles, the conflict between exertions of independent analysis and pressures to imitate, is an important part of understanding our behavior and the powerful role they play in our investment decisions.

In order to learn how to invest well, therefore, we must acquire sharp insights into our inner lives. We must acknowledge, among other things, that we are emotional beings and that we are products of the many overlapping social groups that influence how we think and how we make choices.

For investors, the mass phenomena of interest are those characterized by heightened emotion, where deliberate individual action is overwhelmed by the pressures built into the situation. It is not simply that we as individuals make mistakes in our decisions; more important is the fact that individual errors often become highly correlated to produce large-scale moves and errors.

The Serbs' emotion about their history and their future, or the dieters' feelings with regards to their personal health, these were the key ingredients that transformed a collection of everyday people into an active mass that erupted onto the scene with notable impact. Being all too human, investors are prone to similar periodic bouts of euphoria or panic when emotions of fear and greed overwhelm sound analysis.

There are, of course, many theories as to why people behave the way they do when in large numbers. There are theories that invoke our biological heritage that puts emotion at the center of our very being. There are theories that point to our fundamentally social nature and the influence that those around us exert on us. There are theories that insist that the computational power of the human brain is limited, and so, rather than try to objectively evaluate everything, we find it convenient to just go along with what others may be doing. There are also theories that say that it is rational for people to join the herd, lest they be trampled by it.

Whatever the theory, it is clear that investors, like people in many other endeavors, have an innate and very human tendency to herd. Such tendency is at least partly responsible for the speculative bubbles and large scale swings in prices that we see periodically in the stock markets.

What is a savvy investor to do with this knowledge? How do we incorporate this knowledge to become better investors?

In later chapters, I will develop a decision-making framework and associated techniques with which to guard against and perhaps even take advantage of these kinds of built-in human tendencies. But first, we need to understand how the inclination of people to herd and, by implication, of investors to get caught up in speculative manias, has been understood through history and how this understanding has been used sometimes to manipulate the masses into doing things against their own interests.

3

The Dark Arts

———

It is bad enough that we are so prone to making errors in judgment and so very vulnerable to holding all variety of faulty opinions and beliefs; it is worse that our built-in biases open us up to being manipulated. The big secret of modern societies is that our habits and ways of thinking can be used to influence *what* we believe and to shape which products and services we consume, what choices we make in local and national elections, which causes we choose to support and oppose, and where we look to invest. But what is perhaps most disturbing is that knowledge about our systematic biases and psychological vulnerabilities is sometimes used to instigate behaviors that are against our very own interests.

Years upon years of thinking about human reasoning and mental processes has helped build powerful insights into how to influence people *en masse* so as to modify their thinking, their choices, and their behaviors. These insights have gradually evolved into practices that are now routinely used to work our common biases and collective errors to someone else's advantage, so much so that we sometimes undermine our own interests.

Whether it is to sell a product or an idea, whether to have us vote in a particular way, or to join one cause or oppose another, armies of influence peddlers of all varieties are ready to persuade us into doing something we barely understand at the conscious level, or worse, only think we understand. Because these mass-persuasion tactics rely on effective manipulation of psychological factors that reside below the level of awareness, I call them the dark arts.

Below I review the history of how the techniques of mass-suasion came into being and how they have been practiced over the decades up into our own times. By understanding how we are persuaded into doing one thing or the other, by understanding how the dark arts are practiced upon us, we will be better prepared for the later chapters in which I develop methods to defend against them in the arena of investing.

Note that the practice of the dark arts is through the medium of language and symbols, through the clever use of words and images to focus attention on some issues over others, and then integrating the message with the natural subconscious tendencies of the target. But we are getting ahead of ourselves. Let us start in the beginning.

Ancient Foundations of the Dark Arts

Many ancient civilizations, such as those in Mesopotamia and Egypt, valued skill with words or verbal artistry; the Homeric myths, as is well known, attest to the high regard in which shrewd language and rhetoric were held in pre-classical Greece.

But, like many other things, the formal development of the art of persuasion did not quite begin until classical Athens, and especially around the time Plato put his stylus to the wax-coated tablet. In his wide-ranging writings, Plato explores, among other things, the differences between substance and form and between seeking truth and avoiding falsity. In one of his works, *Gorgias,* Plato sets up a dialogue in which he pits Socrates against a sophist named Gorgias to explore the difference between truth and mere belief. Sophists were the wandering intellectuals of the period, and they were much in demand as teachers because of their skill in making compelling arguments irrespective of the facts at hand. Plato was both distrustful and contemptuous of the sophists, as he saw them conjuring up language to distort truth and to prove or disprove whatever caught their fancy.

Among the pre-eminent sophists of his time, Gorgias was a pioneer in the art of rhetoric and manipulating public opinion through persuasion. He considered rhetoric as a performance art that included both a play on words and the sounds or the manner in which carefully chosen words were delivered.

Like other sophists, Gorgias recognized the power of rhetoric to move people into pursuing any course of action. As such, he argued, rhetoric was a supreme art of persuasion and it enabled mastery over others.

Sophists seemed to believe that there was no absolute Truth, only what one made of the facts at hand. Both sides of an issue needed to be fully argued, in their view, to understand the pros and cons, to discover the best course of action. For this, they were seen as obstructionist and as using clever rhetoric to muddy the facts and lead people away from Truth. They were eventually much maligned, especially through the writings of Plato and Aristotle, and were even accused of lacking morality. Over time, sophistry acquired a derogatory meaning and it is now universally equated with trick argumentation to accomplish unpalatable ends.

At the time, though, the sophists were much in demand as teachers, and they earned their livelihood by instructing students on how to use words to produce desired emotions and effects in others. In a democratic and litigious society that was then Athens, skills of persuasion were highly sought after by elites, statesmen, and orators (demagogues), and they were widely used in debates and jury trials.

As teachers for hire, the sophists fine-tuned the techniques of oral persuasion and gave their disciples general arguments that could be adapted to a variety of purposes. For instance, a common technique of persuasion that the sophists taught to demagogues was to flatter the audience in order to gain their favor. Also in the training were techniques such as modulation of voice and its projection, humor, and even-balanced use of body and gesture to accompany carefully chosen words and argumentation. The emphasis was not only on logic and pure reasoning but much more on invoking emotions such as anger and fear, pride and pity, as the occasion demanded.

Opposed to the falsely persuasive powers of rhetoric, Plato was afraid the sophists were teaching their knowledge of the passions and pleasures and their techniques of manipulation. That, to him, was immensely dangerous, as masses were easily led and prone to believe in skillfully made but false arguments. Moreover, as masters at twisting logic to suit their purpose, the sophists appeared to have no moral compass. So, to Plato, the sophists were tricksters and mere opinion shufflers; they taught for pay and were, therefore, corruptible. More importantly, by selling their tricks of manipulation, the sophists hurt the reputation of true philosophers.

In modern terms, sophists can be seen as viewing knowledge as relativistic or socially constructed and knowledge creation as requiring flexibility of thought and social discourse. In that sense, they anticipated some of the more advanced social thought of our own times. But back in their times, the newly found fascination with the search for absolutes lowered tolerance for word play and dissent against the established order, so that little by little the sophists faded from the scene. Soon after the Peloponnesian War, perhaps as a result of nationalistic feelings and the need for social solidarity, most of the sophists were put out of business and their writings burned.

Although despised, the sophists had, however, set the stage for later developments in rhetoric. Aristotle was to formalize the art of persuasion in his *Rhetoric*, in which he noted three essential elements of effective persuasion: *ethos*, indicating credibility of the source; *pathos*, indicating psychology and emotion of the audience, and *logos*, indicating visible logic and reasoning in the arguments. In other words, even though personal credibility and logic were important, Aristotle insisted that the emotions of those in the audience also counted. He went on to describe emotions in detail and encouraged the persuader to understand how to stimulate desired emotions in the other person. Like Plato, Aristotle seems to have understood the powerful effect that a good speaker could have on the emotions of the audiences.

What the Greeks started, the Romans built on. Especially well known for advancing the techniques of rhetoric is Cicero, the orator and lawyer who is still very much present in high school curricula across the country. Well versed in Plato, Aristotle, and other classical Greeks, Cicero developed an expansive style that he freely practiced in courts, in the senate, at funerals, and on other public occasions. He relied not only on *logos* or pure reason, but on a range of formal techniques to appeal to the *pathos*, the emotions of his audience. Storytelling, humor, digression, and imagery, among other things, were in his arsenal when he stepped in front of an audience. He deftly used praise and blame in his speeches, and generally brought the art of persuading and dissuading to new heights.

A more lasting contribution came later from Rome in the works of Quintilian, also a lawyer, who became the first officially funded teacher of rhetoric.

Setting up an institute to train orators, he formalized rhetoric in education and emphasized that his students learn the doctrines and practices of earlier influential rhetoricians. The program of study included the staged process for learning to become an accomplished orator. His emphasis was not necessarily on politics and demagoguery but on developing ethical and virtuous orators who would serve the public good.

Even so, the techniques of rhetoric were spreading through Rome and were finding their way into the broader culture, social critique, and entertainment. Reminiscent of Plato's position, this latter development was seen by purists, such as Quintilian, as an unfortunate victory of style over substance, and as the second coming of the sophists.

The Middle Years

Formal study of rhetoric faded into the background for centuries after the breakup of the Roman Empire, yielding to more formalistic training with emphasis on repetition and rote learning. Yet, remnants of old style rhetoric remained in letter writing and quickly found expression in sermons. Considered a pagan art, rhetoric was nevertheless developed by the likes of St. Augustine in the service of spreading Christianity. If it could be applied with ease and effect to plead right or wrong, the thinking went, then why not apply it for a just cause such as that of Christianity? Rhetoric in sermons became commonplace and, justified by the righteousness of the cause, formalized over time into *homiletics*.

It was not until the early sixteenth century that rhetoric began to regain prominence, beginning with the works of a Dutch Catholic priest, Erasmus, and his friend, Juan Luis Vives, a Spaniard living in England. Along with other contributors in that century, they further developed the art and continued to emphasize the connection between words and emotion.

By the end of the seventeenth century, formal study of rhetoric was firmly established in England and a clear shift had taken place from Greek and Latin scholastic traditions to vernacular English. There was a movement to let go of the eloquence and amplifications in favor of more straightforward words and sentence structures. Fine speaking was a disease, John Dryden said, and needed to make way for a simple and direct style that took account of the occasion, the subject, and the audience. These efforts to separate style from substance, although successful, curtailed the study and teaching of rhetoric.

The rise of democratic institutions in the 18th and 19th centuries spurred a revival of rhetoric in education. The increasing importance of language and persuasion were instrumental in this revival; knowledge gained over the previous centuries provided a good deal of ammunition that could be subjected to serious study using the emerging methods of scholarship.

By the twentieth century, as in classical Athens and Rome, rhetoric was once again indispensable to liberal education in Western Europe and the United States. Today, in the second decade of the twenty-first century, rhetoric is a well-developed field of study and well ensconced in high school curricula and in communications departments in most major colleges and universities. Scholars engage in discourse to develop new techniques and students take courses that apply not only newer concepts but also trace the historical development of rhetorical studies all the way back to the ancient origins.

Increasingly of interest both in the classroom and outside is the role that cultural symbols and images play in persuasion. Speeches, essays, and poetry aside, the modern world is now full of persuasive messages that are packaged with a full complement of audio and visual aids. Far from the world of Plato and Aristotle, ours is a world ripe with rhetoric in its varied forms, and through all possible mediums.

Wherever there is a need to persuade the public or segments of the public, people trained in rhetorical techniques are at work in ever larger numbers. Lobbying firms, law firms, public relations firms and corporations, newspapers and magazines, radio and television, Internet, marketing and advertising agencies—these are some of the most eager employers of those who have the training and sensitivity for rhetoric.

The Vulnerable Investor

Clearly, Madison Avenue is more than just a street in New York. It is, in principle, an intellectual home for the vast number of professionals in advertising and public relations everywhere. It is associated with the art of mass persuasion, with the creation and delivery of messages that are designed to influence beliefs and generate action. Whether those messages have substance or not, form and presentation are critically important, as they have always been.

Facilitated by deeply institutionalized knowledge of rhetoric, the art of persuasion is well entrenched in all aspects of life in modern societies. Emotion remains a key lever in the design of persuasive or dissuasive messages.

The rapid rise of financial news media in the last few decades has brought Madison Avenue lock, stock, and barrel into the world of finance. Print, radio, television, and now the Internet and social media are common channels though which much information, news, and opinion are packaged and delivered to the masses of retail investors; advisor networks, offices, and customer support centers are geared to deliver advice and financial products in a more personal fashion. All these create opportunities for potential investors to access large amounts of relevant and useful information that would have remained mostly inaccessible only, say, two decades ago.

Yet, with the modern means of delivering vast quantities of information and opinion come opportunities for those skilled at constructing clever persuasive messages. As such, investors remain vulnerable to manipulation on a large scale and to make choices that are a product of questionable influences rather than objective analysis of facts.

So, next, let's turn to understanding how the techniques of mass persuasion, or the dark arts as I have called them, have developed over the past hundred or so years. An understanding of how these ideas and techniques have evolved in recent history will show how and perhaps why investors are vulnerable to acting against their own interests.

4

Purveyors of the Dark Arts

————

Even as the resurgence of interest in rhetoric has intensified and gained momentum in recent centuries and especially in the last few decades, the emphasis appears to have remained mostly on the rhetorician, or on the theory and practice of making persuasive arguments. The analysis of the intended audiences has always been an important part of rhetoric studies, but practical insights into mass audiences and how to manipulate them came from altogether different sources. Such thinking is relatively more recent, originating in late nineteenth century France and then quickly making its way across Europe and into the United States.

In this chapter, I tell the story of mass psychology through reviews of three seminal books on the subject. Separated by geography and time, and operating independently of each other, the authors of these three books popularized the theories and practices of mass persuasion. Their influence is very much with us today and it behooves students of investing to understand what these writers made visible through their labors.

The Psychology of Peoples

The nineteenth century was one of much turmoil in Europe in general and in France in particular. After the bloody revolution of 1789 and the dark days following it, the country fell under Napoleon and entered into a series of bloody and ultimately disastrous wars with the European neighbors. When Napoleon was finally removed from power in 1815, things settled down for a few years but massive upheavals returned with the revolutions of 1830 and 1848, followed by a particularly devastating war with Germany in 1870 and then a bloody civil war the following year. Also starting in the mid-century, the industrial revolution brought millions of people from the countryside into Paris and other big cities, making the streets fertile grounds for all nature of disturbances.

In this context of recurring revolutions and wars, and with a growing and an increasingly assertive industrial proletariat, much debate arose about the nature of the masses. There was a sense of urgency to try to understand why men behaved so badly when in large numbers, and to see if any natural laws that governed mass behavior could be found.

Starting in about the early 1870s, therefore, several different arguments began to emerge about the psychological characteristics of humanity, especially of human aggregates such as groups and crowds. An especially important insight developed from the increasing influence of Darwin's first book, published in 1859 and translated into French in 1860.

Darwin's theory of evolution had connected humanity to the animal kingdom and led to the belief that underneath the modern human were hundreds of millions of years of biological evolution. Following *On the Origin of Species*, man was now clearly seen as a product of deep time, a product that was made in layers such that the most primordial core was overlaid with the more recent in succession up to modern times.

Very soon after the publication of Darwin's book, the psycho-biological view of humanity gained rapid currency. There was wide agreement that powerful psychological and biological forces governed human behavior. In fact, a section of the French intelligentsia became convinced that while behavior could be modified somewhat with strong discipline, long education, and selective breeding, the animal was still at the core of man. Civilization, according to this view, was but a fragile and thin veneer, barely containing the strong primordial impulses.[46]

This jaundiced view of mankind was put forth and used to explain social upheavals of the previous 100 years. Many intellectuals of the period argued that large human aggregates, or crowds, were even more dangerous than individuals because they multiplied the animal impulses. Any collection of individuals was, in other words, a powerful destructive force. Moreover, the argument went, crowds could be, as they often were, manipulated by ill-intentioned demagogues and enemies of the state. Reminiscent of how the classical Romans saw them, crowds were seen as beasts that if left unchecked could destroy everything in their path, including the very institutions that made civilized social life possible.

Thus began the search for understanding how crowds could be controlled, the endeavor spearheaded by the hope that, perhaps, control was possible because of what was thought to be the susceptibility of people to manipulation by skilled rhetoricians and other students of human behavior. This was the origin of crowd theory that became hugely popular during the last two decades of the nineteenth century.

The most popular rendering of the above view was by Gustave Le Bon, the French writer who used this theme to produce four international bestsellers in just eight years from 1894 to 1902. Le Bon was strongly ideological and vehemently opposed to the increasing tide of socialism sweeping through France at the time. He was (and remains) highly controversial, and he is rightly accused of being an elitist and a bigot because of his open contempt for women and minorities, and anybody opposed to the established social hierarchy.

Still, Le Bon had good instincts as a writer. He popularized the idea that masses of people could be manipulated, and that their manipulation by the ruling class was necessary for social order and survival of the state.

Along with many of his compatriots, Le Bon wrote that because of savagery hidden deep within him, man could not be rational. Volition and conscious choice could be no match for animal passions. Not rational thought but instinctual life, or the urges and feelings from below, were fundamental to the human condition; they governed daily existence. Without natural psychological guideposts and driven largely by instinct and habit, Le Bon agreed with the conservative French historian Hippolyte Taine, man is essentially an irrational creature, prone to mental imbalance and hallucinations.

The animal nature of man, the argument went, was mostly restrained by social controls in everyday life. But, under special situations, such as when people gathered in a crowd, the beastly impulses were let loose and men became mad. The social pressures of belonging to a group made the civilized individual a dumb animal; careful, deliberate, conscious thought went out the door and animal cravings dominated behavior. That is why, Le Bon argued, crowds were extremely dangerous to social stability and their periodic rampages inevitably pushed civilization down a couple of pegs back into the animal kingdom.

It was not simply that each individual had an animal core; it was that any gathering shook that animal into action. That, to Le Bon, was the reason why crowds were basically irrational and prone to collective hallucinations, and, therefore, easy to manipulate. The following, in brief, are Le Bon's prescriptions for manipulating crowds or any large aggregation of people, whether physically assembled or only mentally connected:

Men, according to Le Bon, are dominated by a diverse jumble of unconscious aspirations of which they are only dimly aware. Such aspirations are touched by fleeting images of various kinds but remain elusive and outside the grasp of consciousness. And therein lies the mysterious power of words, which when carefully used can evoke and crystallize grandiose images that flow in and out of the minds of men. These forever-passing images produce anxiety from which people seek relief by holding onto whatever beliefs are easily accessible.

The need to believe is so strong in people that, Le Bon wrote, "Were it possible to induce the masses to adopt atheism, this belief would exhibit all the intolerant ardor of a religious sentiment, and in its exterior forms would soon become a cult."[47] The object of sentiments may change, but the people need to believe and to be fascinated.

Therein rests the psychological basis for manipulating crowds.

Any sort of synthesis of the fleeting jumble of images and the hope of their realization is what gives the demagogue power over people. When in a crowd, Le Bon wrote, men

—must have their illusions at all cost, they turn instinctively, as the insect seeks the light, to the rhetoricians who accord them what they want...[T]he masses have never thirsted after truth. They turn aside from evidence that is not to their taste, preferring to deify error, if error seduce them. Whoever can supply them with illusion is easily their master; whoever attempts to destroy their illusion is always their victim.

In essence, Le Bon argued that the leader of a crowd instinctively relates to the unconscious aspirations of his fellows. He is himself hypnotized by a single dominant idea, becomes its apostle, preaching it to those who would listen, speaking to their aspirations, helping them imagine its realization. Strong conviction, not reasoning, is his strength and any opposition or contempt only makes his cause greater, slowly but surely leading him to exercise despotic control over the masses. For the qualifications of such leaders, Le Bon had choice words: men of action, not gifted with foresight; morbidly nervous, excitable, half-deranged, bordering on madness; immune to contempt and persecution; sans instinct for self-preservation; seeking martyrdom.

Persuasion, Le Bon argued, is not to be achieved by speaking to the intelligence, as the crowd has no reasoning power. Persuasion is more effectively achieved by invoking sharp images and a shrewd choice of words, Le Bon wrote, just as—in Shakespeare's rendering—Mark Antony had roused the crowd by cunningly reading aloud the will of Caesar and pointing to his corpse.

In terms of the actual techniques of persuasion, Le Bon argued that stirring up an already expectant crowd requires imagery and suggestion by a prestigious person. What the crowd needs is affirmation of vaguely felt aspirations, for someone to give form to formless ideas and to stabilize those unconsciously fleeting images that torture the minds of men. Affirmation by itself is not enough, however, as any mildly tangible images just beginning to take root are liable to be washed away by the torrent of chaotic and unformed notions. Affirmation needs to be followed up with repetition in rapid succession. He explained,

The repeated statement is embedded in the long run in those profound regions of our unconscious selves in which the motives of our actions are forged...[W]hen an affirmation has been sufficiently repeated and there is unanimity in its repetition—as has occurred in the case of certain famous financial undertakings rich enough to purchase every assistance—what is called a current of opinion is formed and the powerful mechanism of contagion intervenes.

Once affirmation and repetition give the idea some traction among those most susceptible, it spreads through contagion to rest of the crowd, gaining in strength with the increase in the number of converts. He wrote, "Ideas, sentiments, emotions, and beliefs possess in crowds a contagious power as intense as that of microbes." It is not reason that captures the attention of the crowds, Le Bon explained, it is the subtle and blunt messaging to the unconscious that is the *modus operandi* of leaders; flattery of the base instincts arouse the faith of the masses. He wrote,

> Orators who know how to make impression upon [crowds] always appeal in consequence to their sentiments and never to their reason. The laws of logic have no action on crowds.

> Logical minds, accustomed to be convinced by a chain of somewhat close reasoning, cannot avoid having recourse to this mode of persuasion when addressing crowds, and the inability of their arguments always surprises them.

In fewer than 100 pages of his short book, *The Crowd*, Le Bon had speculated at length on the psychology of the masses and presented plausible arguments as to why they were susceptible to manipulation. More importantly, he outlined how leaders could manipulate the masses.

Le Bon was extremely successful as a writer, with a knack for simplifying and popularizing complex ideas. Although he was despised as a reactionary by progressives and intellectuals, his writings provoked intense debate in academic circles then and as they do now. Le Bon was a hero to the conservatives, and he was much in demand by political figures wanting to learn his theories for their own advantage. Eager followers applied his ideas in business; for a time up to World War II, his thinking also found its way deep into the battlefield doctrines of both the French and American militaries.[48]

Le Bon reinforced the power of rhetoric in persuading the masses, especially those that were already predisposed to being persuaded. Men are governed by instinct rather than intellect, he argued, and their unconscious sentiments overpower the ability to reason.

Le Bon died in 1931, leaving behind a strong influence. Modern thinkers reject many of his assertions, as they were indeed colored by bigotry. Still, he had planted the seed of an idea that influenced a large number of political figures and intellectuals in his own time. More importantly, his ideas and ways of thinking found their way into the writings of other influential people of the twentieth century. One such person was Ed Bernays.

Engineering Consent

Ed Bernays came to Le Bon's writings through those of his uncle, Sigmund Freud. Already a prominent figure by the time he wrote *Group Psychology and the Analysis of the Ego* in 1922, Freud had accepted Le Bon's premise that people become less intelligent and less rational when they are part of any human aggregate, whether committees, juries, assemblies, or crowds.

Yet, it was Bernays who carried many of Le Bon's ideas into politics and business in the United States; he was the one to coin the term *public relations* and was instrumental in developing the field through the middle part of twentieth century. He took many of Le Bon's prescriptions indirectly from the theories of his uncle, and made manipulation of the masses into a highly successful art form that is to this day widely practiced and, in fact, now deeply institutionalized in many parts of the world.

Bernays wrote several books on public opinion, but ones that made him famous and captured his basic thinking were *Crystallizing Public Opinion* (1923) and *Propaganda* (1928), both early in his career and only a few years after Freud published *Group Psychology*, in which Le Bon features prominently. As was Freud, Bernays is respectful of Le Bon and agrees that the group, large or small, has "mental characteristics distinct from those of the individual, and is motivated by impulses and emotions which cannot be explained on the basis of what we know of individual psychology."[49]

Bernays took the art of rhetoric to a completely new level. In his book, *Propaganda*, he paraphrased Le Bon and wrote:

The group mind does not *think* in the strict sense of the word. In place of thoughts it has impulses, habits and emotions. In making up its mind its first impulse is usually to follow the example of a trusted leader. This is one of the most firmly established principles of mass psychology. It operates in establishing the rising or diminishing prestige of a summer resort, in causing a run on a bank, or a panic on the stock exchange, in creating a best seller, or a box-office success.

But when the example of the leader is not at hand and the herd must think for itself, *it* does so by means of clichés, pat words or images which stand for a whole group of ideas or experiences.

In writing *Propaganda*, Bernays noted the immense success of the techniques for mass manipulation, such as that of the Committee on Public Information (CPI) set up by the Wilson Administration to gain support for America's entry into the World War I. Much later, Bernays was to acknowledge that his early work had helped the Nazis build up their propaganda machinery. To his mind, the term "propaganda" was damaged by the negative associations with the Nazis. He therefore introduced the term "Public Relations" and so gave birth to a modern profession that is well-respected even as it continues the very old practices of using clever rhetoric to persuade the masses.

Bernays developed such new techniques as focus groups to uncover the habits that were developing among people. He pioneered product placement, deftly placing the products of his clients in news stories and in movies. He was among the first to use tie-ins, the first to advertise the product simultaneously in multiple channels such as radio, magazines, television, and department stores. Playing on the idea of the need of the masses to look for a strong leader, he pioneered the practice of celebrity endorsements and fake authority such as a spokesperson in the garb of a doctor and insinuating that "research has shown" the value of a product.

Among the most famous of Bernays' campaigns was to make public smoking acceptable for women. That was a time when smoking by women was a cultural taboo—there was a well-reported incident in 1922, when a woman was arrested for lighting up on the streets of New York. On hire by the American Tobacco Company, Bernays studied the issue and uncovered deep aspirations for liberty as well as strong social undertones that supported more rights for women and immigrants

In order to execute the project, Bernays deftly combined the cultural undertones and aspirations into the 1929 Easter Parade, during which a group of debutantes marched down Fifth Avenue lighting up Lucky Strikes. He had, of course, already alerted the media to make sure that the event received wide coverage. The campaign was immensely successful, as in one fell swoop he broke down an age-old taboo against women smoking in public. In effect, he had leveraged a growing social movement and carefully inserted powerful cultural symbols in his persuasive message. He had choreographed social change.

Labeled *Torches of Freedom*, the campaign is a classic in the annals of mass persuasion, but it was hardly the only one in which the master manipulator applied the ideas of Le Bon and others to have his way with the masses. Over a career spanning from 1919 to about 1963, Bernays had numerous successful campaigns for big-name corporate clients, such as General Electric, but also for non-profit institutions, such as the National Association for the Advancement of Colored People (NAACP), and even for President Calvin Coolidge to help uplift his dour image among the electorate. To his credit, once the harmful effects of tobacco became clear, Bernays worked to support the anti-smoking campaigns.

But perhaps his most important client was Bernays himself. He used all the tricks of the trade to be seen as "America's No. 1 Publicist." The constant reference to his uncle Freud, self-presentation as a psychoanalyst to troubled corporations, and a steady stream of books and articles, all appeared to be coordinated to establish himself as a credible spokesperson in the minds of his various audiences.

The trademark Bernays campaign was one in which he would leverage existing cultural beliefs or ongoing social movements, in which specific issues as well as symbols were already on the minds of people, widely shared and strongly believed. Things like equality, anti-discrimination, liberty, equal rights, communism, and dictatorship were the resident ideas that he invoked in carefully crafted messages.

The key was not that such ideas were universals, as ideals and aspirations are always in flux; rather, Bernays uncovered those undercurrents through focus groups and with a keen personal understanding of what was happening in his world at the time. Then he orchestrated his discoveries in his messages, using images and language that could be easily understood by his target audiences.

There were no quick fixes in the methods used by Bernays. He was systematic; he took his time doing the research and assembling facts and opinions, always exploring the underlying currents of widely shared beliefs of the moment. The final message was artfully constructed and its delivery was a culmination of much work; it was a production. Yet, the effect on the audience was always derived from invoking deep emotion. Logic could be seen in hindsight, but logic was always secondary to and in the service of emotion. Clearly, Bernays was more Gorgias than Plato.

Yet, Bernays had turned mass-suasion into an art form and, in the process, he spawned a whole new industry that we know today as public relations.

The Hidden Persuaders

By the time Bernays was easing himself out of his active career in the early 1960s, the practice of mass-suasion was gaining momentum and was in many ways already entrenched in some quarters. The methods he had so effectively pioneered and used were now widely applied in politics, business, and elsewhere. The print and the airwaves and the highways were full of attempts to have people buy this way and vote that way. The life of an average American was already under constant bombardment, with appeals for everything under the sun, often loudly but also more softly and in insistent whispers.

All this was not lost on the targets of these newly evolving practices of mass-suasion. An air of cynicism had developed among the people, and it was often expressed in books and articles. People sensed they were being sold to and they generally took the sales pitches for what they were worth, the usual innuendo, half-truths, and outright lies. That America was a consumer culture was simply accepted, and trying to have people part with their money for this thing or that was just part of the setup, with its usual pros and cons. After all, the targets of advertisers and salesmen were in some cases themselves practitioners of those crafts. Still, there was an underlying anxiety that there was more to it than what met the eye.

The most impactful of the critical analyses of the period was a book-length exposé published by Vance Packard in 1957. Titled *The Hidden Persuaders*, the book critically reviewed the practices of the advertising industry; it exposed in a somewhat wild-eyed, scandalous way how the social sciences were being applied to hoodwink people. He even went so far as to suggest that the advertising industry treated consumers and voters like "Pavlov's conditioned dog." In making his point, Packard obviously exaggerated some of his claims, especially in making it seem as though the methods he criticized worked perfectly.

In spite of some shortcomings by academic standards, and vehement criticisms by the champions of the advertising industry, *The Hidden Persuaders* made a strong impact on the public. It was the most commercially successful of the many books that Packard wrote in a span of about forty years. There were three million copies reported to be in print by 1975 and, for those interested in the art of mass-suasion, it remains an indispensable read to this day.

The reason for the success of the book lies, of course, in the fact that there was much uncomfortable truth in it. People had begun to feel that they were being scammed by the ever more creative pitches; Packard exposed some of the methods by which those pitches were being developed. He begins by telling the reader that the book was,

> —about the large-scale efforts being made, often with impressive success, to channel unthinking habits, our purchasing decisions, and our thought processes by the use of insights gleaned from psychiatry and the social sciences. Typically these efforts take place beneath our level of awareness; so that the appeals which move us are often, in a sense, 'hidden'.

Packard reports that the techniques of commercial mass-suasion had been in practice since the 1930s, and that they were based largely on Freudian psychoanalysis. Interchangeably calling it the *Depth Approach* or *Motivational Research*, he gave numerous examples of what marketers and advertisers were doing to induce beliefs and change behavior so that people would buy the goods as they were told. Packard wrote:

The use of mass psychoanalysis to guide campaigns of persuasion has become the basis of a multimillion-dollar industry. Professional persuaders have seized upon it in their groping for more effective ways to sell us their wares—whether products, ideas, attitudes, candidates, goals, or states of mind.

Many of the manipulators, indoctrinators, thought-controllers, persuaders, and probers as he variously called them, were "systematically feeling out our hidden weaknesses and frailties in the hope that they can more efficiently influence our behavior." The psychiatric probing techniques were being used on little girls, on graduates, on administrative personnel, and on anyone who needed to be sold to. Nothing was sacred and off-limits, he lamented.

And what did these probers think of those that they were probing? Did they think that Americans were thoughtful and sensible, rational individualists? Not at all! Packard noted:

Typically they see us as bundles of daydreams, misty hidden yearnings, guilt complexes, irrational emotional blockages. We are image lovers given to impulsive and compulsive acts. We annoy them with our seemingly senseless quirks, but we please them with our growing docility in responding to their manipulation of symbols that stir us to action. They have found the supporting evidence for this view persuasive enough to encourage them to turn to depth channels on a large scale in their efforts to influence our behavior.

What is more, Packard reported that the persuaders were learning their tricks "by sitting at the feet of psychiatrists and social scientists." Researchers from such well-known universities as California, Chicago, Columbia, Connecticut, Harvard, Indiana, Michigan, New York, and Virginia were eagerly working with the people-manipulators, or setting up their own private consulting practices. He had reasons to be concerned. The *American Psychological Association* had only recently (1953) published its first edition of the *Ethical Standards of Psychologists*; the monitoring of personnel in the field was still in its infancy, and the appropriate codes of conduct were neither fully developed or uniformly enforced.

There were those in the industry, however, who were skeptical about Packard's account of the new methods of persuasion. The critics argued that the depth approach was a pseudo-science, and that the motivational researchers were overselling themselves to Madison Avenue and, perhaps, exploiting the exploiters.

Even the most enthusiastic practitioner, Vienna-born Dr. Ernest Dichter, was cautious. He agreed with the critics that explaining why people made the decisions they did was extremely difficult. There was open acknowledgement that both rational and irrational factors were important in the decision process.

Yet, the use of motivational research continued to grow unabated. The main comeback of its proponents was that this new method of psycho-persuasion was still experimental. The pull of the hidden persuaders was just great. The very perception that the depth approach helped corporations sell their products and services was validation enough. That people seemed to respond to subtle manipulations was indicative of the usefulness of probing techniques. In spite of the mysteries surrounding it, there was wide agreement among both supporters and detractors that probing into the psyche of the masses was an approach that had much potential and staying power.

Packard was troubled by the use of social science to invade the privacy of peoples' minds. Of the psycho-suaders, he wrote:

They are mostly decent, likable people, products of our relentlessly progressive era. Most of them want to control us just a little bit, in order to sell us some product we may find useful or disseminate with us a viewpoint that may be entirely worthy.

But when you are manipulating, where do you stop? Who is to fix the point at which manipulative attempts become socially undesirable?

The soul searching notwithstanding, Packard had brought to light the techniques first noted by Le Bon and then, through Freud and Bernays, had found their way deep into the political and commercial culture. To an average person, what Packard had to say validated the suspicion that there was more to advertising than met the eye; it was a frightening thought that the seemingly free choices were not free after all.

Packard did, however, exaggerate his case. He implied that the persuasive techniques were so effective that they determined our behavior; that we are indeed like Pavlov's conditioned dog and respond to persuaders like puppets to the puppeteer. Clearly, that is not the case. Persuasion then was an art and it remains so now, with a good deal of variability in how different people respond to the machinations of clever persuaders.

Ironically, in conveying his message, Packard used the same techniques he had exposed. He used many concrete examples to encourage imagery of vicious corporate interests manipulating the unsuspecting masses. He built on peoples' deep anxieties that advertisers and marketers were using sophisticated techniques of mind control to deceive and accomplish their commercial ends.

And he used repetition, lots of it. For instance, in just about 200 sparsely-populated pages of his book, Packard used the word *manipulation,* or a variant, more than 177 times. Similarly, he made very liberal use of loaded words such as *motivation* (130), *deep* (48), *depth* (162), and *probe* (50). In addition, perhaps to gain credibility, the then famous Viennese psychologist, *Dr. Dichter,* is inserted more than ninety times, and another commercial psychologist selling his wares to corporations, *Dr. Cheskin,* shows up twenty-seven times. Similarly, Packard uses the word *university* or *professor* about forty-five times, and variants of the words *anthropology, sociology,* and *psychology* more than 200 times.

Packard was, of course, only the latest in a long line of thinkers who had written about mass manipulation. As we have seen, Le Bon and Bernays had already written extensively about it as an art form and developed it in the spheres of politics and business. But whereas the previous writers had mostly wanted to impress the social elites to help them accomplish their political and commercial goals, Packard's wild-eyed exposé opened up the techniques for consumption by the masses. Now the masses knew how they were being manipulated.

Even more interestingly, Packard also showed how deeply institutionalized the techniques of mass manipulation had become in the commercial culture of the United States. It was no longer just a few elites manipulating the ignorant masses; a broad swath of society, including professionals and academics, were now engaged in practicing the art and refining it further for better effect.

Well-developed though the art of mass persuasion (or manipulation) was by the time Packard wrote his best-seller, it was to evolve into a multi-faceted and much more formidable weapon in the arsenal of those who understood its true potential.

Clearly, like Le Bon and Bernays before him, Packard had made astute empirical observations that masses of people were highly susceptible to being swayed or mislead. Yet, also like them, he did not have a clear understanding of *why* we, as humans, were so inclined to be pulled into acting and behaving as if part of a larger crowd, even when such a crowd is invisible and we may not quite see ourselves as belonging to one. Several decades after Packard wrote, however, we now have a much better understanding of how mass-suasion works and how masses of people are swayed or manipulated. Insights from modern social sciences—especially social psychology—have shed much light on perceptions, personality, and identity as the basis for mass phenomenon. We will not go here into the social theories that specifically apply to mass phenomenon, but suffice it to say that mass-suasion or mass-manipulation are now a highly developed art form that is widely practiced in all civilized societies. Investors should take note.

5

Victims of the Dark Arts

———

More than fifty years after Vance Packard's exposé, the practices of mass-suasion have, if anything, become even more pervasive. The channels through which messages are delivered have proliferated far beyond those available during his time. Not only have print, radio, and television expanded their reach, but also cable and satellite television are now well established. Plus the new mediums of the Internet and increasingly the wireless technologies are making it possible to deliver customized messages to millions, directly on their smartphones.

More important than all of the above, commercial mass-suasion has become deeply embedded in our culture and economy; it is taken for granted that we are being sold to, perhaps as a way to fulfill the needs we never thought we had and certainly as a right of those selling the goods to make a living.

The persuasion industries are now supported by large professional organizations, with the teaching of the necessary skills deeply institutionalized in the educational system as well as in corporate training programs. Smart and ambitious individuals compete with each other on career paths where success depends on skills in creating messages that persuade. Personal and mass selling is now a highly developed art form, providing for high-powered careers and lucrative rewards. Professionals in a range of different industries apply the knowledge built over many decades of tinkering and fine tuning to tactfully construct and deliver persuasive messages.

Modern living, as Douglas Rushkoff's documentaries show, is saturated with messages of all kinds.[50] If the din was growing louder during Packard's time, it is now deafening and getting louder still. Not only are the airwaves blanketed with all kinds of messages, with emergent new technologies the persuaders are coming straight at us through our computers and cell phone screens. More important, the din is not all just sales pitches or even irrelevant noise; in it are truly effective messages that tug at our most secret fears and desires, and as Packard pointed out, sometimes at the wants, needs, and aspirations of which we are not even aware.

Of course, not all persuasive messages are sinister in their intent or effect. Advertising copy, whether in print or on-screen or deftly embedded in sitcoms and movies, is entertaining and informative. A lot of good comes out of information about such things as health and education. Even advertising for simple products is informative, as it provides solutions to real needs, and creates demand that keeps factories humming, workers employed, and societies functioning. It is no exaggeration to say that even a breakthrough cure for cancer needs to be correctly messaged for it to gain trial and acceptance and to work its magic.

In a way, then, the sophistication of messages and the mediums used to deliver those messages are both necessary and integral parts of advanced societies. Censoring persuasion or severely restricting persuasive techniques would likely bring the economy and society to a grinding halt. At least to some degree, a society that restricts persuasion with a heavy hand or forces monopoly on delivery of persuasive messages is so much the worse for it.

Yet, delivering straightforward information and education is not the whole story; there is much more to persuading than the simple presentation of facts. From lessons learned over the centuries, it is clear that emotions play a central role in how people absorb information. *Word-smithing* is now a highly developed art form, as evident in the works of contemporary artists such as Frank Luntz and George Lakoff. It is no longer a secret that facts are subject to different interpretations depending on how they are presented and on who is doing the interpreting.

Clearly, persuasion is a double-edged sword. It can be used for good but also for not-so-good. Persuading people to give up smoking or to be culturally sensitive or to contribute to charity surely are all desirable ends. In contrast, persuasive messages that urge consumption of unhealthy foods or to be hateful toward others can do a lot of damage. In both cases, in using persuasion for good or for bad, the role of emotions cannot be understated. As the sophists understood at the dawn of civilization, the unfortunate fact remains that there is no clear line dividing when clever messaging is for the good versus when it is simply to induce people to do things that are clearly against their own interests.

So, in spite of the potential for much good from modern techniques of mass-suasion, people remain vulnerable to being led astray by deceitful messages, especially at the hands of unscrupulous operators. We remain vulnerable because of who we are, both biologically and psychologically. After all, in the long span of biological evolution, we are virtually unchanged from the people that Le Bon and his contemporaries were observing in the late nineteenth century. We may be more educated and more technologically sophisticated and perhaps even smarter than people of that era, but we share with them the basic bio-psychological makeup. Emotions continue to have a powerful hold on us; emotions color everything we see and hear and feel; they make us who we are.

The Irrational Animal

Recent developments in behavioral psychology have uncovered additional reasons why people find it difficult to make even straightforward choices: reasons why an average person remains highly vulnerable to scams and frauds. To understand these obstacles to good decision-making, imagine a scenario in which you are making choices about how to eat well. Let us say that in making those choices you are factoring in nutrition, quantity, taste, aroma, color, presentation, and perhaps other considerations like who you eat with, the environment in which you dine, and other things such as service and comfort.

In normal circumstances, you will try to make choices that are consistent with your desire to eat well, and you will carefully avoid foods that are not nutritious or those that don't taste good. There will be times when you may splurge or make a poor choice by mistake, but by and large you will want to maintain a good diet as planned. Now suppose that you are very hungry. Let us say you have not eaten all day. What will happen to your plans to eat well?

Chances are you will be slightly irritated, in a somewhat bad mood, and ready to eat what's available. What if you are extremely hungry and on the verge of starvation? Then what? In that case, not only will you be irritable, but hunger will become all-consuming and drive out all considerations except the need to find food, any food.

Cravings for food, drink, and sex, psychologists say, are visceral factors. So is the smoker's need for cigarettes and an addict's need for drugs; so are moods such as happiness and sadness, emotions such as anger, fear, and greed, and the sensation of physical pain. Especially at high levels of intensity, these factors often make people behave in a manner that is not in their own long-term interest, even though they know at the time that their immediate actions are not good for them in the long run.

These visceral factors are always present, as a residue from our animal past. Under normal conditions, these factors are generally muted. But they are always there, lurking in the background and powerfully shaping our daily routines. After all, our need for food has to be periodically satisfied and subtly governs where we go during the day. Similarly, we can't be too far away from water for very long, as recurring thirst reminds us that we cannot do without it.

Yet, at high levels of intensity, these same visceral factors tend to dominate our very being. George Loewenstein of Carnegie Mellon University has proposed that the first effect of intense visceral factors is the very strong urge to satisfy them.[51] So, an intensely hungry person wants to satisfy hunger, above everything else. All other considerations fade into the background and have little impact on decisions in the moment of extreme hunger. The focus narrows on finding food.

The second effect of intense visceral factors is that they need to be satisfied immediately. That is, the time dimension shrinks to such an extent that long-term thinking becomes an easy casualty. Even when the person is aware that the choice made in the moment will be against his own long-term interest, the need to satisfy the powerful urges simply trumps those remote considerations. Here and now reigns.

The third effect of intense visceral factors is that they go away as quickly as they come. Once the hunger is satisfied, there is no way to remember the power it had over you until the next time it comes around. So, intense craving or emotion is accompanied by a loss of memory and perspective about life outside the moment. For a starving person it is very difficult to recall how he felt when not hungry, and for a satiated person it is very difficult to recall how it felt when he was last intensely hungry. As a result of not remembering the previous intense experience, it is very difficult to anticipate and prepare for moments of intense hunger in the future and it is difficult as well to fully comprehend the behavior of someone else who happens to be in the grip of hunger.

As with hunger, so it is with other visceral factors such as anger and fear, envy and greed, and extreme sadness. The result of all the cravings, moods, and emotions is that when active in their full intensity, they override rational deliberation, or "cool-headed" thinking. People who are deliberative in normal circumstances make incredibly odd decisions when in the grip of the visceral urges.

So, not only are we encumbered by such obstacles as belief persistence and confirmation bias, our own biology also at times works against us when it comes to making good decisions. Together, all these factors make us highly vulnerable not only to making bad decisions by ourselves but also to being sold to or to being taken advantage of by unscrupulous others.

Perhaps the best and extreme examples of how we are led into making bad decisions are the scams and swindles that occur all around us with shocking regularity. It is when being scammed that our biases, emotions and, our animal nature in general are all on perfect display, and all available for skillful manipulation. So, here in brief is what we know about how people fall prey to frauds of different kinds, and in broad outlines the tactics that scammers and swindlers typically use to accomplish their unworthy ends.

Manipulation and Fraud

In reporting the results of a survey conducted in 2005, the Federal Trade Commission (FTC) noted that 30.2 million people, or 13.5 percent of adults in the United States, self-reported as victims of fraud.[52] The most common fraud (4.8 million) was related to weight loss products. The other frauds on the list were foreign lottery scams (3.2 million), unauthorized billing and buyers' clubs (3.2 million), prize promotions (2.7 million), work-at-home programs (2.4 million), credit card insurance (2.1 million), unauthorized billing—Internet services (1.8 million), advance-fee loans (1.7 million), credit repair scams (1.2 million), and business opportunities (0.8 million).

Of the medium used to reach their marks, the fraud perpetrators used print advertising (27 percent), Internet and email (22 percent), television and radio (21 percent), and telemarketing (9 percent). Other means, presumably such as word of mouth, were used the remaining 30 percent of the time.

Typically, victims are vulnerable populations such as the elderly and the lonesome, in the lower economic strata. But studies have shown that people even from affluent and socially active groups fall victim to scams because they are unable to identify them.

The fact that even relatively affluent and sophisticated people routinely fall prey to master emotion-manipulators, the con artist, is clear from a visit to the Securities and Exchange Commission (SEC) website.

Consider, for instance, the Ponzi scheme. Made famous by their originator, Charles Ponzi, about ninety years ago, the fraud involves the age-old trick of taking from Paul to pay Peter and swindling them both in the process. These kinds of frauds are widely understood, but they keep happening nonetheless.

The usual *modus operandi* of Ponzi schemers is to manipulate emotions, especially greed, by promising very high returns with no risk. In reality, Ponzi schemes work because money taken from later investors is used to pay the earlier ones, and it collapses when new investors can't be recruited anymore or when existing investors want their money back in a hurry, as during panics or steep recessions.

The most well-known of recent Ponzi schemes is the one operated by Bernie Madoff. Unlike the usual victims who are poor, elderly, and uneducated, the people whom Madoff swindled were generally wealthy and financially sophisticated. Yet, even these people, including hedge fund managers, royalty in Europe, and affluent retirees, all fell victim to an elaborate ruse. Taking advantage of his high status in the financial community, Madoff conned his marks with the promise of moderate but steady and relatively risk-free returns. More important, he seems to have cruelly manipulated their trust in him, their apparent greed, and their lack of ability or motivation to do their own due-diligence.

Like other master manipulators, Madoff seemed to be well versed in such common human emotions as greed for more money, desire for security, awe of authority, fear of asking questions, hope that everything was all right, and blind faith in a prestigious figure. Working deftly as if an expert puppeteer, he manipulated the emotions of his associates and clients, and bilked them of their life's savings.

But Madoff is only the most famous of the fraudsters who populate our world, seeking out the potentially most gullible and trusting souls, no matter their station in life, and manipulating their emotions to induce actions that are voluntary but against their self-interest. In 2009 alone, the SEC prosecuted 60 cases of Ponzi or Ponzi-like schemes in which con artists had beguiled people into parting with their money.

Such frauds have continued unabated. In October 2010, for instance, the SEC (2010-195) charged a Minnesota businessman, Thomas Peters, with a Ponzi scheme into which two Florida hedge fund managers funneled more than $1 billion. The press release from the SEC stated that the managers used lies and deceit, portraying themselves as guardians of the funds of their investors, when in fact they facilitated the fraudulent scheme of Peters and pocketed $58 million in fees for themselves. It was an elaborate scheme deftly inflicted on hopeful but unsuspecting marks.

Similarly, in June 2010, the SEC charged that two Canadians living in Florida were the perpetrators of a $300-million international Ponzi scheme (2010-99). After an FBI investigation, the SEC alleged that Milowe Allen Brost and Gary Allen Sorenson of Calgary promised investors 18 to 36 percent annual returns from investing in the gold mining companies they had "discovered." The two men were alleged to have orchestrated a complex scheme to move money around and live a high life, but in the end they bilked their investors by selling shares in a series of shell companies, and then paying them interest from monies extracted from late comers.

As yet another example, in June 2010 again, the SEC (2010-112) charged a Daniel Spitzer of St. Thomas Island with running a $105-million Ponzi scheme. Spitzer fooled about 400 investors, promising them high returns and having them believe that he was using a sophisticated investment strategy when none really existed. Similarly, in March 2010, the SEC (2010-33) reported having stopped a $14.7-million Ponzi scheme that had targeted retired bus drivers in Los Angeles.

The list is endless. Reading through the website of the SEC is sobering if for no other reason than seeing the frequency with which "investors" get taken in again and yet again by their greed for high returns and security. Even though the SEC was asleep at the wheel while Madoff built his fraudulent empire, the cases that they do bring to light reveal the vulnerability of investors and the danger from unscrupulous operators.

What is particularly disturbing is that Ponzi schemes are now sophisticated operations involving teams of people working as if in a formal organization. Unlike the solo operation of Charles Ponzi, the scams nowadays are in many ways similar to the organized efforts that companies put in place to sell genuine products and services. This insertion of organization into the Ponzi scheme creates a special danger to the unsuspecting public.

As Arthur Leff once argued in his brilliant book, *Swindling and Selling*, there is little difference in the tactics that good salesmen and shrewd fraudsters use. Both are masters at gaining confidence and subtly manipulating the emotions of their targets. Now, with organized scamming, there is another difficult distinction to make between genuine companies and those that only pretend to be so.

Yet, the Ponzi is just one of its kind. The world is full of other kinds of swindles such as pyramid schemes, affinity scams, pump-and-dump operations, and virtually infinite variations in which people are parted with their money, willingly at first and then with regret. The con artists, the SEC website warns, are experts at gaining one's confidence. Beware.

New World Old Biology

Some research is now available on what specific techniques fraudsters use on their marks and, in addition, why people tend to fall victim. In a Fraud Forum organized by the Federal Trade Commission (FTC) in February 2009,[53]

56

researchers noted that even though scams come in a wide variety of forms and they change over time, their structure can be identified. "It is possible to identify the most common persuasion tactics used in fraud," they write. To that end, the Forum participants presented the results of their research, the data for which were obtained from, among other things, 300 undercover audios compiled by the American Association of retired Persons (AARP) and the Financial Industry Regulatory Authority (FINRA).

According to the FTC analysis, the most common tactic used by fraudsters is what the researchers call *Phantom Fixation*. This is to create a phantom reward and tell the marks that they have won something big, simply to fix their attention on the reward and inhibit their ability to carefully evaluate the offer being made. The trick used here is an old one, and that is to raise the emotions of hope and greed and undermine the ability to reason.

The second psychological tactic used by fraudsters is to create a perception of *scarcity*, by insisting that the deal of a lifetime is available only for a little time. Here the psychological trick is to make the victims feel rushed and decide in a hurry, once again to inhibit their ability to logically analyze the situation and to make careful decisions.

The third psychological tactic used by scam artists is to gain *credibility* in some way. As Le Bon long ago noted, prestige impresses people. Swindlers know this instinctively. Madoff, of course, had prestige from being a successful investment professional and he cultivated that carefully by keeping his distance from clients. In fact, he relied on a network of third-party agents and feeder funds, who sold his services by creating and reinforcing a myth about him as a brilliant investor. While Madoff had legitimate experience in the industry, prestige is sometimes faked by swindlers who may claim far more education and social status than they actually have.

In addition, credibility is also attained by outward displays of wealth and an expensive lifestyle. As John Kenneth Galbraith explains in *A Short History of Financial Euphoria*, people seem to have a strong tendency to equate wealth with intelligence, often thinking, as the saying goes, if you're rich, you must be smart. Displays of wealth and of being well-connected are, therefore, a common tactic used by swindlers as a means of gaining credibility and building trust as part of the con operation.

The fourth psychological tactic used in the committing of fraud is to use *comparisons* in the sales pitch. The comparison may be genuine but more likely fake, and swindlers use it to create the impression that what is being offered is so much better than anything else that the mark could get. The psychological trick here is to create an anchor or a benchmark against which the phantom offering looks much better. Here, again, the tactic is to interfere with the reasoning process, to force attention on the benchmark and away from the offer, hiding it in plain sight.

The fifth psychological tactic used by scam artists is to create, if necessary, imaginary *social proof*. This is in the spirit of strongly hinting that there are lots of other people already buying the opportunity or waiting to get a chance to buy it. The psychological trick in this tactic is to give the impression that others have already evaluated the offer favorably so there is obviously something good in it. The subtle message being conveyed here is that the mark does not need to spend time and effort trying to evaluate the offer; he should forego evaluation and just believe in it.

The same FTC study showed, moreover, that not all of the five persuasion tactics worked equally well in all situations. Source credibility and phantom fixation, for example, were the most common tactics used in investment frauds, although social proof and scarcity also played an important role. In travel-related scams, on the other hand, source credibility appeared to play no role at all but phantom fixation and scarcity dominated as tactics. The same two tactics also appeared to be heavily used in sweepstakes and lottery scams.

One important reason for the success of the five persuasion tactics, as discussed in previous chapters, is that we are burdened with strong biases in how we think and those biases make us vulnerable to scams. The need for us to believe and to confirm what we already know or think we know are the chief obstacles to seeing the tactics for what they are.

Sometimes, in addition, there is a basic inclination to trust others and take things at face value. This trust instinct is, of course, very important for living a stable and happy life but it is one that unscrupulous operators are keen to exploit. Then there is sometimes the illusion of control or invulnerability, with people thinking that they are just too smart to be taken in, not realizing that the illusion itself creates the vulnerability, as fraudsters often feed a sense of self-importance and navigate their way into a position from which to shape behavior.

As shrewd manipulators of emotions, con artists appear to be well aware of human frailties, not to mention the visceral factors that so powerfully influence our behavior. Loewenstein notes that they are experts at "rapidly invoking greed, pity, and other emotions that can eclipse deliberation and produce an override of normal behavioral restraints."[54]

Moreover, knowing that visceral influences subside rapidly, skillful persuaders emphasize immediate action. Get on board now, they say, the train is leaving the station. It's a limited-time opportunity, or this house is going to get snapped up, so buy it now. Students of human behavior, as con artists are apt to be, they understand that visceral factors are always present in the background, and that they must be invoked to do the persuading. It is their skill at noticing which factors are ripe in a given situation and which emotions to manipulate that makes them so effective in their trade.

In the Stock Market

People lose money not only because of direct operations against them as discussed above. They are also parted with their money by being induced to make poor choices through pervasive mass-suasion, whether intended to deceive or not. Whereas Ponzi schemes and other swindles typically involve operators who select their marks and organize to fleece them, the general climate as portrayed in the media can result in similar effects for millions of those who invest in the stock market.

Evidence about how investors make bad choices is scrupulously compiled in a series of impressive studies by Professors Brad Barber and Terrence Odean. The authors have been analyzing the behavior of investors for well over a decade and they have built an impressive body of work that shows the many ways in which people make bad investment decisions.

In a 2006 paper, for example, Barber and Odean show that individual investors generally purchase only attention-grabbing stocks. These are stocks that are in the news, perhaps pitched on television or in cyberspace, and stocks that become noticeable because of high trading volume or recent extreme price movements. That is, investors often consider buying only those stocks that first attract their attention either because of wide media coverage or simply because of rapid price movements. Consistent with the primacy effect, once a stock captures their attention, investors then are liable to seek evidence that confirms their initial hunch or thesis about its suitability as an investment.

The authors build on the work of behavioral psychologists to argue that investors make identifiable, systematic mistakes in their stock market decisions. For instance, they show that investors have a strong tendency to avoid regret, because of which they tend to sell their winners too soon but hold on to losers too long. The authors also show that investors are unnecessarily optimistic and overconfident in their abilities to make the correct decisions, and are therefore subject to easy manipulation. Barber and Odean report that people trade too much and lower their returns, in one study, by as much as 7 percentage points per year compared with what they could have attained by simply purchasing a broad market index.

Concerned only with investor behavior but not their motivations, the authors did not delve more deeply into why people thought they could do better by trading so much. Yet, it is no secret that our airwaves are filled with messages urging people to buy and sell stocks, generally encouraging the gullible, tantalizing them with the possibilities of quick riches and perhaps even flattering people in their ability to "beat the market" when evidence clearly shows the inability of most to do so. In addition to the encouragement all around to trade, the marketplace is overflowing with easy-to-use tools that facilitate trading. As such, for those willing, not only is there a good deal of encouragement but also the means with which to do the buying and selling; a couple of key strokes and the monkey is in the market!

What Next?

What all of the above means is that, to a lesser or greater extent, we are all vulnerable to making bad decisions and being taken advantage of, especially when in the grip of any of the visceral factors. Deep biases in decision-making and the ease with which persuaders penetrate our minds make for formidable obstacles to good decisions.

So, the task for us next is to understand how to overcome the various obstacles to good decision-making, to guard against our emotional vulnerabilities, and to build good defenses against manipulative attacks originating in the financial media or elsewhere. In the next few chapters, therefore, I develop a conceptual framework for countering our many biases and vulnerabilities to being manipulated.

Book II

Verity

Chapters

———

6. Defense Against the Dark Arts

7. Logic–Data–Doubt

8. Investing as a Negative Art

9. How to be a Wise Investor

10. The Art of Looking

———

6

Defense Against the Dark Arts

With our own biology acting against us and with others wanting to systematically take advantage of our many psychological vulnerabilities, the question becomes: How can we defend ourselves? How do we make good investment decisions when faced with enemies internal and external? How can we overcome the bio-psychological limitations embedded deep in our own being? How, in short, do we defend ourselves against the dark arts of mass-suasion?

There are three lines of defense to use in making decisions, each displaying an increasing level of sophistication in overcoming the internal and external obstacles to clear, independent thinking. Let us discuss these.

Defense 1: Slow Down

The first line of defense is simply to recognize the power of visceral urges and to make every effort to avoid making decisions when under their influence. Respecting our collective heritage as biological beings and the power that our animal passions have over us, it is helpful to be aware that when operative in their full intensity, visceral factors override careful deliberation by narrowing attention to information that is most directly related to solving the immediate problem at hand. As such, a key element of good investing practices is to make important decisions *only* when the visceral factors are under normal restraints, and never do so in a hurry.

Clearly, visceral factors are very much part of what makes us human; they are necessary for both survival and profit. It is likely that, at times, circumstances will force your hand and the decisions will need to be made in the heat of the moment, with visceral factors like hunger and fear operational in their full glory. There will also be times when visceral urges will motivate action (e.g., a search for food when starving) that is necessary and useful; lack of attention to those urges would be disastrous.

Yet, these same urges can be costly in investing. When unsatisfied, visceral urges accompany a feeling of vulnerability and intensify a range of emotions, such as greed and fear. The ability to reason diminishes when hunger or thirst or other cravings go unsatisfied for long, when greed or fear dominate consciousness—making us vulnerable to grave errors in judgment and forgoing even simple analysis altogether.

Since visceral urges peak in intensity and recede very quickly with satiation or changes in circumstances, sometimes it may be just enough to let the moment pass and normalcy return before making those important decisions—after regaining the ability to think rationally and analytically.

Visceral urges are part of our biology and they are always with us, ready to be activated when conditions are ripe. As such, even though each of us is vulnerable to them at the individual level, such urges can also be activated at a large scale when the general environment creates shared feelings of greed or fear or any of the many other emotions. In fact, the larger social mood can make people especially vulnerable to visceral factors. When the social mood is positive, euphoria can suppress deliberative processes; when the social mood is negative, intense irritability may undermine the ability to reason.

For instance, during the technology bubble in the late 1990s, when people thought that prices would forever rise, even worthless companies were going public and finding a market for their stocks among people giddy with the paper profits they had made from years of rising prices. At the peak of the technology bubble, according to a report, individuals and households invested more than $180 billion in the stock mutual funds. Because of years of rising prices, it appeared as if a little hope had amplified into greed and people fell into buying the stock funds at rapidly rising prices.

A few years later, after the market had fallen sharply, people appeared to be frozen by fear of further loss. The stock mutual funds attracted just over $7 billion, indicating a sharp turn in mood against stocks even as the economic fundamentals were rebounding.[55] Greed for more, or fear of being left out perhaps, inspired people to pay too much at the peak of the market; fear of losing or perhaps greed for better bargains kept them from investing in bargains that were available after the decline in prices.

For investors, therefore, the message is to slow down and make important investment decisions only when the visceral urges are firmly under control. A simple rule of thumb is that, to the extent possible, you should not make investment decisions thirsty" or tired or in physical discomfort. Nor should commitments be made when in the grip of anger or fear or panic, or aroused by intense greed or envy or anxiety. By limiting yourself to "normal" conditions when the visceral factors are firmly under control, through rest and satiation, you allow the deliberative processes the room necessary to enable rationality. Restraint makes you rational.

Defense 2: Beware of Common Mistakes

Accommodating and managing visceral urges is not enough, however, for good decision-making. It is also necessary to be aware of psychological vulnerabilities, even when visceral influences are well under control. Let us look at some of the typical biases and the systematic errors with which we are burdened.

From memory failure to incorrect attributions, from blind compliance to eager conformity, from misperceptions to simply not remembering, and from over-simplifying to just believing the stories we hear, our failures as decision makers have been well documented with volumes of careful research. As such, the second line of defense is an appreciation of at least the most common biases: anchoring, framing, overconfidence, hindsight bias, and overreaction.

Research has shown that we anchor purchase and sale decisions on arbitrary prices and to round numbers; similarly, we are inclined to frame an investment prospect as positive or negative and then seek information that is consistent with such framing.

We tend to underestimate the risks and uncertainties that surround us. We need to be able to not think about all that can go wrong in the next instant. Constant and full awareness of the bad things that can happen to us is bound to create such a high level of anxiety that we would not be able to function. So, nature induces us to push uncertainties and risks under the rug, perhaps as a psychological defense so we could live relatively anxiety-free.

Maybe as a result of perceiving risks and uncertainties to be lower than they often are, we are generally overconfident in our choices and optimistic about the outcomes of those choices. Technically, this shows up as more than justified confidence in our abilities and as a fairly narrow view of what can happen and not happen.

So, for instance, when driving at eighty miles an hour, some people assume that there will not be any sudden surprises on the highway and, if there are any, they would be able to control the vehicle and avoid a mishap. Clearly, the risk of nasty surprises at high speeds depends on where in the world you are, but even in developed countries it is more than some may think it is, especially if the driver—or someone in another car on the same road—is intoxicated or distracted. The very fact that accidents at high speeds don't happen all the time lures people into thinking that they will not happen when they are behind the wheel.

The combination of optimism and overconfidence not only leads us into poor choices, it also makes us vulnerable to manipulation by others. It allows unscrupulous persuaders to encourage us to underestimate risk and downplay the potentially negative consequences. Similarly, scammers play on the exaggerated and faulty belief that you may have in your ability to control events that may be essentially uncontrollable.

Researchers have also found that optimism and overconfidence notwithstanding, people tend to take their mistakes in stride. No matter that what they had expected turns out to be wrong, researchers say that people just forget what their initial expectations were or simply fail to reconstruct what they had previously thought. Even more common is the hindsight bias, or the tendency to see an unanticipated event and think that they could have predicted it, that the event was inevitable and they would have seen it coming if only they had been paying attention.

The hindsight bias makes investors highly vulnerable to manipulation, of course, as it strengthens the misperception that they can predict correctly. In fact, persuasion often involves the recasting of a wrongly predicted event into something correctly predicted. Because of the difficulty people have in reconstructing the logic that was used to make the original prediction, they can be convinced of their own or someone else's ability to correctly predict events, when in fact all they are doing is distorting the facts after seeing the outcome. It is little wonder that predictions fill our airwaves, and there is nary a financial commentator who does not correctly predict what happened yesterday.

Coupled with the hindsight bias is the tendency for people to see patterns or regularities in random events. We are incorrigibly pattern-seeking animals, and we are prone to see patterns where none may exist. Thinking erroneously that a particular event or an observation is part of a pattern, we extrapolate and react accordingly. There appears to be an inbuilt bias among us to react strongly to what may be chance events.

Unjustified pattern-seeking makes us vulnerable to all kinds of claims for this product and that, all asserting that the past experiences with their product or services show a pattern of high performance. These kinds of assertions are especially common in (although not limited to) the financial services industry, where many mutual funds routinely market themselves by noting the superior track record based on cherry-picked data so as to highlight periods of good performance. Our tendency to seek out patterns creates vulnerability in the subtle expectation that the showcased past performance would be repeated in the future.

In sum, the second line of defense against the internal and external enemies of good decision-making is an ability to recognize and compensate for many natural biases, including those discussed above.

Investing wisely requires that, among other things, we be realistic about our capabilities and our ability to control circumstances, be more cautious than optimistic, be careful about extrapolating the past into the future, and more pointedly question the patterns that we think we may be seeing around us.

In effect, as the heritage of our animal past are imprinted deeply into us by the powerful forces of evolution, visceral urges and psychological biases cannot be eliminated. They are part of us, always in the background, occasionally bursting onto the scene and then fading again, only to resurface without warning. As we have seen, when not properly controlled and managed, the urges and biases become obstacles to rational, deliberative decision-making.

So, part of setting up for investing wisely is to recognize the ease with which our perceptions are distorted; and try to spot the distorting influences so we may be able to defend against them.

Defense 3: Do the Doubt

The third line of defense against the dark arts of persuasion is none other than doubt or, more accurately, active skepticism. Doubt, after all, is that ambiguous space between belief and disbelief, where one is not sure of what seems to be true, or of what is presented as fact.[56]

In his famous aphorism, "I think, therefore I am," René Descartes implies that the very fact that he doubted proved his existence. Perhaps the strongest doubter of all time, Descartes refused to believe anything of which he could not be certain, even doubting his own senses, including what he saw and touched and tasted.

So that he could get at the essence of things, he used doubt as the key to building firm knowledge, arguing that by rejecting that of which he could not be certain, he would eventually get to the foundational issues that could not be doubted and then start building from there a more robust body of knowledge. It was like digging in the sand with a shovel called doubt until hitting the solid rock buried deep down, and then building a foundation for a structure that could withstand doubt.

It turns out that, like sophists of a bygone era, Descartes rejected everything that came to him through his senses. Not trusting anything he experienced directly, it was as though he dug up sand by the bucketful. Finally, he was left with only one thing that could not be doubted. He knew he was thinking, so that was the only sure thing; everything else was possibly a mirage.

In a famous thought experiment, Descartes used the hypothetical piece of wax that, his senses tell him, has certain characteristics such as color, aroma, weight, and texture. Once that wax is brought very close to a flame, of course, those characteristics appear to change even though it is still the same wax; color, aroma, and so on seemed to be different than what they were originally. His senses deceive him, Descartes argued, and could not be trusted to convey that he was still looking at the same wax. Yet, even though color and aroma were now different, reason told him that it was the same wax nonetheless. It was not sensory perception, he concluded, but thinking that helped him grasp the essence of that piece of wax. Reason and deduction were more powerful than observation and perception. To him, therefore, the mind was a better instrument of knowledge than the senses themselves.

But thought cannot be separated from me, Descartes argued, as I cannot really separate myself from myself. Thinking is the very essence of who I am, but then how do I know that I exist outside of my own thinking, separate from my own mind? The only way I know I exist, he concluded, is when I have doubts about my own thoughts, my very existence. So, in effect, it came down to: "I doubt, therefore I am."

Doubt had, of course, been at the center of Western philosophy ever since Plato made Socrates a central character in his writings. Yet, Descartes revived doubt as a formal method to be used in the search for truth. Like Socrates and Gorgias, Descartes was highly skeptical of the senses that brought information to him, fully aware that sensory perceptions could be distorted. Our senses can easily fool us, he argued, and cannot be trusted. What we think is true may be simply a figment of our imagination, or our distorted perceptions deceiving us such that we see what we hope to see.

So, Descartes is credited with developing *methodological skepticism*, a method in which doubt is used as a path to uncover and discard things that may seem to be true but are not really so. For us, therefore, active doubt is the third line of defense against the dark arts.

It can be argued that doubt already plays an important role in life around us. Reasonable doubt, for instance, is firmly established as a principle of American jurisprudence, at least in part to protect the innocent from collective passions of the public and the jury. Similarly, the adversarial processes of modern democracies largely use doubt to sort through different claims made by the various parties and interest groups.

Yet, we also know that some forms of doubt can have severe negative consequences for people and can be debilitating at times. Doubt about one's abilities or about relationships can be devastating in personal life. Using misinformation to instill doubt for the purposes of propaganda can also have unfortunate consequences for open and honest exchanges of ideas in public discourse.

My objective here is not to debate doubt in its various forms. But I do want to use *active* doubt as the third and, in some ways, the most sophisticated line of defense against the various internal and external forces that lead us into bad decisions. Remember that, in the first two lines of defense discussed above, the approach was to try to escape the stranglehold of visceral urges and psychological biases that so distort our thinking and make us vulnerable to manipulation. In contrast, the emphasis in this third line of defense is to seek out and actively build processes that strengthen and formalize our natural tendency to be skeptical of or doubt what we see and hear.

In effect, the lesson here is to encourage our built-in ability to disbelieve, doubt, and formally disconfirm what we think we already know. So, in the next chapter, let's discuss how methodological skepticism can be a powerful conceptual tool for investors.

7

Logic–Data–Doubt

———

In this chapter, I briefly review four thinkers who wrestled with and clarified the process with which to separate truth from falsehood. You may wonder why we are continuing with, even belaboring, abstract philosophy when this book is really about the very practical problem of investing wisely. Bear with me.

The thinking reviewed here is crucial to understanding how to invest well. Finding, evaluating, and recognizing good investment opportunities is about thinking clearly and seeing them for what they really are. By understanding how people over the centuries have tried to separate fact from illusion, investors can learn how to separate genuine investment opportunities from those that seem to be so but really are not. Investing, in many ways, is a mind game; learning how philosophers have thought about how the mind works is perhaps *the* most important thing for investors to learn and appreciate.

So, the desire to distinguish truth from falsity, reality from perception, substance from form, and value from hype, has been with us since at least the time of the ancient Greeks. The skill of the sophists, as we saw in an earlier chapter, was in blurring the lines between seemingly polar opposites and frustrating the claims of what seemed like straightforward truth. Perhaps instinctively, the sophists recognized that perceptions could be distorted, that the same thing or idea could look very different depending on the perceiver.

Sophists made many enemies, of course, by openly questioning conventional wisdom and teaching for pay their techniques of rhetoric and argumentation. As discussed, frustration is clearly visible in the writings of Plato, who seems to bristle at the sophists' penchant for countering the arguments of other professional philosophers. He also may have been concerned that the sophists were spreading their obstructionist ways to the citizenry at large and thereby undermining people like himself who were in the serious business of finding truth.

Logic and Deduction

Ultimately, as discussed in chapter 3, it was not Plato but his student Aristotle who developed formal methods to try to separate truth from falsity. In *Sophistical Refutations*,[57] Aristotle clarifies the various ways in which what appear to be refutations of an argument could really be only fallacies. "That some reasonings are genuine," he wrote, "while others seem to be so but are not, is evident. This happens with arguments, as also elsewhere, through a certain likeness between the genuine and the sham."[58] He discusses at length how word games and manner of delivery were used by sophists to create false arguments that appeared to be true.

There are six tricks of language, Aristotle wrote, that sophists used to refute genuine arguments and seven tricks that were independent of language. The six linguistic fallacies were *ambiguity* (same expression may mean different things), *amphiboly* (seemingly straightforward sentence may have a secondary hidden meaning or suggestion that the listener may understand at a subconscious level), *combination* (words when combined have a different meaning than what they mean by themselves), *division* (parts of an expression may have different meaning when separated), *accent* (emphasis changes meaning), and *form of expression* (figure of speech).

The seven non-linguistic fallacies, Aristotle wrote, were *accident* (general rule is misapplied to a specific situation), *improper use* (an expression applied beyond its usual constraints), *ignorance of refutation* (using any random argument to contradict and then tacking on the desired conclusion at the end), *false reverse causality* (if A follows B, then B must follow A), *circular logic* (the conclusion is "proved" by its assumptions), *false causality* (A causes B, but this relationship is not true or cannot be proven), and *jumble of questions* (ask many and complex questions to put the opponent on the defensive with no chance of a satisfactory answer).

The thirteen fallacies that Aristotle painstakingly outlined clarified the structure of refutations used by sophists to dispute the claims of others and to create false argumentations as they attacked and refuted claims of knowledge. The way to ward off such attacks, Aristotle suggested, was to understand the kinds of tricks the sophists used.

Also necessary, however, was a systematic approach to creating knowledge, to formally arrive at conclusions that could be defended against false attacks. To that end, Aristotle insisted that philosophical claims of knowledge were an enterprise in which the method was really the key and much more important than knowledge itself.

In a collection of six writings which his followers later pulled together under the title of *Organon*, Aristotle presented a system of logic for making formal inferences. Now called Term or Traditional logic, this system contained three parts: 1) terms which represent something, such as "tree" or "stock" but don't by themselves indicate right or wrong, 2) premise in two parts, comprising a major premise and a minor premise, and 3) inference that necessarily obtains from a logical combination of the major and minor premises.

That is, Aristotle argued that if you define terms properly and then take some things related to those terms as given, then you can draw conclusions that are different from those suppositions but which naturally fall from them. So, if you suppose that all men are pious (major premise) and Rob is a man (minor premise), then Rob is pious (conclusion). Conversely, every valid conclusion must have within it underlying premises that are held to be true and those premises must themselves be built on well-defined terms.

Syllogism, the kind of logic developed by Aristotle, has been influential in Western thought ever since it was first developed; it was the dominant mode of thinking until being eventually supplanted by modern versions of logic, most notably by predicate logic and other higher logics that encode much more complex reasoning and make liberal use of mathematical notation. Even so, syllogism persists and is still useful in formalizing problems of logic.

Syllogism was also crucial to how Descartes formalized his thinking and developed his method. Calling it *deductive reasoning*, Descartes extended Aristotle's argument that a conclusion is valid if it necessarily follows from a set of two or more premises. That is, deductive reasoning is properly used when a conclusion is drawn by combining existing statements, which themselves are taken as true or given.

So, up until the early seventeenth century, and the time of Descartes, the dominant mode of trying to understand reality was still strongly influenced by the ancient Aristotelian doctrine of deriving conclusions from pre-supposed statements taken as given. By and large, however, this method was a mind game. Because of the suspicion of sensory data, and the recognition that the senses were extremely vulnerable to distortions, the syllogistic or deductive method of knowledge discovery was driven by pure logic, by thinking alone.

As such, the problem with syllogism and more broadly with deductive logic was that the premises underlying the conclusions were based in pure thought, in conceptions of reality and not in direct experiences of it. But the premises themselves could be subject to biases and prejudices, as they often were. They were for a long time based on mysticism or blind faith, yielding conclusions (often delusions) that were largely unsupported by reliable facts. We can imagine how distorted premises can be used to defend preferred conclusions.

If it turns out that *not* all men are pious, the conclusion from the original syllogism that Rob is pious would be wrong, even though it is consistent with the (faulty) premise that all men are pious. In other words, if the major premise is taken as a given but is, in fact, a faulty product of your imagination or some pernicious bias, then the conclusion would be logically correct but still an outright mistake.

Data and Induction

This pre-scientific approach to the search for truth remained a big impediment for a long time, and knowledge creation was chronically stunted by over-reliance on mystery and myth. Descartes' valiant efforts notwithstanding, premises were often heavy on abstractions and vulnerable to severe distortions from biases and prejudices of those desiring particular conclusions. After all, once you reach a desirable conclusion, you can always reach back and design premises that logically support your conclusion.

For an eternity, then, human action was routinely incited by passions and glibly justified by pre-existing beliefs, or worse. Once the public decided that the accused was a witch, as in Salem, Massachusetts, for example, it was then quite easy to come up with supporting but faulty premises to confirm that the accused was indeed a witch and, therefore, deserving of torture and execution.

But the significance of sensory data was not lost on all. Just as Descartes was a continental philosopher in the tradition of *rationalists*, there was an opposing camp of thinkers who went about as *empiricists*. Among those who put faith in observation and data from the real world was the English polymath Francis Bacon. A restless intellect and a brilliant thinker, Bacon applied his significant talents to the dissatisfactions he had with the Aristotelian dogma. Where Descartes was questioning his own ability to use direct observation to distinguish fact from fiction, Bacon questioned the validity of conclusions derived from purely deductive reasoning. Where Descartes bowed to Aristotle, Bacon felt it was time to move on. In the methods of *rationalists*, who put so much faith in pure thought but ignored the world around, he saw vulnerability to preconceived notions.

Playing on Aristotle's writings on logic, Bacon wrote *Novum Organum* (The New Instrument), in which he presented the method of induction and detailed how scientific knowledge ought to be created by a formal process of verification. Instead of ignoring data because of concerns about sensory distortions, he argued that systematically gathering, organizing, and evaluating data was at the center of building good knowledge. Instead of taking premises for granted and deducing conclusions from just plain logic, Bacon insisted that real data be used to verify the premises. Empirical verification needed to be at the center of scientific inquiry.

"Those who simply assert the laws of nature do great injury to science and philosophy," Bacon wrote in the preface to the book.[59] Inducing belief by professional affectations, with claims that could not be verified outside of pure logic, was harmful; it created empty dogmas and quashed inquiry. Empirical verification was necessary, he argued, precisely because the human mind is highly vulnerable to sundry influences; the claims of knowledge derived from pure logic could be grossly misleading.

Pure deduction was inadequate for true understanding, Bacon explained, because the minds of men are beset by deep-rooted false notions. He then discussed four such notions (or, *idols*, as he called them) in some detail:

Idols of the Tribe are the false notions that our reasoning is free of limitations which our humanity necessarily bestows upon us. There is, in effect, no universal truth that can be ascribed from what we know at a given time; nature is too complex and particulars change from time to time. That which we know is necessarily limited by who we are.

Idols of the Den are the false notions that we are free of our own culture or social group. That is, everyone lives in and is shaped by his or her own experiences and, inevitably, limited by those. Family, friends, neighbors, and colleagues all shape who we are, what we prefer, and how we think. The books we read, the television shows we watch, the celebrities we admire all collectively influence the range of possibilities in which we reside. In other words, Bacon wrote that we live in our own private den and can only see what we can see from inside it. We are not free from the influences that shape our worldview and color our thinking.

Idols of the Marketplace are the false notions that arise from associating with others whose words can change how we think. Echoing Gorgias, Bacon wrote that words impose meaning and shape understanding, even overruling the understanding we once had about something. Words can also create confusion about something that we may have once thought was perfectly clear. It is not just our own biases, he explained, but also the words of others that obstruct understanding.

Idols of the Theater are false notions that arise from prevailing dogmas and the systems of thinking that men have been persuaded to believe by the various acts that make up the drama of life. Specific ideas and the whole systems of belief become accepted, Bacon wrote, because of tradition, eagerness to believe, and even laziness or negligence.

After discussing at some length the four idols, Bacon presses on with more troubles for thinkers. It is natural for men, he argued, to look for more order and regularity than may exist in the world. The need for order creates dreams and fancies that reinforce both false notions and rigidity. Once men adopt an opinion, they are drawn to all things that support and agree with it, and despise, reject, and suppress those that are contrary to their opinion.

Men are most impressed by those things that enter the mind simultaneously and suddenly and fill up their imagination; these things then impose an image that colors everything that follows immediately after. Men's minds are unquiet and always in motion; as such, they always seek something beyond, some explanations about universal laws when in fact they are confined by the natural limits of their own understanding. Man, Bacon argued, is inclined to believe readily whatever he wishes.

> He rejects difficult things from impatience of research; sober things, because they narrow hope; the deeper things of nature, from superstition; the light of experience, from arrogance and pride, lest his mind should seem to be occupied with things mean and transitory; things not commonly believed, out of deference to the opinion of the vulgar. Numberless, in short, are the ways, and sometimes imperceptible, in which the affections color and infect the understanding.

Bacon quite agreed with Plato and Descartes that the senses were prone to "dullness, incompetency, and deceptions."

"The things that strike the sense," he wrote, "outweigh things which do not immediately strike it, though they [may] be more important."[60] The senses can mislead, so sensory data cannot be taken at face value or trusted. This is even more so because the human mind is prone to abstractions and flights of fancy; it gives substance and form to things that that may not even exist, while at the same time paying no heed to those things that are enduring and real.

The limitations of the human mind are so extreme, Bacon insisted, that simply willing them away was impossible. So deeply entrenched are such limitations, that the only way to prevent them from corrupting the scientific enterprise was to develop good methods that systematically attended to them. He agreed with Aristotle, that the focus ought to be not on knowledge *per se* but on the method of its production, but he strongly disagreed on what those methods ought to be.

Bacon was among the first to so clearly articulate the many flaws in our ways of thinking. His insights are important for investors to understand because such deeply embedded flaws are often the reason for costly mistakes in investing.

I discuss below how Bacon suggested such fundamental limitations and flaws in our ways of thinking could be overcome. In later chapters, we will see how specifically to correct for these flaws when investing. For now, let's continue this somewhat abstract discussion so that we can appreciate what we really are up against as investors.

The most pressing problems in investing, it should be evident by now, are within us. Given that we are prone to distorting facts to our liking or ignoring them altogether, the principal task for all investors is to understand how to manage and correct the deep flaws within us.

Once he had articulated the difficulties that people have in seeing clearly and thinking independently, Bacon then went on to discuss how to overcome those difficulties. Instead of relying on pure thought, he argued, real-world data were central to producing knowledge. Certainly, distorted perceptions create problems, but instead of ignoring the world around, thinkers needed to develop new methods to make sure that the data were not corrupted. A robust, data-driven method was the key.

The necessary defense against the natural distortions in our thinking, Bacon argued, is in what he called *inductive reasoning*. Rather than relying simply on imaginings and instead of pulling premises out of one's opaque beliefs or prior givens based on faith or tradition, he urged that premises be based on empirical evidence, on data. That is, as much as possible, researchers should collect facts from direct observation and then use those facts to generate axioms before deriving general laws.

Bacon's emphasis was on collecting and organizing data, and on drawing inferences from those data in a systematic fashion, being aware always of the possible distortions and systematically correcting for them. By repeatedly going to data and getting additional evidence to support the premises, one could obtain more robust conclusions and get closer to the truth. Once sufficient evidence had been corralled, one could have greater confidence in the scientific laws one may be uncovering.

Wholly empirical, the Baconian (or scientific) method was quite different from the deductive reasoning it sought to supplant. Although he did not entirely reject syllogism and deduction, Bacon urged empiricism, in which direct observation informs premises, and these data-driven premises are then logically combined to produce conclusions. Rules of logic still apply, but the logic is now buttressed by carefully gathered and catalogued data from the world around. That is, general laws and understanding were to be uncovered not from purely logical thinking but from application of logic to carefully compiled data.

Suppression of Belief

Bacon's contribution was, of course, significant and his insistence on planned procedure constitutes an indispensable element of scientific inquiry to this day. Results, to be sure, are invalid if the methods used to obtain them are corrupt, if evidence did not exist or is shoddy. Naturally, the scientific method has been much refined over the centuries, but the basic acknowledgement of natural biases and the need to guard against them is certainly owed to Bacon.

Yet, the story does not quite end here. Over a long stretch of time, inductive reasoning has drawn a strong contingent of skeptics who have opposed it on two grounds. First, they argue, the supposition that you can uncover general laws by marshaling empirical evidence is suspect. How could universal truths be uncovered by examination of particulars? When you collect evidence, how are you to know that the particular sample you are examining does indeed adequately represent the entire population to which the results would be generalized? How much evidence do you need to be able to say what the underlying truth is?

If there have been no devastating accidents in the nuclear arsenal of the American military, can we be sure that there will be no such accidents in the future, or even in the very next moment? Europeans had once thought that black swans did not exist. The more white swans they saw over the centuries, the stronger became their taken-for-granted assumption that swans were of no other color. Yet, viewing all the swans in Europe could not be taken to mean that swans of other colors did not exist. True enough, as is now widely reported, a Dutch explorer eventually discovered the black swan in the southern hemisphere.

In effect, the first objection to inductive reasoning is that all the empirical evidence you collect may mislead you by drawing attention to what is available as evidence at the expense of truly important facts that are simply not available or observed at the time of analysis. Even if the methods are sound, in other words, the evidence may be insufficient for you to draw conclusions or it may be sufficient for you to draw wrong conclusions.

If stock prices have generally gone up in the long run for the hundred or more years for which we have data, does it mean that they will always do the same? Do patterns in the data represent some underlying reality that stock prices should always go up in the long run? Could the past be exceptional and not a reflection of the future that is about to be revealed… in the future?

The second, more important, objection to inductive reasoning, as we saw in an earlier chapter, is in the strong confirmation bias that plagues decision-making. Bacon clearly saw the tendency for people to try to *confirm* what they already believe. Yet, he underestimated the strength of such bias and overestimated the ability of induction to overcome it. The method of induction, as Bacon conceived it, fell short of overcoming the very biases and distortions that he had outlined.

As Bacon strongly implied and research in recent years has shown, our belief structures are complex and we don't always know why we believe what we do. In the midst of constant bombardment of messages from any number of sources, beliefs are shaped in ways both subtle and obvious, to such an extent that we don't so as much believe what we see but see what we believe. There is a strong tendency, in other words, to look for confirmatory evidence to support prior beliefs, especially in those instances in which emotional stakes are high.

The careful methods that Bacon so insightfully articulated can, in other words, be easily corrupted. The collection of evidence itself can be distorted such that the data that support prior beliefs may attract and consume attention while the data that contradict expectations are ignored. Hence, yet again, while the results of an empirical inquiry may be consistent with the available evidence, they may be faulty because of the bias in the data and in the biased interpretation of those data.

The Falsification Way

Objections to induction were forcefully articulated by such 18th-century thinkers as David Hume. But it was the 20th-century Austrian living in England, Karl Popper, who formally articulated the chief problem with induction. Trying to marshal evidence to prove your prior beliefs or expectations is, he showed, full of pitfalls. If you were committed to prove something, there is no end to the "correct" evidence you could collect and, based on that, make claims that appear justifiable, even though the evidence may be grossly biased and even though you could never collect exhaustive evidence.

Reminiscent of Aristotle's desire for separating good reasoning from false argumentation, Popper was concerned with "distinguishing between a genuinely empirical method and a non-empirical or even a pseudo-empirical method—that is to say, a method which, although it appeals to observation and experiment, nevertheless does not come up to scientific standards."[61]

In a 1953 chapter on how he solved the problem of induction, Popper explained that data collection and analysis alone did not make something worthy of being called scientific knowledge. Astrology, for example, was not a science even though it was characterized by a stupendous amount of data based on observations of horoscopes. It was more myth than science.

To argue his point, Popper used the examples of Marxism, Freudian psychoanalysis, and Adler's individual psychology. These he described as being less science, like astronomy, and more primitive myths, like astrology. This is how he explained his thinking:

I found that those of my friends who were admirers of Marx, Freud, and Adler, were impressed by a number of points common to these theories, and especially by their apparent *explanatory power*.... [T]he study of any of them seemed to have the effect of an intellectual conversion or revelation, opening your eyes to a new truth hidden from those not yet initiated. Once your eyes were thus opened you saw confirming instances everywhere: the world was full of *verifications* of the theory.... [T]he most characteristic element in this situation seemed to me the incessant stream of confirmations, of observations which 'verified' the theories in question; and this point was constantly emphasized by their adherents.

This, again, is the problem of confirmation bias turning people into believers, and corrupting our ability to see the evidence for what it might actually be. To Popper, this was a grave problem. How do you distinguish claims based on legitimate empirical methods from those that may be corrupted by our many human frailties?

Popper's response to this long-standing problem of inductive reasoning was to turn the tables on Bacon. Instead of collecting evidence to prove your hypothesis, Popper argued that the correct scientific approach is to try to *falsify* your expectations. In a brilliant twist, he correctly noted that while there is always a strong incentive, but never enough evidence, to conclusively prove your hypothesis, a single counter-example is sufficient to disprove it.

That is, trying to prove a belief is highly vulnerable to being corrupted by confirmation bias. The correct approach, therefore, in the spirit of Descartes, is to doubt and try to negate what you already believe. Instead of justifying or verifying, try to falsify.

What distinguishes science from non-science, Popper reasoned, is not simply that one is empirical and the other not. Empiricism says nothing about the quality of thinking. The real difference is that scientific knowledge is clearly expressed so that it can be empirically falsified. It needs to take that risk of being disconfirmed. The emphasis is still on observation and data, but the shift is in what to do with those data.

Popper says the data should be used to try to challenge your beliefs. The reason that psychoanalysis is not science, he wrote, is that the data gathered during clinical sessions is used to apply rather than falsify its basic premises. The more you see the data confirming what you already believe, the more likely it is that you may be falling prey to confirmation bias, and greater the caution is warranted, through empirical falsification.

By shifting the scientific approach from justifying to falsifying, Popper at once noted the conservative nature of the knowledge-building enterprise. As with Descartes, doubt once again was at the center of knowing. Yet, unlike Descartes, Popper also made a modified version of Bacon's empiricism central to his method.

At the same time, however, by insisting on falsification Popper also made truth inaccessible. You can never be sure about the truth of a situation. The inability to falsify a hypothesis at a given time does not mean that the next effort to falsify will not succeed; even repeated failed efforts to falsify do not mean that the next effort at falsification will not succeed. Since a single valid counter-example would be good enough to cast doubt on a scientific belief, there can be no confirmed truths.

This is not to say that repeated unsuccessful falsification tests are not helpful; they are because they increase confidence in your hypothesis. Yet, you can never be sure what the next moment or next piece of evidence will bring. All scientific laws or "truths" are subject to the risk of disconfirmation, in other words, and all scientific knowledge is tentative by its very nature.

Logic, Data, and Doubt

So, through the labors of a long line of thinkers spanning more than 2,000 years, we now understand that good decisions require careful application of logic, data, and doubt. Together, these provide some protection against the many corrupting influences on our ways of thinking and making choices.

Following Aristotle, careful logic and well-constructed deductive analysis remain central to good decision-making. Yet, however careful one might be, logic devoid of data remains vulnerable to biases and prejudices that are deeply human.

So, logical reasoning imposed on good data is another layer of protection against our all-too-human vulnerabilities. Finally, because of our apparent need to seek validation, to avoid dissonance with our wishes and desires, logic and data are not by themselves enough. Both are corruptible and easily recruited into the service of what we already believe or want to believe.

As such, logic and data best serve the path to knowledge when they are used not to confirm but to challenge our beliefs. What we need is a mental orientation of skepticism, the search for well-constructed empirical evidence that refutes or negates or disconfirms what we think we already know. Systematic empirical skepticism, or falsification, incorporates both careful logic and good data.

More than 2,000 years removed from the labors of Plato and Aristotle, half a millennium after Bacon wrote his masterpiece, not quite a century after Popper began his studies, we now have a method with which to tackle the frailties of our human mind. As investors, we must take heed.

How to Think Right

Important to note, however, that Popper was articulating the method of empirical falsification to help strengthen *scientific* research. He had in mind theories in the natural sciences such as physics and astronomy, where the hope is to uncover fixed laws that are not alterable by human action; his methods can be only approximately applied in the social sciences and the humanities. This is because unlike the natural sciences where plethora of objective data can be collected and analyzed, the social sciences seek to understand social phenomenon that are themselves generated by human behavior.

When empirically studying social phenomenon, therefore, uncritical application of falsification methodology is troubling because the data and patterns themselves are transient products of human behavior. Some have claimed that social phenomena are objective social facts,[62] but surely they don't claim that social data are as objective as, for example, magnetic waves and solar radiation.

Investing is a human endeavor and the data or patterns generated in the financial markets are really a result of the aggregate behavior of millions of investors. As such, the price and other data relevant to investing are not objective as are the data typically available in the natural sciences. Applying the methodology of empirical falsification, as Popper had originally intended, is not particularly well suited for investors.

Yet, Popper's falsification is but a special case of the larger *principle of negation* that has been a consistent if not always visible theme in Western thought. It is a particular form of and draws from the broader orientation to be skeptical and cautious about beliefs. This inclination to doubt, even self-doubt as we have seen in the previous pages, has clearly been present among thinkers at least since the sophists in classical Greece. Skepticism and doubt remain relevant outside the natural sciences.

Almost five decades after Popper's 1953 chapter, researchers are generally in agreement that good decisions require a deft combination of tentative verification and outright disconfirmation to gradually build up confidence in a given point of view. Using sound logic and evaluating relevant data are the keys, but both ought to be done with caution and in the spirit of trying to disconfirm whatever the initial and emergent beliefs may be. Objective data and clear benchmarks are to be desired, as they can clearly invalidate a belief; but subjective evaluation of fuzzy data is also helpful in such attempts to cast doubt on your own beliefs and those of others. Repeated attempts at disconfirmation, if unsuccessful, give you greater confidence in the decisions that you ultimately make.

This is the state of knowledge after eons of thinking about how we humans reason. This is the approach we will take, therefore, to frame how to make good investment decisions. In the chapters that follow, I will show how to set up an investment hunch as a thesis and how to then try to cast doubt on that thesis using both quantitative and qualitative data. If the investment thesis survives serious efforts to create doubt and disconfirm, it is then a good basis for confidently making investment decisions.

8

Investing as a Negative Art

———

Thinkers both ancient and modern have taught us that our belief structures strongly influence how we relate to the world around us. We have implicit theories about how the world works and we need these theories to help structure the overwhelming amount of information that confronts us every moment. But our belief structures also act as blinders of sorts, restricting our field of vision, powerfully guiding attention to data that are consistent with our prior beliefs, and easily distorting our evaluation of those data.

It is for this reason that clear thinking when investing rests largely on our willingness and ability to disconfirm the prior beliefs we bring to an evaluation. That is the method of the philosopher and, arguably, a method of sound investing.

In the writing of their classic, *Security Analysis*, Graham and Dodd spend considerable effort discussing the problems of investment analysis, problems that become quite daunting because of the array of confusing cues emanating from the churn of the markets and the noisy coverage in the media. Their approach to solving those problems is worth noting because *how* they understand and define the task of analysis is as important, if not more so, than *what* they may think about any particular investment situation.

To these two authors, the method of analysis was the key, as it incorporated not only good technique but also a correct temperament to seek and approach data with appropriate skepticism.

Given the noise of the market and the hubbub in the psyche of the analyst, Graham (the senior author) is suspicious of pure deduction, of logic alone.

Instead, like Francis Bacon, he insists on empirical verification, on collecting data, on quantifying, and on establishing standards and benchmarks. He understands that data can be faulty and misleading, but expects that a good analyst ought to be able to detect faults in the reported information, to be able to read all manner of company literature.

Graham relies strongly on quantification, or marshaling evidence and making decisions based not on conjectures and vague premises but on judgments that are grounded in good data. He is at once quantitative and, knowing the hazards of investing, he is also guarded in his evaluation and interpretation of the facts.

To the extent that the standards and benchmarks may be tentatively established given historical experiences, Graham's methods of verification are quite sound. But, as we have been discussing, care must still be taken about that old nemesis, the confirmation bias.

For a variety of reasons, you may begin to believe that a particular investment opportunity is a good one, and, before you know it, all the evidence appears to support that belief. As we will see when we discuss valuation techniques later in the book, it is indeed quite easy to justify the price you are willing to pay for a stock.

Graham understands this problem and is, therefore, quite suspicious of qualitative factors, those premises that do not have a basis in clear, quantifiable facts. He is comfortable with historical numbers and much less so with future projections; more with quantitative factors and less with qualitative expectations.

It is in these situations, where analysis is vulnerable to corruption from confirmation and other biases, that refutation and disconfirmation can be useful. Instead of trying to verify or prove that a given investment is good or bad as we may be inclined to believe from hearsay, half-truths, and initial impressions, we must use sound judgments to try to disconfirm our prior beliefs. And, as much as possible, we must do that empirically, with good data.

Disconfirmation is key, method is king, and a conservative orientation is indispensable for investing wisely.

As we have been discussing above, of course, it is impossible to know for sure the incontrovertible truth about an investment opportunity. There will never be enough evidence to know for sure. All the evidence from the past may be moot in the very next moment. Yet, it ought to be relatively easy to negate or disconfirm our prior beliefs if we were to find robust logic or data that contradict expectations.

Graham did not explicitly mention disconfirmation as an approach to investment analysis. I suspect he knew about it instinctively, but not enough to articulate it as succinctly as Popper tagged falsification to be central to the scientific method. Born in 1894, he was deep in a productive career on Wall Street when Popper (born 1902) was just beginning to develop his ideas in the 1920s. Although they were contemporaries, the two men occupied very different and unconnected spheres.

Graham was a practical man of money; Popper was an academic philosopher. Graham was inspired by the need to cut through the noise and systematically working his way through the haze of the stock market; Popper was driven to understand the nature of knowledge and the correct means to build intellectual integrity. Graham wanted to solve the age-old problem of trying to make a buck without being run over by the herd; Popper wanted to solve an age-old philosophical problem of knowing: how do we know what we think we know?

Two very different men, Popper and Graham, but both with the same deep desire to find and draw that line of demarcation: between science and non-science for the philosopher; between investment and speculation for the investor.

It is left to us to flesh out what the principle of negation means for investors and how doubt and skepticism ought to be formally applied to investment decisions. For now, let it simply be said that efforts at formal refutation and disconfirmation provide a measure of protection against the hazards and the seductions of investing in the financial markets.

Investment versus Speculation

So, Popper used falsification as a line of demarcation between science and non-science, arguing that while knowledge comes in all forms, scientific knowledge demands testability and empirical falsification. Similarly, for those seeking to make good choices when investing, systematic disconfirmation is the line of demarcation between investment and speculation. That is, investments are those opportunities that can be formally refuted or disconfirmed, those that risk being rejected based on specific quantitative criteria or on the basis of clear qualitative judgment such as poor quality of leadership or incoherence of their narrative.

It follows, then, that those opportunities that do not risk rejection, those that may be justified in one way or another but which cannot be formally set up for refutation, they are speculative.

Disconfirming Investment Thesis

Yet, as in all practical endeavors, care needs to be taken that refutation and disconfirmation are done judiciously. It is naïve to simply reject an investment opportunity on the basis of a single observation. To take each evaluation criterion individually and make a yea or nay decision solely on that one criterion independent of all others is not the true intent of disconfirmation.

Instead, disconfirmation is a process that formalizes a mental orientation of skepticism. It helps systematically evaluate investment opportunities by carefully organizing quantitative and qualitative data specific to those opportunities. These data, when cautiously interpreted with the aim of trying to refute the investment thesis, help make judgments about the safety and suitability of the investment being scrutinized.

A systematic disconfirmation approach is meant to attain a deep and holistic understanding of the investment under scrutiny. So, for instance, if it turns out that the firm under consideration has low profitability or that it has high financial leverage, these are not by themselves sufficient reasons to refute the investment thesis.

Instead, the spirit of disconfirmation and all its power is in evaluating an investment thesis on the basis of a hierarchy of criteria, with each individual criterion being part of a group of related criteria. Rejection of the investment thesis is based not on a single piece of evidence but on the basis of the violation of some key principle about what makes for a good investment. As such, evaluation of an investment thesis requires consideration of the overall evidence and leads to the judgment whether or not the thesis ought to be discredited.

So, for instance, if you have a thesis that a particular stock is a good investment, then you evaluate that thesis by deriving and setting up a related sub-thesis about, among other things, the financial strength of the company. This sub-thesis is tested by systematic evaluation of a set of quantities (e.g., cash flows and debt capacity) that indicate various aspects of the financial strength of the company. The sub-thesis need not be rejected if any one of the many quantities indicates financial weakness when all other indications of strength are good. If it turns out that the company is financially not particularly strong, there may be other sub-theses, such as yield and stability or business model and leadership team that may lead you to a different conclusion.

Financial weakness will, however, cast doubt on the thesis and this doubt you will carry through the analysis to be eventually evaluated in light of all subsequent evidence.

In essence, then, you to try to disconfirm the investment thesis on the basis of your overall judgment based on the totality of tests, rather than reject it based on a single quantity or even a set of quantities that operationalize the investment thesis. As we will see from examples later in the book, it is important not to lose sight of the overall picture when applying this approach of trying to refute and disconfirm your prior or emergent beliefs about an investment.

Even more importantly, disconfirmation is an exercise in sorting through a large number of investment candidates that may look equally attractive. Descartes, you will remember, doubted everything and used doubt as the key to questioning and rejecting false knowledge. Metaphorically, his method was akin to scooping out bucket loads of sand until he hit firm ground, the solid rock on which to then begin building a foundation for true knowledge.

In a similar vein, the method of disconfirmation is to scoop out by bucketloads investment candidates that are only seemingly attractive but not quite. Refutation is an inductive method of doubt; when used well, its purpose is to help systematically lead you to investment opportunities that are truly attractive because they have survived systematic and well-calibrated skepticism.

So, the task ahead of us is to define what kinds of criteria ought to be used for refuting and disconfirming investment theses, and then to outline how such an approach ought to be applied in practice. We will get to these issues in due course, but in the meantime, in the next chapter, I present some thoughts on how investors ought to think about investing.

9

How to be a Wise Investor

———

For a beginner to think that he is a smart investor just because he knows how to buy and sell stocks is like imagining that he can execute a battle plan just because he knows how to shoot a gun. Far from it. However talented someone may be, investing wisely demands mastery of certain analytical skills and, perhaps more importantly, a sound method to help control destructive internal urges and external inducements for thoughtless action.

New investors usually start out with wild, frenzied buying and selling. They are attracted to popular names, impressed by the seemingly infallible expertise of commentators, and fascinated by the thought of striking it rich. Unaware of the many hazards that await them, they alternate chaotically between hope and fear, getting fixated on one stock after another in quick succession…and trade too much. Their distracted, disjointed plays inevitably lead to steep losses, sooner or later, and a realization that there is more to investing than meets the eye. Eventually, drained of resources and in financial pain, they begin to develop a greater appreciation of the complexity of the endeavor. Caution follows, and alert novices begin to learn the importance of reasoned restraint when investing.

As novice investors mature into adolescence, their choices become more deliberate. Yet, their buying and selling is still burdened with too many ideas that they chase simultaneously. They remain enamored with quick wins and sell whenever there is an opportunity to lock in profits or when gripped by fear of loss. They lack a systematic approach and have little by way of an overall game plan that would give coherence to their actions.

Although more deliberate, intermediate level investors don't quite grasp the importance of organized buying and selling such that individual transactions help build positions that transcend daily fluctuations in prices and periodic bouts of euphoria or panic in the markets. Slowly and painfully, they realize that personal experience by itself is insufficient to master the art of investing. As Jesse Livermore once said, there are just too many different kinds of mistakes that investors can make for them to ever be confident that their experiences are sufficiently educational. Hence, the most alert investors eventually recognize the importance of good conceptual frameworks that would help them deal with the complexity of investing. They begin to see the value of playing for position and, furthermore, the need to not only develop good analytical skill but also an ability to manage and stabilize emotions.

As investors mature and make it a habit to play for position, they also learn that investing wisely is not just clever buying and selling. More than that, investing is about making sound positional plays such that each trade firms up the foundations of their investment program and sets them up for future investing actions, both deliberate and opportunistic. That is, each trade is more than just a transaction; it is part of a larger investment puzzle that they may be trying to solve. In order to accomplish such, advanced investors become much more interested in developing a method—a systematic approach—to guide them through the chaos of the financial markets.

The path from ignorance to wisdom in investing can be long and arduous, and not everyone who embarks on it ends up at the right place. But those who do acquire the correct analytical skills and mental attitudes, they find that the self-knowledge they gain along the way pays very good dividends, both as outsized investment performance and as personal satisfaction.

Investment Errors

A large part of investing wisely is to understand and manage the errors that are inevitable when making decisions under uncertainty, as investment choices are apt to be. The principle of negation, as we have developed in the previous chapters, can certainly help reduce self-inflicted mistakes that investors are liable to make when investing. But even as cautious an approach as guided by the negation principle cannot eliminate mistakes altogether; there are just too many factors to fully take into account in even the most comprehensive analysis. Hence, a key to good investing is to understand and broadly frame the kinds of errors that investors are likely to make in spite of good analysis.

Trying to refute or disconfirm an investment thesis can generate two kinds of mistakes: errors of commission and errors of omission. In order to understand how these errors come about, consider the following simplified example.

Assume that you are considering a major commitment to buy 'S' units of company 'A' at a price of 'P' per share. You do your analysis and believe that buying the stock is a good idea. You make the investment and later find out that the stock did very well, in which case your thesis turned out to be correct. In figure 9.1, that would put you in Cell 1: you thought that investing in Company 'A' was a good idea and it turned out to be so. It could have turned out that your investment in the company did poorly, in which case your purchase of the shares of the company would turn out to have been a bad idea. That would put you in Cell 2: you thought that the stock of Company 'A' at price 'P' was a good investment but it turned out to be bad.

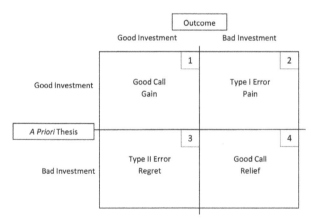

Figure 9.1: Error trade-off. Errors of commission (Pain) versus errors of omission (Regret)

On the other hand, your initial thesis could have been that investing in Company 'A' was a bad idea. If it turned out that it was actually a good investment, then you would be in Cell 3: you thought that the stock was no good and it turned out to be good. Conversely, if it turned out that the company was a bad investment, then in figure 9.1 you would be in Cell 4: you thought that it was a bad stock and it did turn out to be so.

All in all, four possibilities exist in the combination of your thesis (Good or Bad) and the outcome (Good or Bad): 1) Good—Good [Gain], 2) Good—Bad [Pain], 3) Bad—Good [Regret], and 4) Bad—Bad [Relief].

Scenarios 1 and 4 are where what you had expected was consistent with what actually turned out to be the case. You either make an investment gain or are happy that you avoided the loss.

The other two scenarios are much less rosy, however. Scenario 2 is where your disconfirmation analysis led you to think that the investment was a good idea but it turns out that the investment was bad. Here, you made a false-positive or Type I error: you incurred an investment loss by mistakenly being unable to disconfirm or refute the thesis that this was a good investment. In the worst case, that mistake would be as if investing in the likes of Enron or Lehman Brothers or AIG or any of the busts over the years that looked good but were, in fact, bad investments.

Scenario 3, on the other hand, is where you disconfirmed or refuted the thesis that the stock was a good investment. You decided not to make the investment, only to find out later that it was indeed a good investment. Here you make a false-negative or Type II error: you disconfirmed what was, in fact, a good investment and you suffered an opportunity cost from not having invested. That error would be like letting go of the likes of Home Depot or Dell or Microsoft or many other breakout companies in their early years. With Type II errors comes the regret of not catching the winners, so there may be an emotional cost as well.

The problem for investors is that the type of error committed is a function of how the disconfirmation analysis is set up and used. If you design loose filtering screens (investment thesis is hard to disconfirm), then you increase the chances of committing Type I error and catching poor investment targets. If, on the other hand, you design stringent screens (investment thesis is easy to disconfirm), you increase the chances of committing Type II error and letting good opportunities slip by. Loosening the screens will allow more garbage into your investment program; conversely, tightening the filtering screens will squeeze out good opportunities.

Error Trade-Off

A further problem for investors is that the two types of errors are the exact opposites. Reducing the chances of making Type I error increases the chances of making Type II error, and vice versa. Sure, you would like to reduce both errors by doing good analysis, but that can be done only up to a point. Beyond that point, there will be unavoidable trade-off between Type I and Type II errors. It is then up to you to decide which of the two for you is the more egregious error that you'd like to avoid, and which of the two types of errors is acceptable to you.

We will see in chapter 24 that, using portfolio logic, it may be possible to raise total portfolio returns by having an appropriate mix of possibilities for the two types of errors. But, even then, your orientation toward errors of commission (Type I error) or errors of omission (Type II error) plays an important role in how you construct your stock portfolio.

Note that either type of error can occur in spite of very good analysis—when, for example, the market price is driven largely by sentiment or other extraneous factors. In such cases, you lose money even though your analysis was correct. Of course, errors can also result from faulty or incorrect analysis, where you misdiagnose the stock.

Still, powered by the principle of negation, our approach to investing helps highlight the trade-off between the two types of errors—and bring a measure of control to investment decisions. The method also helps clarify your own personal approach and style of investing. If you find Type II error acceptable but want to avoid Type I error at all cost, for example, then your approach to investing is likely to be strongly defensive and valuation oriented. Conversely, if you find Type I error acceptable but want to avoid Type II error at all cost, then your approach to investing is likely to be aggressive and perhaps even adventurous. In either case, you will calibrate your approach to the mix of possible errors that are right for you.

In this sense, wise investors shape their investment programs in accordance with their underlying preference for either of the two types of errors. Even when seeking outsized investment performance, advanced investors usually develop well-conceived filtering screens so as to avoid at least the most egregious errors that have the potential to undermine their otherwise carefully-constructed investment program.

10

The Art of Looking

———

Much of what happens in investing seems to be driven by a strong inclination of people to focus too much on what others say and not enough on their own analysis of facts at hand. Both professional and lay investors fall easy prey to this tendency to rely on what others think and do in the stock market.

Blithely following others is so rampant among analysts and money managers, in fact, that researchers now recognize imitation as a central feature of the financial markets.[63] Sometimes called *rational herding*, such imitative behavior among professional investors is said to arise from, among other things, the pressures to produce returns for anxious clients who demand quarterly performance when, in fact, the nature of markets is such that performance simply cannot be guaranteed.

The problem of not paying attention to facts and relying instead on what others say is much more pronounced in lay people, who typically do not have the time or skills to do their own confident analysis. Most lay investors, therefore, look to media personalities and other authority figures in order to form opinions about where to invest and how.

The Urge to Imitate

What encourages copying and complicates investing is that in the short-term at least, driven largely by the unpredictable forces of buying and selling in the aggregate, prices move randomly.[64] So, even those investors who think they are doing good analysis can suffer poor results because prices can move sharply against their well-informed expectations. There is little if any connection, in other words, between careful analysis of fundamental factors and the short-term movement of prices.

Then there is always the chance that the analysis itself is incorrect because of misinterpretation of facts, leading to investments that turn out to be mistakes. Since prices do move randomly in the short-term and analysis can be wrong, reasonable people may think that it is easier to just ignore the facts and follow what everybody else seems to be doing. Going along with the herd can be profitable, after all, even if getting caught going in the wrong direction can create losses.

Imitation is often also an easy, if dangerous, solution to the problem of noise in the markets. With so many stocks, bonds and other securities to choose from and with so many opinions and marketing pitches to sort through, potential investors are vulnerable to utter confusion. As they gaze over the noisy markets, a sense of paralysis can set in and induce either no action at all or one that is drastically against their own self-interest.

If not disciplined in the art of picking and evaluating one stock at a time, both lay and professional investors can easily succumb to the impossible task of trying to understand everything and, as a result, see nothing. Such a state of confusion and bewilderment is an inducement for many investors to simply copy what others may be doing, especially when those others have prestige and credibility.

So, the focus on the short-term and the inclination to copy others go hand-in-hand with the facts that prices are unpredictable in the near term and the markets are incredibly noisy. These are reasons enough for people to not pay attention to important attributes of the investments—and be easily incited into gambling and unfettered speculation.

It is no surprise, then, that imitation and speculation drive the markets. With the lays following the experts and the experts following each other, investing often becomes an exercise in which everyone follows everyone else with few, if any, carefully evaluating fundamental drivers of economic value. It is easy, in such an environment, for fragments of disjointed data and opinions to so fill the airwaves that facts get inextricably mingled with fantasy, and thoughtful analysis becomes increasingly difficult. The sea of noise that surrounds the would-be investor drowns out, in effect, the important nuggets and insights. It is not easy in such an environment to look for, find, and stay focused on key facts that may be salient to the investing opportunity at hand.

Already disoriented by the maddening cacophony, aspiring investors are further misled by modern finance theory that says the markets are efficient and prices incorporate all relevant information. As such, they are told, analysis will not help because efficient markets make it impossible to find profitable opportunities.

In effect, overwhelming noise and the inclination to imitate together induce people to herd, perhaps with the thought that others might know something they themselves do not. It is when the gaze so shifts, from facts about the investment to the behaviors of those around, that speculation becomes pervasive. What others will do next or where prices will go next becomes a question of supreme importance.

Not doing careful analysis appears to have become so widespread that people hardly know much about what they trade or own. Those who buy mutual funds don't usually know what mutual fund managers really do, let alone what they own. People who buy stock index funds don't seem to know the stocks that make up the index. Hedge funds and their trading practices are black boxes. The millions of individuals who buy stocks often do ad hoc analysis of poorly organized data or know very little about the companies in which they invest. Still many more simply get a thrill from chasing prices up and down, and couldn't care less about what they are trading.

From Imitation to Analysis

Yet, for thoughtful investors interested in opportunities to put their capital to use in fundamentally sound businesses, ignoring the facts is fool-hardy. Fundamentally good businesses produce good and growing profits over a period of time and, when carefully chosen, they have the potential to provide excellent returns over time.

Certainly stock prices of even good companies fluctuate a lot and are essentially unpredictable in the short run. But good managers and their enduring ability to generate strong returns on invested capital make good companies worth careful scrutiny. Investing in such companies can be highly profitable over the long-term but it requires that the investment thesis is clearly set up and subjected to a rigorous process of disconfirmation.

As opposed to gambling or speculation, in effect, investing requires that investors re-learn the art of looking, of honing in on important facts, and then cobbling a diversity of clues into well-informed thesis about each entry into their investment portfolio. Intellectually demanding though good analysis is, it is only as good as the analytical skills and the temperament that you bring to the task. It demands consistent focus on facts instead of what others may be doing.

It pays for you to learn how to dig into the facts precisely because most people care not to do so. Where others may be focused on prices and trying to figure out which of the plethora of opinions to follow, those with the correct temperament and analytical skills have a leg up in the world of investing; their choices are anchored in the enduring fundamentals of wealth creation rather than in the fickle sentiments of the moment.

You need to learn, therefore, how to evaluate companies, to know what to look for, to know how to dig up useful data, to interpret the data and make guarded judgments from it, and to patiently wait for good results to come in over time. Be a capitalist—invest on the basis of sound data and analysis, with an eye out for what could go wrong.

Yet, sound analysis is not easy. As discussed, the many biases we have in our ways of thinking easily distort perceptions and lead us astray. The key to looking, therefore, is to be aware of the inclination to confirm beliefs and counter it with formal skepticism: a systematic process of disconfirmation, a way of seeking and approaching data so as to try to refute whatever hopeful thesis you may have begun to form.

The formal process of disconfirmation acts as a check on fascination with price movements or with the careless pronouncements that so fill the airwaves. It forces attention on crucial facts with which to try to refute that the quoted price of a stock is sufficiently different from reasonable expectations of its economic worth. Trying to refute and disconfirm wishful thinking brings forth important data that you may have secretly wanted to ignore for any of the many reasons. It encourages a careful but cautious look, fully acknowledging the possibility that the eagerness to prove a point, bolstered perhaps by hopes for quick riches, can get you to do foolish things. The skeptical orientation and the process of disconfirmation helps you make good choices.

How to Look when Investing

Investing is based on the search for divergence between valuation and sentiment, and the ability to clearly see such divergence when it does occur. It is based on the view that, at least for *some* stocks, reasonable estimates of economic worth can be made *independent* of both the market sentiment and the prices at which those stocks trade.

Three things need to be kept in mind when looking for investible opportunities: (1) estimates of the worth of a stock may be ascertained with a reasonable degree of confidence, although never with precision, (2) such estimates can be made without factoring the prevailing price into the equation, so that it may be possible to compare the prevailing market price with approximate economic worth, and (3) estimates of worth can be made for some but not all stocks.

As discussed in later chapters, the techniques of valuation—for estimating economic worth—are only moderately complex. The arithmetic that drives valuation analysis is fairly straightforward and can be learned with a modicum of effort. The assumptions behind the numbers that go into the analysis are an altogether different matter, however. As we have seen, the assumptions are powerfully shaped by personal biases and emotions overlaid with the seductions of the marketplace. Bad assumptions can make analysis pointless or, worse, dangerous.

The first task in the process of disconfirmation is to formalize your hunch by setting up the investment thesis that, in any particular case, price has indeed deviated far from intrinsic worth. This thesis could be based on a variety of reasons. You may think that the shares of Home Depot, for example, have been beaten down because of apparent reasons that have little to with the fundamental attributes of the business. A market-wide panic or overreaction to new information that is only seemingly harmful could have driven the prices down. You may think that a tip you received from a respected friend needs to be formally investigated. Whatever the reason, you begin to form a hunch that Home Depot is undervalued and, therefore, set up a formal thesis that the stock of the company is an attractive investment.

Next, instead of trying to prove or confirm the thesis that Home Depot shares are an attractive investment, you try to disconfirm that such is the case. If the process of disconfirmation were successful, then you know that your initial hunch was incorrect and you reject the thesis about undervaluation. By doing so, you avoid making a mistake of buying Home Depot, thinking that it was underpriced when, in fact, it was not. If the disconfirmation was *not* successful, on the other hand, then you accept the thesis tentatively; still, you remain cautious and continue trying to disconfirm the thesis. If repeated attempts to disconfirm fail, then you have a degree of confidence in your initial thesis and, perhaps, you commit and invest.

The important point of setting up a clear thesis and executing tests to try to disconfirm it is that by doing so you risk the outcome that the belief you had begun to form about the stock could be rejected. This very *risk of rejection* makes the investment worthy of being evaluated as a possible opportunity.

Refutability is the Key

Unlike investment thesis, a speculator's thesis requires no risk of rejection. Speculative activity is based on hope or expectation that the prices would move up or down within a certain time period. There may be good or bad reasons for expecting such price movements, but no easy way to set up adequate tests in order to refute such expectations.

Consider gold, for instance. If you were to think that the price of an ounce of gold would rise 10 percent, how would you disconfirm that? Market prices of gold are driven by the forces of supply and demand. While approximate supply may be estimated with some effort, the demand for gold is in large part driven by non-economic factors, especially fears and hopes about the unknowable future. So, absent any reasonably firm estimate of worth against which to evaluate the price of gold and the inability to set up a clear refutable thesis that risks rejection, it is in practice not possible to disconfirm claims about what the price of gold might be in a given period of time.

Disconfirmation is possible, on the other hand, for stocks whose approximate intrinsic worth can be estimated with inputs that are based in a good understanding of the economics and leadership of the companies in question. In such cases, pitting the prevailing price against estimates of worth derived from careful valuation and related analytics allows the possibility that the investment thesis can, indeed, be disconfirmed.

As we have discussed in the previous chapter, the risk of rejection, or disconfirmation, is the fundamental difference between investment and speculation; it is the line of demarcation between them.

Indeed, for some stocks and in certain situations, intrinsic economic worth is *indeterminate*. In those cases where reasonable estimates of worth simply cannot be made from available information, the prevailing prices are without an anchor and we move into the realm of speculation.

That is, stocks whose worth is equated wholly and squarely with the quoted prices are purely speculative in character. This would be if no track record of steady performance exists, for instance, or the underlying economics are simply those of uncertain supply and whimsical demand, or the business model is opaque, or it is too complex to be clearly articulate. Investible stocks, on the other hand, are those that have enough of a track record and such information as would help ascertain the approximate economic worth with a reasonable degree of confidence.

Ironically, the same stock could qualify both as a speculation and as an investment. An investible stock is one whose approximate value can be estimated with credible data and analysis but *without* reliance on the prevailing market prices at which it is selling at a given time. The same stock would be speculative, however, if there was no reasonable data-driven conception of its potential intrinsic value independent of the prevailing prices.

So, imagine that you were to purchase shares of Home Depot at a given price with the expectation that the price was approximately half the estimates of intrinsic worth. In this scenario, you would be considered to be investing. If, on the other hand, you were to purchase the same shares of Home Depot with no conception or estimate of intrinsic value but with the hope that the price would go up in the future, then you would be speculating. The ability to make and the very act of making reasonable estimates of economic worth separates investment from speculation.

Yet, worth and value are elusive concepts. As such, the conventional tools of valuation are liable to be misused to justify preconceived notions of what the underlying value of a stock might be. Estimates themselves are liable to be shaped by hope, fear, and greed; commentary by television personalities and the plethora of well-written "free" advice available in print and on the Internet all have powerful effects on investors trying to make estimates of value.[65]

So, what separates investing from speculation or gambling is the ability to ward off the extraneous influences by being deliberate and measured with the help of a formal process of refutation. Formally trying to refute or disconfirm your investment thesis is, in essence, the art of looking.

Book III

Foundations

Chapters

———

11. Price and Value

12. How to Value a Business

13. Risk and Uncertainty

14. The Simple Math of Valuation

15. Yield–Stability–Strength

———

11

Price and Value

———

In our cautious approach to investing, we are making the essential assumption that the prices of a given stock can be compared with robust estimates of true economic worth. That is, we assume that there exists an identifiable standard or a benchmark (economic worth) against which we can judge the market prices of a given stock. If there was no such benchmark, the entire enterprise of investing would be thrown into disarray: How would you then know what the correct price *ought* to be? If Wal-Mart stock sells for, say $55, how do you know that it is worth that much? How would you know that it is not worth $25, or $95 for that matter?

Now, the prices could be driven purely by expectations and counter-expectations about capital appreciation—such that they go up or down as expectations about future gain change. But what are the expectations based on? Are they driven solely by sentiment or do identifiable economic factors anchor expectations and, therefore, prices? Even if sentiments play a role, as they surely do, expectations and prices must have some basis in economics so that markets can function and transactions can occur. Otherwise, driven by the mood of the moment and periodic amplification of emotions to either extreme, the markets would likely experience spectacular booms and busts and, ultimately, seize up. This would especially be the case because of the amplifying effects of program trading that so defines our times.

As John Burr Williams long ago pointed out in *The Theory of Investment Value*, economic fundamentals must play a role in pricing. Assessing those fundamentals and their impact on prices is, therefore, an essential part of investment analysis—as is the ability to estimate the approximate economic worth with a reasonable degree of confidence. Once a range of such estimates are available, then it is a matter of comparing with prevailing prices to see if the opportunities may exist to invest profitably. That is, investment opportunities occur when sentiment or other extraneous factors drive prices far and away from confident estimates of true economic worth.

The confusion for those who wish to invest arises from the short-term fluctuations in prices and, given the many uncertainties about future prospects, a lack of confidence in their own analysis. Instead of taking prices as in-the-moment collective wisdom of a very large number of people, investors can sometimes equate any and all prevailing prices with true economic worth. It must be remembered, however, that collective wisdom can sometimes be a form of pure sentiment, or crowd psychology, which changes frequently and often without notice.

In the short run, stock prices are shaped by a complex of factors that influence buying and selling decisions of individuals and institutions. Depending on the social mood of the moment, both intrinsic valuation and sentiment influence prices to varying degrees. Sometimes, especially when emotions are high, sentiments dominate pricing and valuation takes the back seat. At other times, cooler heads prevail and prices gravitate toward approximate valuations. Prices, as Graham aptly noted, are subject to both neglect and prejudice.

Intrinsic worth of a stock may have little or no consideration in buying and selling, for other reasons as well. It is not uncommon, for example, for mutual funds and money managers to sell a stock when it is taken off an index and buy another when it gets on, with no consideration for its underlying valuation. Similarly, individuals and institutions often buy and sell stocks to re-balance their portfolios. Some may sell stocks to cover margin calls or to send their kids to college or any number of other reasons. Stocks and other securities are bought and sold for a range of economic and non-economic reasons, in other words, and such transactions may or may not have anything to do with underlying economic worth.

More important, during periodic euphoria or panic, masses of individual investors and institutional decision makers lose their independence of thought and can become part of a crowd joined in thought by the fear of loss, or the greed fueled by seemingly easy money. The diversity of opinion is severely diminished during such periods of high emotion, and large numbers suddenly coalesce effectively into much smaller numbers; the laws of large numbers no longer apply when that happens. Prices in such situations can deviate substantially from value, especially if the emotions of the moment drive collective attention sharply in one direction or the other.

As Benjamin Graham once wrote, the market is a voting machine in the short run but a weighing machine in the long run. Emotion and imitation influence stock prices in the near term; yet, over time, as investors adjust their expectations to realities on the ground, they do gravitate towards economic fundamentals.

For alert investors, therefore, sentiment-driven short-term fluctuations of prices can provide attractive investment opportunities. To the extent they can get reasonably good estimates of the intrinsic worth, investors may be able to evaluate the extent to which prices provide such opportunities.

In practice, estimates of economic worth are replete with subjectivity, and emotion can easily penetrate the veil of objectivity that valuation formulae may suggest. Worth and value are elusive concepts and they shift with the changing assumptions about the nature of the underlying asset.

As such, estimates of economic worth are prone to errors. Worse, the tools of valuation are liable to be misused to justify preconceived notions of what the prices of a stock might do in the near future, especially those notions that are subtly or strongly shaped by prevailing prices and by unrealistically hopeful or fearful expectations of the future. Indeed, the prudent attitude toward valuation is to assume that all estimates are just that; they are estimates.

What Good Is Valuation?

Valuation is an argument. It is an argument in which you bring estimates of economic worth to the negotiating table, to haggle with all the other buyers and sellers about the price at which you are willing to do business. If you get the price that makes sense in light of what you think is a good deal, then perhaps you do business. If you don't like the price, then perhaps you have the courage to walk away. That is the discipline.

It is often hard to say whether or not you made the correct decision by doing the business or walking away from it. This is because the price of shares of any company is driven not by your analysis but by the acts of multitudes of other people buying or selling. The price of a stock will go up/down if the demand for shares is greater/less than the supply of those shares. As for any other product or service, the laws of supply and demand also drive the prices of shares in the stock market.

Since the supply of the shares of a company is limited at any given time to the number of shares outstanding, prices are in effect driven by the demand for those shares. There may be instances in which the supply is affected by the buying and selling done by large shareholders or institutions who tend to own big blocks of shares. But, by and large, on a day-to-day basis, it is the demand side of the equation that drives the prices.

But the demand side of the market for a company's shares is driven by all sorts of motivations and perceptions, which in turn are subject to a variety of influences and manipulations. That is, people buy and sell stocks for reasons that may or may not include diligent analysis of available facts.

As you go to the market with your analysis in hand, you will find that other parties may or may not be as prepared as you are. Some of them may have better information than you do, or their analysis may be different so as to give them a different assessment of worth and value. Some may not even look at the fundamentals of the company and only rely on the movement of prices, or on tips from friends, or on the urgings of an influential television personality. Others may not do any analysis at all and may be acting on a hunch, or even no hunch at all but simply on hearsay, or hope, or hype.

The theory is that the buyers and sellers of all stripes will somehow negotiate prices so as to make trades, such that the underlying worth is ultimately discovered through prices. The errors that different people make are both on the upside (overpricing) and downside (underpricing); those errors simply cancel out in the aggregate and what you get is the clearing price that mirrors the correct value of the shares.

Now, the law of large numbers sure does apply when millions upon millions of shares change hands in short order and thousands upon thousands of decisions are made. In that it allows decisions to buy and sell to be quickly implemented, market liquidity is fundamental to healthy functioning of the capital markets and is essential for the law of large numbers to work.

But, also critical for markets to function properly is a wide diversity of opinions. This is because the law of large numbers only works when enough decision makers are independent of all others—in which case the independent errors are expected to cancel out, such that, over time, prices find the central or correct value.

Yet, we know that buyers and sellers in the capital markets are *not* independent of each other; they are exposed to a whole lot of the same information and influences and, given the concentration of media in the country, often from the same sources. As such, market participants are often joined in thought.

In spite of great diversity in preparation and motivations, in other words, large numbers of people are drawn to think and act similarly; their errors tend to become highly correlated. As a result, instead of converging on whatever may be true worth, prices can on occasion move away and stay away for varying periods of time.

Now, it is often argued that correlation of errors can be corrected if the smart money moves in and bets against the deviating prices. It seems reasonable that, seeing the deviation, investors may want to take advantage of the situation and arbitrage the gaping difference in prevailing prices and underlying worth. This is the mechanism that is said to regulate, in theory, the prices in the markets and, when it works, markets are generally quite efficient.

But there are several reasons such arbitrage may not be possible without serious risks to the arbitragers. After all, if thousands of investors are driving billions of dollars in one direction, what arbitragers can effectively resist that movement? Single arbitragers don't have much of a chance no matter what their resources; they have about as much chance of reversing the direction of deviating prices as you standing on the beach and trying to stop a tsunami. Only when the momentum has run its course and the directional move begins to lose steam can arbitragers effectively unite and ride the receding wave in the hope of making profits.

So, the markets being efficient may be a myth that relies if not on omniscient investors or on the law of large number then on phantom arbitragers fighting valiant battles to bring prices back in line with some underlying economic worth. In fact, prices don't so much as correctly reflect the true underlying worth as they are rough approximations of worth based largely on the sentiments of buyers and sellers at a particular point in time.

What the pricing mechanism does do is search for value, with prices running up and down looking to settle on a central value—even if they sometimes do the searching only in vain. Clearly, markets can on occasion efficiently price assets, such as stocks, but they cannot necessarily do so all the time for all different kinds of assets. This does not mean that there is another better system for finding the true values of assets and for allocating resources in the economy; the pricing mechanism is still a much better and more equitable system than, say, central planning. It's just that the best system we have is vulnerable on many levels and especially to the force of collective human emotion.

In essence, then, prices ought to be seen as being generative from the behavior of people buying and selling shares; such behavior is in turn influenced by a good deal more than simple considerations of immediate economic worth.

So, what use is analysis? What use especially the kind of analysis we will be doing in this book going forward? If prices move hither and thither because of emotion and seemingly random behavior of the multitudes chasing each other, then what good is careful analysis going to do for you?

Turns out, the power of analysis is in the fact that it forces you to ground decisions in the facts of the case, to look before you jump. It allows you to control your impulses, to slow down before you commit. Given the tricks that your mind can play on you, and given that a whole army of influencers is trying to persuade you to do this or that, you can be easily drawn into the emotions of the markets, to be seduced by the stories of how this stock is going to go up and that one down. Analysis helps you resist the temptations to do foolish things.

The power of analysis is in that it focuses you on the meaningful facts and to ignore the rest, to allow your mind to process the information intellectually rather than emotionally. All this so you can negotiate intelligently and commit wisely. Analysis makes you a rational investor.

Valuation and Negation

In the following chapter, I show how to estimate the economic worth of a business. You will see that the techniques of making the estimates are only moderately complex and can be learned with little effort. Yet, the techniques can be misused easily, as small changes in the key assumptions produce big differences in estimates.

As such, estimates of value must be made cautiously and with care, defensively and with humility in the knowledge that valuing a business is, in the end, more of an art than a science. Prudence requires that estimates of value be made using assumptions that are consistent with observable facts and are logically defensible.

More to the point in relation to what we have done in the first part of the book, the key to good valuation is that you try to refute your thesis that the stock you want to evaluate offers an attractive investment opportunity. That is, since emotion and the desire to justify a particular price can corrupt analysis, the key to good valuation is a careful application of the principle of negation.

You must try to refute!

12

How to Value a Business

———

Although many different valuation techniques exist for estimating how much a business may be worth,[66] we will focus here on two common ways to do so: (1) Market Valuation, and (2) Intrinsic Valuation. Before we discuss each in turn, however, think about how valuation plays a role during a common transaction in which many people engage, or aspire to, at least once in their lifetime: housing purchase.

If you wanted to buy a house for $100,000, for instance, and apply for a mortgage to finance the purchase, the bank would get an appraisal for the value of the house. The appraiser collects data on similar houses sold in similar neighborhoods in the recent past, makes adjustments based on space, location, number of rooms, quality of construction, et cetera, and estimates the approximate market value of the house at the time of the appraisal.

That is, the appraised market value indicates how much similar houses have sold for in the recent past. The bank then loans money, usually up to about 80 percent of the appraised value so as to have a bit of a cushion in case the housing prices take a drop, but also to make sure that you have skin in the game. The appraiser may also give you a replacement value, or how much it would cost to rebuild the same house if it were to be destroyed in a fire or such. Sometimes called cost-basis value in housing parlance, the replacement value is used by insurance companies to write homeowner's insurance policies. If you were to rent out the property, then you could also estimate the intrinsic economic worth by appropriately discounting the future net cash flows from rental income.

Similar logic is applicable for transactions involving businesses. Replacement value is rarely used in such transactions but it is common to use the *market value* or *comparable method*, where the value of a business is estimated using the sale prices of similar businesses. The approximate economic worth, or intrinsic value, of a business may also be obtained by estimating and appropriately discounting the expected future net cash flows. Let us discuss both the techniques.

Market Value: Capitalization Ratios and Benchmarks

As in the case of appraisals done in the housing sector, market appraisals of business are based on the market pricing of "similar" businesses or, specifically, normalized ratios.

The value of a business, in this way of thinking, is approximately what someone has recently paid for a similar business. The challenge in this kind of analysis, however, is to find market transactions involving businesses that are similar to yours in such terms as specialization, geography, demographics, size of markets/clientele served, size of business in gross revenues, and profitability. No two businesses are exactly alike and trying to find an identical twin in the world of business is quite difficult indeed.

Hence, once you locate several transactions involving similar businesses, necessary adjustments then need to be made to account for unique attributes or circumstances of the particular business being evaluated. As in housing appraisals, moreover, these adjustments are subjective judgments based on your understanding of the particulars.

Typically, therefore, market value can be assessed using ratios such as price/sales, price/earnings, price/book, price/cash flow, etc. The idea is to hone in on the ratios that best capture how value for a particular kind of business is actually being assessed out there. It may be, for instance, that similar businesses have been selling at a price that equals revenues. In valuation parlance, this means that the market is *capitalizing* revenues by a factor of one—or one dollar in market value for one dollar in revenues. On the other hand, the market may be capitalizing not revenues but free cash flows and by a factor of, say, four. In that case, the market value of a business with, say, $10 million in annual free cash flows would be something in the neighborhood of $40 million. It is difficult to generalize as to what exactly the market capitalizes without knowing the specifics of the industry. Hence, you have to be quite familiar with the nature of business and with buying-selling activity in the marketplace to know which ratios to use as rules of thumb in particular cases.

Let us consider the above using the example of Wal-Mart and also include Target in our analysis for the purpose of comparison. See table 12.1 for the key numbers and the computed ratios as discussed.

As of the fiscal year ending in January 2010, Wal-Mart had a total market value of about $211 billion. For that year, it had total sales of $408 billion, net income of $14.3 billion, and it generated just over $14 billion in free cash flow. The company had $70.7 billion in common equity.

Computing capitalization ratios from these figures, as shown in the column to the far right, the market was valuing the company at 0.52 times the revenues, just under fifteen times its earnings, just over fifteen times free cash flow for the year, and about three times common equity.

To put these numbers in context, it is best to compare them with those for another similar company in similar businesses, and then also with the company's own numbers from some years ago.

Although Wal-Mart is a company unlike any other, let's compare it with Target in order to illustrate a point. [67] There are many differences between the two companies, both in terms of size, reach, and geographical scope, but they also have a few notable similarities which make them suitable for side-by-side comparison at least for our purposes here.

Although the two companies are much different in size, the ratios on the right of table 12.1 tell the story that they are priced relatively similarly as of the end of their fiscal years ending the early part of 2010. For each dollar of revenue, the market price of Wal-Mart was 0.52 and that of Target was 0.58. They were both selling for just about 15 times their total net income. Wal-Mart was selling for about three times the common equity and Target at about 2.5 times common equity. Wal-Mart was selling for about 15 times free cash flow for the most recent year and Target about under 10 times the free cash it generated during the year. This last number looks good for Target until you factor in that they reduced capital expenditures during the year, whereas Wal-Mart increased their reinvestments.[68]

Table 12.1

(Data in $mm)	WMT	TGT		WMT	TGT
Market Value (MV)	211,529	37,951		Ratio	Ratio
Revenues (Rev)	408,214	65,357	MV/Rev	0.52	0.58
Net Income (NI)	14,335	2,488	MV/NI	14.76	15.25
Common Equity (CEQ)	70,749	15,347	MV/CEQ	2.99	2.47
Free Cash Flow (FCF)	14,065	4,152	MV/FCF	15.04	9.14

Using such cross-sectional comparisons between the two companies as above indicates the degree to which the market is pricing a company in line with how it is pricing other similar companies. But the story does not end here. We also need to see how the capitalization ratios compare with historical valuations. To that end, let's see in table 12.2 how Wal-Mart was being priced, say, 10 years earlier in 2001 and compare it with 2010 market valuations as reflected in the capitalization ratios.

Table 12.2

	WMT	WMT		WMT	WMT
(Data in $mm)	2010	2001		2010	2001
Market Value (MV)	211,529	228,819		Ratios	Ratios
Revenues (Rev)	408,214	191,329	MV/Rev	0.52	1.20
Net Income (NI)	14,335	6,295	MV/NI	14.76	36.35
Common Equity (CEQ)	70,749	31,343	MV/CEQ	2.99	7.30
Free Cash Flow (FCF)	14,065	1,562	MV/FCF	15.04	146.49

As is evident from table 12.2, with revenues of $191 billion in 2001, Wal-Mart was a smaller company then than in 2010, when it reported revenues over $408 billion. In addition, as the ratios in the table show, the company was being priced much more aggressively in 2001 than it was in 2010. The market was paying $1.20 for every dollar of revenues and more than 36 times every dollar of net income. Price as multiples of common equity and free cash flow were also aggressive.

Ironically, the company grew revenues from $191 billion in 2001 to $408 billion at the end of 2010; yet, those who invested in the company at the beginning of the period did not benefit because the subsequent growth was already incorporated in the stock price back in 2001.

The numbers in the tables above indicate that as of the end of fiscal 2010, Wal-Mart was priced quite similar to Target and the pricing was much more reasonable compared with what they were at the end of 2001.

Needless to say, this technique of capitalization and comparable metrics requires a good deal of guesswork and subjective decisions on which ratios to use and which companies to compare with. Although capitalization ratios can give a quick sense of how the company is being priced in the market, it is important to understand that the market can value the same company very differently depending on the larger sentiments at work.

In 2001, Wal-Mart was seen as a high-growth company and investors seem to have overpaid based on their optimism about future prospects. As such, those who had bought Wal-Mart in 2001 saw their returns severely compromised for the next decade. The company continued to improve its performance but the capitalization ratios actually went down! The stock price of the company hardly even budged from an average of about $44 in 2001 to an average of $50 in 2010.

Capitalization ratios can provide investors insights about reasonableness of prices. But if valuations across the market are low or high, then it is difficult to judge the reasonableness unless the capitalization ratios are evaluated in an historical context. It is easy for capitalization ratios to be distorted by sentiments about the company or the market at large.

Intrinsic Value: Discounted Cash Flow (DCF) Analysis

Let us now turn to the alternate way of valuing a business. To illustrate the methodology, I use a hypothetical business that is up for sale. Valuation of publicly traded companies requires a similar thought process.

Say you wanted to buy a small medical practice for $1 million from a friend who wanted to retire after having built that practice over an entire career. You figure that the practice was well established, although by no means was it at its full potential. You would like to update the capital equipment with an additional $300,000 by the end of the first year. Then with some savvy marketing and tie-ins with large hospitals in the area you could grow that practice at an average rate of at least 10 percent a year for the foreseeable future.

Your dear friend Leon Shaky is willing to lend you the $1 million at a 20 percent annual interest charge plus a 25 percent stake in the business. You think you'd give it a shot for about ten years at the end of which, well, you'll see how it goes.

Your due diligence shows that the practice was healthy financially. It had no debt and was generating about $1 million in annual revenues and about $300,000 in free cash flow. You figure that additional upfront investments, increased expenses, and new interest charges would reduce your free cash flow to $247,000 at the end of the first year. Growing this at 10 percent a year for the next ten years, your cash flows would look as in the second column in table 12.3 ($000s).

Note in the "Nom" column that the first year includes a $300,000 cash outflow owing to your capital equipment update. So, since the company is expected to generate $247,000 in cash flow, the net free cash flow during the first year is expected to be –$53,000. You then expect the free cash flow to grow at 10 percent a year for the next ten years.

With the cash flows estimated, you then have to figure the rate at which to discount those future expected cash flows. You ponder that a while and decide that since you are putting a lot on the line, you want to be sure that the investment makes sense at an annual rate of 25 percent. So, using a discount rate of 25 percent, you estimate the discounted cash flows (PV) as shown in the third column in table 12.3.

Table 12.3

Year	Nom	PV
0	-1,000	-1,000
1	-53.00	-42.40
2	271.70	173.89
3	298.87	153.02
4	328.76	134.66
5	361.63	118.50
6	397.80	104.28
7	437.58	91.77
8	481.33	80.75
9	529.47	71.06
10	582.41	62.54
Residual	3,203	275

Nom: Nominal Dollars ('000)
PV: Present Value ('000)

Adding all the discounted cash flows above gives a Net Present Value (NPV) of –$51,932. What this means is that given your feeling of risk as captured in the discount rate of 25 percent, the project is expected to lose money over the next ten years. So, you think, why do all this work only to lose money?

Then, you realize that the practice is likely to have value at the end of ten years, and you can sell it then. But how do you estimate this terminal value? To do that, you assume that if the practice is kept in good order and you continue growing the cash flows at 5 percent a year for a very long time starting year eleven, then your business would be worth over $3 million in year eleven. So including the terminal (residual) value, the nominal cash flow is as in the column "Nom" in table 12.3. Discounted at 25 percent rate, the present values are as in the third column.

The actual NPV now turns out to be a positive $223,227 provided your assumptions hold. You own 75 percent of this value and your friend Shaky owns the rest. Does it make sense for you to buy the practice given this analysis? What would you do? Is this enough of a profit for you to make the investment? Are there ways in which you could improve the value of this business?

This, in essence, is the Discounted Cash Flow (DCF) technique of estimating intrinsic value of a business. It does not give you an answer *per se* but it helps estimate ballpark numbers that can then be used to make good business decisions. You must note that the final NPV number can vary widely depending on the assumptions used. What the future cash flows of a business are likely to be and how risky you think those cash flows are—these can vastly influence the final estimates of value. It is critical, therefore, to take care that your assumptions are reasonable. In such analysis, precision does little good but reasonableness is paramount.

While DCF technique is theoretically sound, note that it has two notable shortcomings. First, since the outcome of such analysis is so much a function of assumptions and gut feel, you can get widely varying NPV numbers depending on the assumptions used. It can be problematic to get a fix on the "true" value using DCF analysis. Second, even if "true" value did indeed exist and it was to be correctly computed, there is no assurance that the sale of the business would fetch the said amount. Depending on market conditions, businesses have been known to sell at prices that deviate substantially from the results of DCF analysis.

It is for these reasons, especially the difficulty of making correct assumptions, that we will turn the DCF analysis on its head so as to make it practically useful for investing. So, in the next chapter, let's build up to that point by first discussing the simple math of valuation, a key formulation that summarizes how to properly discount the streams of cash, in line with what we have done above.

13

Risk and Uncertainty

———

As we saw in the previous chapter, a critical input when estimating the value of a business is the discount rate which, in turn, is influenced by assessments of the likelihood that the expected future cash flows do not materialize. In fact, since estimates are so sensitive to the discount rate, correctly thinking about risk is central to investing. Let us try to understand, therefore, how we should think about risk in the context of valuation.

Imagine that you have three bags marked A, B, and C. Suppose you know that bag A has thirty red balls and seventy green balls. You know the total number of balls in bag B, but don't know how many are red and how many green. Finally, you know that there are red and green balls in bag C, along with an unknown number of black and white balls as well, but you don't know how many total balls and different colors there are in this bag.

Now, assume also that the green ball is worth +$1 and red is worth –$1. So, if you pull out a green ball, you make money and if you draw a red ball you lose money. Let us raise the stakes and make the black ball worth +$10 and the white ball worth –$10, so that the possible losses and gains in bag C are much higher than they are with bag B.

Which of the three bags is the riskiest?

If you are like most people, you think that bag C poses the highest risk. It turns out that your answer is incorrect—because you are mistaking uncertainty for risk. This subtle but important point was clarified by the economist Frank Knight,[69] who argued that risk and uncertainty are two distinct concepts; risk can be quantified and measured whereas uncertainty indicates such unknowns and unknowables that cannot be quantified or measured.[70]

Technically, if you know the frequency distribution (how many of each) from which a particular event (color) is drawn, then you know the risk and can measure it using such statistical terms such as probability and standard deviation. Since you know the count and proportion of the red and green balls in bag A, you can compute the probabilities and know what the odds are that you will pull out a particular combination of red and green. Moreover, since you know how much each ball is worth, you can also compute the probability of making or losing a given sum of money. That is, you know the quantifiable measure of risk for bag A.

You cannot compute the probabilities for bag B, however, since you know neither the count nor the proportion of red and green balls. You face uncertainty, as you do not know even the distribution from which you may be drawing the balls. For all you know, there are only red balls in bag B and all you'd do is lose money every time you reached into the bag. This problem is even more of an issue in bag C, where not only is the distribution not known but the stakes are much larger as well.

If you were an investor, therefore, you would like to reach for bag A, where you know that the odds are clearly in your favor. You would much prefer if all the balls were green, but will accept the challenge because you can quantify the probability of loss and the odds are strong that you would make money. Instead, if Bag A had seventy red and thirty green balls, you would know that the odds are not in your favor and perhaps choose not to draw at all. If you do choose to draw, then you are taking a gamble of sorts in the hope that you would pick green in spite of the odds being against you. In either case, your decision is based on quantifying the probabilities of drawing red and green balls and, therefore, knowing the risk.

As a speculator, on the other hand, you might be inclined to reach for bag B, perhaps in the spirit of experimentation. You accept the possibility of limited losses to see if you might be able to uncover an underlying pattern from the first few draws. That is, you approach bag B cautiously, getting information with each draw, hoping that the true proportions or risk will soon become evident and end up being in your favor. There is also a chance that the underlying patterns don't exist, don't get revealed, or worse, you infer the wrong pattern and get in trouble.

Finally, as a gambler you might be interested in bag C, where the odds cannot be calculated but the prospect of drawing +$10 black balls is appealing; the chances of drawing –$10 white balls brings with it the danger and excitement that makes the game worthwhile. You do not know the risk but are drawn to the uncertainty and the possibility of a big payoff if you were to pick black.

That is, investors, speculators, and gamblers differ in their tolerance for uncertainty and in their desire to know the risk they may be taking. Their motivations could be roughly approximated as the three bags above. Ideally, as an investor, you want to know the risk as precisely as possible and shun situations that are laden with uncertainties.

Resolving Uncertainties

Very often, however, it is not always clear which of the three kinds of bags you are drawing—you do not have enough precise information to know whether you are dealing with risk, as in bag A, or an uncertain situation, as in bags B or C. In most investment analysis, counts, frequencies and objective probabilities about some very important factors are simply not available. Yet, using one-off and situation-specific information that may be available, you try to make educated guesses about the contents of the bag, so to speak, and assess the odds.

You may not know specifically the risk of an investment, but you are confronted with a range of uncertainties that surround the true economic prospects. As such, the essential task for you as an investor is not so much to measure risk as mathematicians or scientists would to, but to understand the key uncertainties and develop well-informed judgments to try to resolve those uncertainties the best you can. Uncertainties that cannot be resolved then temper the confidence with which you can make claims about the suitability or attractiveness of the investment.

That is, your starting position is almost always with something like bag B or bag C: you begin often with a hunch, or maybe it's just a hope. But, then, with diligence and patient analysis, you try to figure out the contents of the bag to the point where you have a very good idea of what may be in it. Since you cannot look inside the bag, however, it is unlikely that you will ever be able to completely pinpoint the context as clearly as in bag A. Therefore, even if it turns out that the odds are heavily in your favor, some uncertainty and, therefore, speculation will remain in your choice. Yet, because your analysis has clarified the odds, your behavior is like that of an investor.

Investment analysis, in other words, is the process of uncovering the odds built into a situation, so that you may commit resources where the odds are heavily in your favor. Clarifying such odds is important for being able to invest wisely.

In practice, it is usually not within your power to resolve all of the many kinds of uncertainties that may surround a particular investment thesis. Uncertainties about the macro-economic events and the environment, for example, cannot be resolved by you; they depend on larger forces over which you have no control. Let us call these *exogenous* uncertainties that you cannot resolve but perhaps only articulate to clarify how they may influence your investment thesis. Whether or not the European Union would be able to satisfactorily resolve the debt crisis, for instance, is an uncertainty that you cannot resolve—although it is still important that you be aware of this uncertainty and understand how it affects your analysis.

The other kinds of uncertainties may surrender to your judgments, however, if they originate not in external phenomenon but in the lack of your own understanding of the situation at hand. Such uncertainties are *endogenous* to your personal knowledge and diligence, and whether or not you resolve them depends to a large extent on the skill and creativity with which you approach the analysis. So, for instance, a company's ability to deliver sustained performance over time may be an uncertainty that you can resolve with analysis of such things as its historical performance and the sustainability of its business model.

Through careful analysis, you can try to resolve the key uncertainties that may be endogenous to your abilities and effort. You still have to make judgments that are well-informed by your analysis of both quantitative and qualitative data relevant to the occasion. The penchant for objectivity should not restrict your analysis to only those few factors for which large quantities of data may be available.

The focus on uncertainty does not mean, of course, that frequencies and objectivity do not have a role in analysis. Where possible, the available objective and quantitative data must be used to form judgments about the uncertainties you face as an investor. Data on past instances of accounting fraud in similar companies may be helpful in forming judgments about the likelihood in a particular case. But the important distinction here is that instead of trying to measure the so-called objective risk, you focus on developing processes and skills that will help you make sound judgments about uncertainties surrounding key issues that impact your investment thesis.

This emphasis on subjective judgments in investment analysis is in sharp contrast to the vain search for objective measures of risk that has characterized modern finance for over six decades. It is worth considering briefly the one seemingly objective measure of risk that has characterized the obsession with objectivity—the market beta (β), which is computed using the variances and co-variances in the past data.

Quantifying Market Risk

The holy grail of investing since at least the 1950s has been the search for a formula or measure that would identify investments that, like bag A, have their risk profile unambiguously specified. One such measure of risk is derived from the size and frequencies of stock returns. When it first came into common use during the 1950s, this quantitative specification of risk—standard deviation of stock or portfolio returns—was seen as an advance over the subjective assessments of risk that business people had been making for eons. Such subjectivity was seen by many as vague and a license to be arbitrary; it lacked precision. Subjective assessments were also difficult to standardize and compare across investment opportunities. So, defining risk as standard deviation became widely popular. Over time, researchers have developed ever more mathematically complex conceptions of investment risk, but β remains the most common measure of risk for stocks.

So, using standard deviation as a base concept, the risk of a stock is measured as β, or the degree to which returns of a stock co-vary with the returns of a benchmark index such as the Standard and Poor's 500 Index. The β is, in a way, simply a summary of the relative frequencies of the green (returns greater than index returns) and red (returns smaller than index returns) balls. In this way, very high β stocks are deemed highly risky; low β stocks are deemed to have low risk. Such quantification of risk for individual stocks is closely related to the idea of portfolio risk, or the standard deviation of portfolio returns, as we discussed in the prologue to this book.

Note that although the theory says to use expected *future* returns, standard deviations are by necessity computed using the past returns from recent history. In practice, therefore, the statistical measures of risk are measures in fact of how returns have behaved historically, anywhere from the past 250 trading days to the past sixty months.

It is easy to see, in fact, the attractiveness of quantifying risk using standard deviation of returns. Since the past returns data are plentiful, computing standard deviation is a straightforward application of elementary statistics; it appears to give an objective measure of risk—and avoids the need for subjective judgments that could be plagued with vagueness. Defined and computed this way, risk of an investment is equivalent to the number and proportion of red and green balls that may be in bag A, to use the example above. Once risk is so quantified, investing is seen as simply figuring out how much risk you are willing to take and choosing stocks accordingly.

Yet, although β is a good indicator of how volatile prices have been in the recent past, quantifying investment risk using only past prices and returns is misleading if not outright wrong. In particular, the shape of the distributions from which past returns appear to be coming remains unclear. In standard theory, the returns are assumed to be normally distributed, but that assumption is strongly contested.[71] What β does reflect is the historical volatility,[72] or market risk—the degree to which the stock returns co-vary with the returns of the benchmark market index. That it may capture broader risk beyond market volatility is doubtful.

Ironically, the focus on quantifying risk distracts investors and weakens the understanding they ought to have about the formidable uncertainties that may be plaguing an investment. Unlike a bag full of red and green balls, companies are dynamic entities, constantly evolving their business models as they try to adapt to a changing environment. Their past stock returns may say little or not much at all about the uncertainties they face or about their future prospects. The past returns may, in fact, be driven by macro events or fickle investor sentiment or something else altogether, but they may have little or nothing to do with the underlying uncertainties related to business, operations, and finance.

Subjective Probability

The fascination with seemingly objective statistics and past returns is largely owing to a deeper fascination with objectivity and precision. Wide availability of past pricing data fuels this fascination, as it allows seemingly straightforward applications of standard statistical tools in order to derive seemingly objective numbers that appear to give a fix on risk.

Yet, such fascination also reflects a bias towards measures of objective probability, as if a true probability is awaiting discovery. This bias is rooted in the methods of research in the natural and physical sciences but it severely limits clear thinking when brought into the world of investing, a world of human affairs in which pure unadulterated objectivity simply does not exist and where the search for precision may actually be more harmful than helpful.

It turns out that the focus on objective probability ignores a long enduring Bayesian tradition that conceptualizes probability in personal terms—that probabilities are not objective but subjective,[73] that they do not inhere in the object or event but are embedded in ideas and expectations of the observer.

In order to understand the subjectivists, think about the odds of getting Heads in a coin toss. Most people would immediately place the odds as one-in-two, arguing that when flipped many times, each of the two possibilities will show up in equal proportions. From a subjectivist's point of view, however, that probability is based on the expectation that the coin is perfectly balanced. Only after observing the results of many coin tosses can you update your baseline expectations about balance and may be able to say what the odds actually are for this particular coin.

The probability does not inhere in the coin but in your expectations about how well the coin is constructed. Subjectivists say that you can start with one-in-two odds of turning up Heads, but then you must update that initial expectation (*prior probability*) either based on new information about how balanced the coin is or from your experiences over several flips of the coin. You learn from experience and then incorporate new learning in your thinking to form updated expectations.

In a similar vein, accepting β as an appropriate measure for risk depends on your expectation that the markets are perfect assimilators of all available information, that they are efficient. This expectation may be based on your unique definition of efficiency or your subjective feeling or interpretation of empirical evidence related to market efficiency. If you do not believe that markets are efficient in general or in a particular case, then you are likely to discount the suitability of β as a measure of investment risk and look for assessing risk in different ways, both objective and subjective.

So, in the world of investing where underlying distributions are not known, where beliefs need to be formed and updated using inadequate or even missing data, where beliefs usually live under the dark shadow of confirmation bias, having a rigorous way of subjectively assessing probabilities is more helpful than the vain search for objectivity and precision. This is especially true in the stock market where trying to capture investment risk with a simple and seemingly objective statistic appears strange and even foolhardy.

Given the complexity of most companies in which you may want to invest, therefore, you need not necessarily measure quantified risk but evaluate subjectively the many uncertainties associated with that investment. These uncertainties are best captured as subjective estimates of probabilities regarding such things as quantifiable prospects for future growth, sustainability of yields, stability of track record, and financial strength. Assessments related to these issues are subjective judgments grounded in simple quantities, as shown in the next few chapters, in your past experiences, and in careful, if idiosyncratic, interpretation of a complex set of clues.

Additional subjective judgments need to be made about such things as the quality of the business model and competence of the management team. For these issues, no large-scale historical quantitative data can be easily tabulated and statistically analyzed in order to yield "objective" risk. Seeking precision in such circumstances can be counterproductive, in fact, as it may remove important but *un*quantifiable information from the analysis.

As discussed in the first chapter of this book, however, forming judgments about uncertain events is full of potential dangers. Subjective probabilities are, in a way, emerging or well-ensconced beliefs about issues that you may consider important to the future performance and valuation of the company. Because beliefs tend to persist irrespective of whether they are correct or incorrect, you are vulnerable to making egregious mistakes. Your subjective assessments can be downright wrong.

Updating Subjective Probabilities

Yet, fear of mistakes should not preclude you from trying to make well-informed opinions and to systematically develop a personal subjective understanding about probable future outcomes. As in any other judgment-driven profession such as law and medicine, subjective understanding is also unavoidable and indispensable when investing. The key is to form judgments conservatively, and to then carefully update them as new information comes to light.[74] Rigorous thinking rather than precision is the key to investing wisely.

Given the potential for gain and the vulnerability to making serious mistakes, therefore, we need criteria for testing the beliefs we already have or may begin forming about a particular company and its stock. Using reasonable but firm criteria would ensure that our subjective judgments about an investment are based on cautious interpretation of knowable and meaningful facts. Such facts can be objective or subjective, quantities or narratives, but they need to be evaluated in light of a deeper understanding of the expectations we may be bringing to the analysis—because those expectation will inform the subjective assessments we may make about the assembled facts.

That is, in order to make good judgments, we need to ensure that our beliefs are reasonable and consistent with well-developed standards of logic and data. More importantly, we also need to have a systematic way of updating our beliefs when new meaningful information comes along. Such updating is critical not only to be rational at first but also to continue being rational once we begin analyzing the investment in detail.

Yet, subjective beliefs must be updated using the principle of negation as developed in chapters 8 and 9. When applied with diligence, as discussed, the framework ensures that our beliefs about attractiveness of a particular investment are reasonable *and* refutable. The correct approach is to update subjective judgments cautiously by trying to refute the thesis with new meaningful information when it comes to light. That is, the thesis must be updated using cautious interpretations of new facts in light of other things we know about the investment.

Developing the ability to assess and update subjective probabilities is essential to successful investing. Perhaps we should think of investment risk not simply in terms of standard deviations but more strongly in terms of the subjective probability of loss or gain. Doing so reduces the reliance on contorting seemingly objective data to produce a statistic, and encourages instead a look broad and deep to make qualified judgments about the investment.

Subjective judgments are to be made using both quantitative and qualitative data, of course. Numerical data are indispensable in investment analysis, and a rigorous consideration of certain quantities is helpful. As discussed in the following chapters and shown below, for instance, bond yields may provide initial clues about some of the quantifiable risks to which particular stocks may be exposed. But even bond yields need to be interpreted subjectively and cautiously, with the initial judgment about the discount rate updated based on additional clues such as financial health and track record of performance.

In effect, the process of refutation enables a cautious and sequential updating of the investment thesis. Such is the rationale for the tests developed to update the investment thesis, as shown in chapters 14 and 15, by trying to refute it using certain quantitative markers. Then, in chapters 16 through 20, I discuss how such updating ought to continue with additional qualitative data about the company.

Assessing Uncertainties Using Bond Yields

One way of beginning to quantify uncertainties when investing is to understand what risk means to bondholders, especially those who hold the bonds to maturity. As discussed further in chapter 14, trying to value bonds raises the issue of uncertainties about interest rates in general and about financial vulnerability of the company in question. What bondholders call the default risk or, more generally, the probability of a downgrade[75] is an assessment of the chances that the issuer would not be able to honor its obligations to the lender. Both interest rates and the financial profile of the company inform the rate at which the future coupons and the eventually-returned face value ought to be discounted.

Bonds can, of course, become quite complex with other things such as recall provisions and liens etc., but the mechanics of valuing simple bonds helps underscore the nature of uncertainties that investors face and the challenges of understanding those uncertainties.

Like bondholders, stockholders too are subject to uncertainties about interest rates and the ability of the company to honor its obligations. Any increase in interest rate hurts companies in several ways. If they hold debt on their balance sheet, then the cost of borrowing goes up with the general level of interest rates. In addition, a rise in interest rates usually accompanies inflation and the cost of inputs for companies can go up as well. If they are unable to pass the rising cost of inputs to customers through price hikes, then their margins are likely to come under pressure. Finally, the rise in interest rates also raises the benchmark bond yields for stock investors and, as shown in chapter 14, the discount rate input into the computation of intrinsic value. So, interest rates affect stocks just as they do bonds.

Similarly, the possibility that the company might default on its bonds would indicate financial difficulty and, therefore, hurt stock prices. Assessing credit risk or the chances of default is an art, in fact, that incorporates both quantitative and qualitative factors that may affect the odds of the company not being able to meet its financial obligations to lenders. Companies with strong balance sheet are generally less likely to default on their bonds, as they have sufficient resources to meet debt service obligations.

Typically, those who buy and hold bonds until maturity are not concerned beyond the assurance that the companies in which they invest will continue to have sufficient resources to service their debts in a timely manner. Once the bonds have been issued and the coupon fixed, any improvements in the financial condition of the company do not benefit the original bond investors except intangibly, in that their coupons become even more certain than they might have been initially. In essence, then, bondholders can avoid the possibility of default by being selective about the companies in which they invest. Yet, they can do little about the uncertainties surrounding interest rates.

Being residual owners whose claims are subordinate to those of the bondholders, stockholders too are unable to do much about interest rates. But by being selective about the companies in which they invest, stock investors too can ensure that their exposure to possible default is minimal. Avoiding default is critical for stockholders because the value of stocks usually goes to zero when a company defaults and/or files for bankruptcy. In fact, even a hint that a company might default can force bond prices to spiral down and stock prices to plummet.

It turns out that stockholders have much more to worry about than uncertainties around interest rates and the likelihood of default. Unlike bondholders and other lenders, they do not have contractually specified coupons or financing charges, as the case may be. Some companies do have a long history and a strong commitment to pay cash dividends, but those are still discretionary and can be cut or eliminated at the discretion of the company. General Electric, for instance, has been paying dividends every quarter for over 100 years. During the financial crisis of 2008, however, they cut their quarterly dividend by two-thirds.

As such, shareholders get no contractual guarantees equivalent to those received by bondholders. Even if we assumed that all residual earnings eventually belong to the shareholders and they are akin to the dividends that will eventually be paid out (in theory), a great deal of uncertainty remains about the company's ability to continue growing earnings well beyond those necessary to satisfy the bondholders.

So, stocks bring with them added vulnerabilities beyond those related to interest rates and the possibility of default. They also have to contend with uncertainties about future earnings and cash flows because of any number of factors internal and external to the firm. In fact, operations of the company could deteriorate only to such an extent that it produces just enough earnings to satisfy obligations to the bondholders but there is nothing left over for the shareholders.

In order to understand how uncertainties influence valuation, consider the discounted cash flow valuation model[76] that we will discuss in detail in the next chapter. The model is best seen as a dynamic representation of intrinsic economic worth being driven by the size and growth of future cash flows and the uncertainties inherent in those flows. That is, imagine the three variables in the model not as fixed and static, but each as a complex of moving parts, with each part being driven by a number of other factors that range from simple to complex, from knowable to incomprehensible, each uncertain in some manner.

As such, for a given level of expected future cash flows, high discount rate lowers intrinsic valuation. Even if the company is expected to produce high cash flows and grow them at a rapid rate, high discount rate bears down on economic worth and can altogether offset high expected cash flows and growth.

A key task for investors, therefore, is to gain insights into the processes that may be driving the rate at which, in the intrinsic value formulation, the expected future flows ought to be discounted. But the discount rate itself is not an objective quantity; it is the subjective assessment of uncertainties that may be inherent in the ability of the company to generate cash flows and the uncertainties that may surround future growth of those cash flows.

If the key uncertainties can be pinpointed and resolved, the discount rate can then be estimated with some confidence. If, on the other hand, the random or stochastic elements are so dominant that the uncertainties about future cash flows cannot be comprehended, then we may not have a good basis for valuation because the discount formulation cannot be then operationalized.

So, even though the formula for intrinsic valuation seems simple and is fairly straightforward algebraically, using it well depends on your ability to understand and resolve the key uncertainties that surround the future cash flows. For the most part, moreover, you assess those uncertainties subjectively. A good part of analysis in this regard is to use quantitative and qualitative data cautiously to make such assessments realistic and reasonable in light of other things you know or learn about the company and its future prospects.

While many often go head-on into situations where unresolvable uncertainties make sound judgment impossible, thoughtful investors remain highly selective about where to make the cautious forays. In fact, success in investing may depend in large part on the degree to which a keen understanding of key uncertainties can help make good judgments about what the discount rate ought to be.

Long-term investment performance is driven, ironically, not so much from seeking gain aggressively but by comprehending the key uncertainties so as to make good judgments about where to invest and where not to.

Know Your Uncertainties

So, uncertainties about cash flows or operations are of fundamental importance to investors. Where a keen understanding of the operations and the business fundamentals is missing, the uncertainties remain high and drive down the valuation because of the need to use a high discount rate. Similarly, where strong leadership and deeply entrenched competitive position define a company and the future cash flows are reasonably assured with few unresolved uncertainties, intrinsic valuation will be high because of the justifiably low discount rate.

It is important to recognize that key operating and other uncertainties are fundamental to valuation and quite distinct from uncertainty about market prices. Derivations of risk using market prices alone undermine the role of judgment in investment analysis, and encourage investors to ignore the many business-related uncertainties that are at the heart of making informed judgments about the quality and the prospects of the investment under scrutiny.

The sole reliance on statistical measures of risk can, in fact, have devastating consequences. Because they appear to be objective and are computed using vast amounts of data generated in the market transactions, such measures give a false sense of security; they encourage aggressive trading models that may actually be vulnerable to fundamental uncertainties that simply cannot be resolved. It is hardly a stretch to say that such seemingly objective measures of risk and the models built around them were at least partly responsible for the mishaps at MF Global and a long list of other spectacular busts, including Long Term Capital.

The trouble with β and other statistical measures of risk is that quantification does not imply comprehensiveness; irreducible uncertainty remains in all statistical representations of risk and the mathematical models derived from them. Worse, the focus on statistics and vast amounts of quantitative data shifts investor attention away from a thorough analysis of the particulars of the individual investments.

In fact, operating and other business-related uncertainties fall well outside the definition of quantified market risk. Investors must understand these uncertainties; to do so, they don't need past prices and returns but a deep appreciation of the factors that may affect the reliability with which the company can generate future cash flows.

We have come full circle from the beginning of this chapter, where we urged investors to draw from bag A, leaving bags B and C to speculators and gamblers. Yet, now we see that investors rarely if ever face situations as well defined as bag A; the search for well-defined risk has misled us all into thinking that we can precisely measure the hazards to our investments. Worse, it has discouraged us from engaging in the essential task of understanding and resolving the key uncertainties that we face when investing in stocks.

As such, investors should accept that they are most likely drawing from bag B or bag C and then work diligently to identify and resolve key uncertainties so that they can appreciate and act according to the true odds built into the situation.

14

The Simple Math of Valuation

———

There are usually two kinds of difficulties investors face when trying to estimate the intrinsic value of a company: the first resulting from not enough skepticism and the second from too much of it.

The first difficulty arises when you try to seek out one or more formulae that would give a precise answer, which you can take as the exact or approximate value of the company under investigation. Unfortunately, once you obtain such an answer, your mind gets anchored to it independent of whether or not the answer is any good. The very process of computing, for some reason, gives the resulting answer certain credibility and, right or wrong, it creates a psychological anchor that becomes an impediment to further nuanced thinking and critical evaluation of the factors that may be driving the economic worth.

The need for such a formulaic approach seems to be quite pronounced in large segments of the population, perhaps because it settles, to some extent, the anxiety that many feel from the ambiguity that surrounds the idea of worth and value.

The need for simple formulations makes you highly vulnerable to mistakes or outright manipulation, as any formula, by definition, focuses attention on a narrow set of variables and hides broader considerations from view. Such vulnerability is especially likely if you are also prone to apply the formulae without fully understanding why and how they were derived, without understanding the embedded assumptions or limitations.

Consider the so-called Graham formula that is widely available on the Internet.[77] The first version of formula (1962) proposes a simple mathematical relationship between the Price-to-earnings (PE) ratio, earnings per share, and expected growth rate, to arrive at an estimate of intrinsic value. The association with Graham gives the formula instant credibility and, unfortunately, a license to apply it uncritically.

It turns out that the derivation of the Graham (1962) formula remains shrouded in mystery; it remains unclear how the formula was developed and why it is a good way to estimate intrinsic value. Moreover, if value is defined as discounted future earnings, then the formula simply breaks down: upon simple algebraic manipulation, it yields a nonsense equation where intrinsic value turns out to be a function of market price!

Graham revised the formula in 1974, but the derivation was still opaque; the combination of variables and constants in the formula appears to be arbitrary.[78] Yet, even though Graham used the formula to illustrate the difficulty of valuation and the foolhardiness of projecting the future, it shows up all over the Internet as if Gospel Truth. People are not sufficiently skeptical about the Graham formula, in other words, and choose to not question its validity.

The other extreme with regards to valuation arises from a deeply felt skepticism that correctly estimating the economic worth of a company is even possible. Valuing a company requires, after all, estimating its projected future earnings and the appropriate rates with which to discount those earnings. But the future is unknown and, for the most part, unknowable as any reasonable formulation of value would necessitate. In theory at least, a virtually infinite list of factors could affect the future earnings of a firm; it may not even be possible to anticipate or measure all such factors.

All sorts of external events, such as supply chain disruptions, competitive forces, natural disasters, internal corruption, new technologies, changing consumption patterns—you name it—can interrupt the activities of the company in question. How could anyone reasonably account for all these factors and, furthermore, incorporate them into any simple formulation? To say that such can be done defies common sense.

Such concerns have merit, as the world is in constant flux and that makes investing quite complex. What appears to stump most people is not that there are no solvable problems in investing but that they don't quite know how to get to them and then navigate through the maze of information, uncover and analyze the salient facts, and make reasonable judgments about economic worth. The absence of concrete answers leads many into thinking that analysis is hopeless, turning them toward gambling and speculating, or out of the capital markets altogether.

Yet, complexity is not unique to investing and concerns about it may be exaggerated in some cases. Professions such as law and medicine address problems as complex or more. The skills needed to address complex problems can be learned and, with practice, improved over time. As in other professions, the problems in investing appear on a continuum from very simple to incomprehensibly complex. You can, however, avoid complex problems and focus on simple ones and only gradually, if at all, move up the ladder of complexity. Being an investor gives you this flexibility that perhaps no other profession does: doctors cannot choose which patients they will see, but as an investor you can choose which stocks/companies you will analyze and which you will not.

So, the ability to make good judgments comes with experience but the skills and techniques to evaluate investments can be acquired on the basis of principles developed with the labor of many over many years.

Instead of gullibility or senseless skepticism, therefore, investing wisely requires a sensible middle ground where quantitative and qualitative approaches help guide judgments about economic worth and value. The skill you need is to recognize and avoid problems that cannot be solved, and focus on those situations that are amenable to competent analysis, given your skillset at a given moment. In this way, quantitative analysis is not so much to get a single number indicating value but to be able to grasp the essence of a situation and surface the fundamental forces that may be driving the economic worth of the company under scrutiny.

In this chapter, I lay out the basic quantitative formulation for valuing stocks. As we go through the process of valuation, note that stocks can be seen as a special kind of bond that has indefinite maturity, variable and discretionary coupon and, perhaps most importantly, residual risk (beyond interest rates and possibility of default). So, let's try to value a simple bond and then see how that translates into valuing stocks.

Valuing a Simple Bond

Let us say that we have a bond of $1,000 face value, and it has a coupon of $50 (5 percent bond yield) to be paid at the end of every year. Let us say also that the bond matures in five years, at the end of which, along with the last coupon of $50, the face value is returned. Row 1 in table 14.1 shows the nominal cash flows from this bond.

Table 14.1

	Year1	Year2	Year3	Year4	Year5
Cash Flow	$50	$50	$50	$50	$1,050
Discount Factor	1.04	1.08	1.12	1.17	1.22
Present Value	$48.08	$46.23	$44.45	$42.74	$863.02
Net Present Value	**$1,045**	(sum of the Present Values above)			

We know from the idea of the time value of money that, in an inflationary environment, future cash is worth less than cash in hand. Assume, for the time being, that the coupons of this bond are deemed reliable, so you set the discount rate for future cash flows at a constant 4 percent. As shown in table 14.1, this assumption leads to $1,045 as the net present value or the intrinsic value of the bond.

It should be clear, however, that the value of the bond will change with the change in the discount rate. For a rate of 6 percent, value of the bond would be $958 and for a discount rate of 5 percent, the bond would be $1,000.

Now, let's consider the same bond as above but with one difference: it has no maturity. That is, the bond continues giving a coupon of $50 per year forever (into perpetuity). For such a bond, the technique for valuing would be the same as in the above table, except the table will keep on going to the right...

It so happens that, in such a perpetual maturity bond, the above table can be approximated by a very simple formula:

Perpetual Bond Value = (C / r)   (14.1)

where C is the constant annual coupon and r is the constant discount rate. So, a bond with a perpetual constant coupon of $50 and an unchanging discount rate of 4 percent can be valued simply as

Perpetual Bond Value = (C / r) = ($50 / 0.04) = $1,250   (14.1 Sol.)

Using equation 14.1, a similar bond with a 5 percent constant discount rate would be valued at $1,000 and one with a 6 percent constant discount rate would be $833.33 value.

Next, let's take the same perpetual bond as above and add one more level of complexity: that the coupon is not constant at $50 per year but that the coupon grows at a constant rate of 2 percent per year for every year into the future. That is, we now have a perpetual bond with a coupon of $50 per year growing into perpetuity at a constant growth rate g of 2 percent per year and with a discount rate of 4 percent. For such a bond, value can be approximated using the simple mathematical equivalent:

Perpetual Bond Value = C' / (r − g)   (14.2)

where C' is the coupon paid out the end of Year 1, r is the discount rate and g is the constant perpetual growth rate. Because of the growth, C' can be re-written as C · (1 + g) to reflect the coupon at the end of year 1. So, the estimated value of the above perpetual bond with fixed coupon and constant growth can be written as:

Perpetual Bond Value = C · (1 + g) / (r − g)   (14.3)

For the bond in our example, with a coupon of $50 growing at a constant 2 percent and discounted at the rate of 4 percent, we compute the value as below.

Perpetual Bond Value = $50 · (1.02) / (0.04 − 0.02) = $2,550   (14.3 Sol.)

Intrinsic Value of Stocks

The same process as above for estimating the value of a perpetual bond is, with care, also used for valuation of stocks. The commonly used Dividend Discount Model (DDM) is the same formulation as above with the annual coupon replaced with the annual dividend. That is,

$$\text{Intrinsic Value} = D \cdot (1 + g) / (r - g) \qquad (14.4)$$

where D is the annual dividend per share paid at the beginning of the first year, r is the constant discount rate, and g is the perpetual constant growth rate of dividends per share.

As an example, consider our ongoing example company, Wal-Mart. As of December 2010, the company had paid an annual dividend of $1.21 per share. Assuming a discount rate of 10 percent and a perpetual growth rate of 5 percent, we get the approximate value of each Wal-Mart share as:

$$\text{Intrinsic Value} = \$1.21 \cdot (1.05) / (0.10 - 0.05) = \$25.41 \qquad (14.4 \text{ Sol.})$$

The key issue in the proper application of the above formula is the estimation of r and g in the denominator. The discount rate r happens to be one of the most intractable problems in finance. So, as indicated in chapter 13, we will work with the bond yields to make initial rough estimates of it. The estimation of g is also a bit of a challenge although, for some companies at least, historical growth rates may provide a measure of guidance on what future growth might look like.

For now, let's focus just on the numerator. Is cash dividend the correct thing to discount to estimate the value of a company's share? What if the company does not pay any dividend? Would the intrinsic value then be zero?

The important thing to remember when answering the above question is that the number in the numerator is what ought to be the property of you, the shareholder. Current and expected future dividend is often only a part of what rightfully belongs to the shareholders. As residual owners of the company, shareholders lay claim to all earnings, after finance charges and taxes and necessary reinvestments in the company.

How to compute the correct cash flows owed to the shareholders can be subject to a good deal of debate and contention. Yet, the key to correctly valuing the shares of a company are the correct cash flows to be placed in the numerator, including those cash flows that are not paid out but retained by the company for various legitimate purposes. Usually, these are the free cash flows that the company generates, net of all re-investments that are necessary to keep the company a going concern.

For the sake of illustration, let's make a simplifying assumption for the time being that the company distributes all its earnings every year. Depending on the situation, we can also use other flows such as earnings less capital expenditures, or free cash flows. For simplicity, let's just use earnings per share in the numerator in the examples below.

For Wal-Mart, annual earnings as of January 2010 were $3.70 per diluted share. If we take the perpetual discount rate as 10 percent and perpetual growth in earnings as 5 percent per year, then the share value is as:

$$\text{Intrinsic Value} = \$3.70 \cdot (1.05) \, / \, (0.10 - 0.05) = \$77.70 \qquad (14.4 \text{ Sol.})$$

The estimate of value as above is highly dependent, of course, on the correctness, or at least the reasonableness, of the numbers in the discount model. As mentioned above, discount rate r and the growth rate g are particularly difficult to pin down, especially since the model requires that the assumptions of risk and growth be constant and perpetual far into the unknown future.

Understand what the above formulation is really saying: the intrinsic economic value of a stock is a function of the company's earning power (e), its future prospects (g), and the rate of discount (r). Sure, the discount model seems like a simple formula with just three variables that we may be able to operationalize with varying degrees of confidence. The logic of the formula, however, is that investors understand the ability of the company to generate a given level of earnings and grow them into the long future—along with an appreciation of the key uncertainties that accompany earnings and growth.

The discount model computes economic value as an algebraic output. But the quality of valuation depends on the reasonableness of the estimates for the three variables—on how well they are derived from a subjective understanding of the company. So, while the discount model is a simple mathematical formula, it is to be understood in terms of the abilities, prospects, and fundamental uncertainties about future performance.

Applying the Simple Math of Valuation

The dividend discount model (DDM) encapsulates in simple form the present value of future cash flows that are rightfully the property of the shareholders. The term "dividend" is used broadly to imply all cash flows that rightfully belong to shareholders, whether those flows are distributed to shareholders as dividends or share repurchase, or are retained in the company for business-related uses.

So, in theory, you could reasonably estimate the value of the shares of a company if you were able to confidently pin down the cash flows, discount rate, and the future growth rate. The DDM model is simple but only deceptively so, as the three components in the formulation can, in practice, be very difficult to pin down. Slight variations in assumptions can make very large differences in the computed value.

To see the sensitivity of this formulation to input assumptions, consider once again the ongoing example of Wal-Mart, using the numbers as above: EPS=$3.70, r=10 percent and g=5 percent gives an economic value estimate of $77.70 per share.

But if the assumption of g is changed to 4 percent, the estimated value drops 21 percent to $64.09 per share. Similarly, if we keep the growth assumption at 5 percent and change the discount rate to 12 percent, then the estimated value drops 40 percent to just over $55 per share.

So, clearly, input assumptions have a big effect on the estimates of value. Being conservative helps but, even then, estimates of value are highly vulnerable to mistakes. It is difficult to refute a stock price because you can always find assumptions that justify it.

Your assumptions could be corrupted if you secretly desire to *prove* that the price is correct or incorrect. If you wanted to *prove* that Wal-Mart is worth much more, simply drop the discount rate to 8.5 percent and the formula then computes the estimated value as $111 per share.

In order to overcome this difficult problem of making the right assumptions, let's look at an alternative approach as below.

A Backdoor to Valuation

The discount model formulation can be approached in a markedly different way to reverse engineer the assumptions that may be embedded in the current price. In this alternate approach, we first make the assumption that the market is correctly pricing the company in question. That is, we assume efficient markets and define our null thesis as Price (P) = Value (V), and then see how reasonable the key assumptions in the formulation look in light of the company's recent historical performance.

This is how the *negation principle* sets up the investment thesis. If you have an initial hunch that the company is under- or over-valued, then you are essentially of the view that the current price does not reflect the intrinsic economic worth. That is, you have the investment thesis or hunch that price is not equal to value (P ≠ V), if you think that the market may be under-valuing the company, then your investment thesis is that the price is sufficiently below value (P << V) and, therefore, offers a potentially profitable opportunity. But, aware of the insidious confirmation bias that could be corrupting your judgment, you do not try to prove your undervaluation thesis; you try to *refute* it with good logic and doubt, applied to important facts of the case.

If you are successful in refuting this investment thesis, then your initial hunch was not correct, and you should no longer say that the company is undervalued. If, on the other hand, you are not able to refute your thesis, then there may be something to your expectation that price is sufficiently below the economic value. Inability to refute, in that case, helps you reach the *tentative* inference that an investment opportunity may indeed exist.

In order to illustrate all of the above, let's go back to the simple algebraic manipulation of the discount model of valuation, where the future cash flows to be discounted are taken simply as the earnings per share (EPS).

$$\text{Intrinsic Value (V)} = \text{Price (P)} = \text{EPS} \cdot (1 + g) / (r - g) \qquad (14.5)$$

That is, we assume that the prevailing price (P) of the shares of a company is correctly reflecting the underlying economic worth or value (V) of future earnings flows, appropriately discounted. Re-writing the above equation:

$$\text{Price-to-Earnings} = (P / \text{EPS}) = (1 + g) / (r - g) \qquad (14.5a)$$

Or, from slightly manipulating the above equation,

$$\text{Earnings Yield (EY)} = (\text{EPS} / P) = (r - g) / (1 + g) \qquad (14.5b)$$

That is, the earnings yield (EY = EPS/Price) equals a simple algebraic relationship between the discount rate r and perpetual growth rate g.

Now, in the above equation, the EPS should be the *earning power*—or the ability of the company to continue earning at a certain level well into the future. The earning power may sometimes be estimated quite reasonably by looking at the historical financial record, but it may remain elusive for some companies because of a lack of historical record or a highly variable performance over the years.

Let us apply the above formula to Wal-Mart. As of November 26, 2010, the company's stock was trading at $53.87, and for a whole host of reasons (e.g., capitalization ratios) we may have a hunch that the company is undervalued. So, we set up the investment thesis that the stock price is sufficiently less than its intrinsic value, or, P = $53.87 << V.

Assuming that current earnings per share of $3.70 correctly indicate the company's earning power, and assuming that the market is pricing correctly, we have the earnings yield (EY) as:

$$\text{EY} = (3.70 / 53.87) = 0.069 = (r - g) / (1 + g) \qquad (14.5b \text{ Sol.})$$

In the above equation, *if* we assumed that the company would not grow its earnings at all, then g=0; in that case, the discount rate r falls out as the earnings yield (6.9 percent). That is, if the company simply sustains the current level of earnings, then its stock is like a bond with a constant but perpetual coupon; for such a company, the discount rate built into the current price is simply the yield, or rate of return on current price.

The question you need to ask is whether the risk profile of the company is correctly represented by this derived discount rate (r = 6.9 percent) in the scenario where it produces constant earnings at the current rate far out into the future. Is this a reasonable approximation given the track record and competitive position in the marketplace?

Alternatively, if the discount rate r was known or reasonably well assumed, simple algebraic manipulation then shows that the future growth rate g could be estimated as follows:[79]

$$g = (r - EY) / (1 + EY) \tag{14.6}$$

where, EY is the earnings yield (EPS/Price), which in this case equals 6.9 percent. That is, the above algebraic combination of discount rate and earnings yield gives theoretical estimates of future growth g that appear to be embedded in the price. You can then try to refute your investment thesis by comparing the estimates of g with the company's historical performance and, we will see later, in light of the subjective understanding of the company's medium-to-long-term prospects.

If we assume for the time being that the discount rate is 10 percent, then we compute g as:

$$g = (0.10 - 0.069) / (1 + 0.069) = 0.0293 \tag{14.6 Sol.}$$

That is, if the discount rate r is assumed to be 10 percent, then a growth rate assumption of 2.93 percent is embedded in the share price of $53.87. At the then prevailing price, in other words, the market was essentially assuming that the company's earnings would grow at the rate of just under 3 percent per year into perpetuity.

Since the discount rate of 10 percent was chosen arbitrarily, let's see what happens to the implied growth rate when we do a sensitivity analysis using different discount rates. The implied growth rate turns out to be 1.06 percent when the discount rate is 8 percent, and it is 4.81 percent when the discount rate is 12 percent.

The range of *implied growth rates* thus derived using different discount rates can now be used to try to refute the undervaluation thesis. Has the company demonstrated a growth rate of 3 percent or more in recent years? Based on the past record and qualitative factors (discussed in later chapters), is it reasonable to expect that the company would be able to grow at this rate well into the future?

It so happens that, over the preceding ten years, Wal-Mart's earnings per share grew at an annualized rate of more than 11 percent; the annualized rate over the previous five years was almost 9 percent. That is, the company's earnings happen to have grown much faster than the growth rates implied in the market price of $53.87 per share. As such, if the range of discount rates chosen were to be appropriate for Wal-Mart, then the expected future growth rate implied in the market price seems to be well within recent historical experience.

Given the rather large differential in implied and historical growth rates, therefore, it is not yet possible to refute the investment thesis that price is significantly below reasonable estimates of intrinsic economic worth. How much greater than the implied growth should the historical growth rate be? The answer depends on how much confidence you have in the company continuing to deliver historical growth rates well into the future. Such confidence is based on subjective judgments about the company's overall health and prospects. For such things, no perfect answers may exist—it depends, as we will see going forward, on your interpretation of important and observable facts about the company.

Even so, for well-established and relatively stable companies such as Wal-Mart, a reasonable threshold is reached when the historical growth rate is twice the growth rate implied in the price. Since the historical growth rate for Wal-Mart in the above illustration is about three times the implied growth rate, it appears that the market is undervaluing the company in relation to its historical performance. As such, we cannot yet refute the hunch or investment thesis that Wal-Mart is undervalued.

The inability so far to refute the thesis gives us some confidence in it, but we are still far from done. That is because we used an arbitrary discount rate (10 percent) to compute the implied growth rate. So, the next step is to understand how to figure out a more realistic discount rate that is grounded in the specifics of the company.

The Discount Rate

The key in estimating the growth rate implied in current price is the discount rate. It is clear from the above tables that the implied growth rate g varies directly with the discount rate r, which in turn reflects the uncertainties about future performance. The greater the uncertainties that surround the company, the greater must be expectations of future growth to justify current prices.

Typically, in textbooks, the discount rate is computed using what is called the *Capital Asset Pricing Model* or CAPM. When done so, the discount rate is directly related to market risk (β) or the degree to which the prices of the company vary with the overall market.[80] This reliance on market risk makes the assumption that the markets are efficient and stock prices fully reflect the underlying value of the company. For those interested in CAPM, any standard textbook should provide a detailed explanation of it. In my view, using CAPM (or other market-based formulations such as the multi-factor model) to compute the discount rates is not a good idea.

First, as discussed previously, we want to evaluate the prevailing prices using markers outside the market mechanism that prices the shares. Since CAPM relies on prices or, technically, on returns from changes on those prices, it is unable to provide for us the independent view that we need for valuation.

Second, the discount rate we use should reflect the risks and uncertainties in the future expected earnings or cash flows. The market risk as incorporated in β is focused instead on changes in returns in relation to the overall market returns. If the markets were fully efficient, then market risk would perhaps fully reflect the uncertainties in the expected earnings and cash flows; if, on the other hand, price changes are only loosely or not at all connected with key uncertainties about the future, then using the market risk to compute the discount rate is incorrect.

Instead of relying on CAPM to compute the discount rate, therefore, let's use a simpler and better indicator of key uncertainties about the future earnings: perceived riskiness of the company's bonds, as reflected in the prevailing yields in the bond market.

To the extent the company has bonds outstanding, the average yield on those bonds reflects the assessments of the bond market about the effect of interest rates changes on bond valuation and the possibility of default by the company. As such, the bond yield incorporates in it the variability in the operating performance and the ability of the company to continue meeting the obligations to its bondholders. Riskier bonds, in general, trade at lower prices to generate higher yields than those bonds that are deemed less likely to default.

I have already discussed the rationale for using bond yields in the previous chapter. Now, in order to estimate the discount rate, let's go to the bond market and see how risky the company's bonds are deemed to be.

Remember that, whereas the company is contractually obligated to the bondholders, equity owners or stockholders are residual owners—who are junior in priority and not contractually guaranteed positive returns on their investments. As such, stockholders have a good deal higher exposure than that to which the bondholders may be exposed. So, assuming that bonds of the company have not turned speculative, the hazards to stockholders are above and beyond the two prominent uncertainties (interest rate and default) embedded in bond prices.

Depending on the company under investigation, therefore, as a rule of thumb we can use a discount rate that is two to three times the prevailing yield on the company's long-term bonds that mature in about ten years from the date of analysis. How much higher than bond yields the discount rate ought to be is neither formulaic nor arbitrary, however. It is based on our subjective judgments about the uncertainties that surround the future performance of the company. These subjective assessments are based on a whole host of quantitative and qualitative information, some of which we will discuss in detail in later chapters. For now, let's do the discount rate as two-to-three times the yields on the company bonds.

Moreover, in choosing bonds that mature in about ten years, we convey a reasonably long-term investment horizon for investing in stocks—with the assumption that stock prices are random in the short run but respond to economic fundamentals in the longer term.

Table 14.2

WMT Sensitivity	
r	g
6.70%	-0.15%
8.38%	1.41%
10.05%	2.98%

So, let's apply the above to our ongoing example of Wal-Mart. As of November 26, 2010, the company had two outstanding bonds maturing in about ten years and yielding an average of 3.35 percent. Using this figure and taking three different multiples (2x, 2.5x, and 3x)[81] we get the implied growth rates, g, as shown in table 14.2.

As expected, the discount rate varies depending on the assessments of multiples on the yields on the bonds that mature in about ten years; and, as a consequence, the implied growth rate varies accordingly. If the company does not have outstanding bonds, then bonds of equivalent companies may be used or multiples of the prevailing yields on suitable 10-year corporate bond composites may be used.

In the above table, we see once again that the growth rate g implied in the share price of $53.87 is well under the historical growth pattern of the company's earnings. This suggests one of two things: (1) either the market is correctly underestimating the future growth prospects of the company or (2) the market is wrong in expecting that the company's future will be markedly worse than what was its recent past.

The truth of the matter is that nobody can see the future and it is, therefore, impossible to fully comprehend the risks and uncertainties that lie ahead. You may assume that the past would have some clues about the future. But such assumptions are just that: assumptions. Sometimes the future may be similar to the past and other times it may be quite a bit different both in degree and quality.

It is prudent, therefore, to analyze those companies for which the future is likely to be fairly similar or better than the recent past. For companies that are in a turnaround or a rapid change mode, the past may be a less reliable indicator of things to come. In such cases, the quantitative analyses that we do in this book are likely only partly helpful.

Using multiples of bond yields as proxy for uncertainties about future performance is not perfect, of course. Yet, this approach has the advantage that the yields reflect independent judgments of the bond market about the uncertainties that the company faces. Bond yields give an outside perspective, in other words, into the company-specific uncertainties that may lead to default.

So, on the one hand, market β is highly mathematical and produces a precise measurement of risk based on price data; historical performance and bond yields, on the other hand, are rough rules of thumb that build subjective understanding about the future prospects of the company.

Yet, the precision of market β is misleading because it ignores the many factors that drive future performance. Estimates of the discount rates that are derived using bond yields, while not as precise, are more meaningful; the very process of making such estimates brings you closer to the operating particulars of the company under investigation. This is because the imprecision of the latter approach encourages you to do a sensitivity analysis and see how the different assumptions change your understanding of the company.

Systematically probing the assumptions through sensitivity analysis, informed by the specifics of the company, is likely to be more productive than sole reliance on statistics and precision mathematics.

Note that, based on the revised estimates of the implied growth rates, we are still unable to refute our original hunch, or the investment thesis, that Wal-Mart is undervalued. Next, we step up our efforts to refute the now-attractive investment thesis that Wal-Mart is a good investment opportunity at about $54 per share as of the end of 2010.

In the next chapter, we do three additional tests using quantitative data from the company's mandatory filings. In the meantime, let's take a moment to try to remember what the stock prices may be telling us.

What Prices Tell Us

As we have seen, the economic worth of a company is simply the expected future cash flows appropriately discounted to the present. If the markets are pricing a company correctly, then prices should be the present value of those future flows. Prices are supposed to tell a story about the future prospects of the company. Yet, the trouble with the future is that it is unknown and all varieties of stories can be told about what the future will bring. The tenor of the stories being told may be less about the true prospects of the company and more about the motivations of the storyteller or about the social mood of the moment. More than future prospects, therefore, prices may actually reflect in-the-moment collective emotions of buyers and sellers.

The challenge for us is to see what the prevailing prices may be telling us, if anything at all: whether they reflect some realistically attainable future or they are just a wild fantasy of people caught up in the moment. Indeed, prices may tell us nothing at all because they drift randomly, as they are known to do in the short run. In fact, daily fluctuations on average mean little other than that people are buying and selling for any number of reasons that may or may not have anything to do with expectations about the cash flows in the long future.

So, the task before us is to tease out any useful information that may be embedded in the price levels over a period of several days or weeks. As discussed earlier in this chapter, one way to do this is to revisit the discount formulation for estimating intrinsic value. Assume for the moment that the market prices reflect correctly discounted future cash flows. Then your goal is to see what assumptions about the future may be built into those prices. By finding your way into the assumptions embedded in the price, in other words, you may be able to see what the market is seeing and then judge whether the market is approximately right or is wildly mispricing the company.

Consider, once again, Wal-Mart as of November 26, 2010. Assuming the discount rate to be between 6.70 percent and 10.05 percent, the growth rate implied in Wal-Mart's share price of $53.87 varied from –0.15 percent to just under 3 percent. That is, in pricing Wal-Mart at $53.87 per share, the market was expecting its earnings per share to grow in the long run at the average annualized rate of 3 percent or less. Since the daily prices don't really mean that much, the correct thing to do here is to compute implied growth rates using the average price of $54.36 for the month of November 2010. In this example, the difference is not much, so the result will be essentially the same as what we get using $53.87/share.

Now, in looking at the historical growth rate we found that the company grew its earnings at an average of about 10 percent per year over the previous ten years. So, if you expect the company to keep growing into foreseeable future as it has in the recent past, then it may seem that the market is being pessimistic about the company's growth prospects. Based on this analysis, we had updated our assessment that the company is likely a good investment at the given price.

So, could we be wrong and the market right? Of course, we may not be seeing something of which the market, reflecting the collective wisdom of all investors, may be well aware. So, we try to understand the reasons why the market may be expecting such a dramatic slowdown in the company's growth rate. Doing so may take digging into the company, and fodder for additional tests to update our subjective assessment. If it turns out that subsequent analysis reveals no indication of growth slowing down in the near term, then we may feel that the initial thesis (P << V) holds for the time being—subject to further efforts at negation.

If further tests are unable to refute the strengthening investment thesis, then we may be confident that we have a good investment prospect. To understand why, consider this: If Wal-Mart's earnings kept growing at the rate of 10 percent per year for the next five years, then they will have grown from the current $3.70 per share to $5.95 per share five years later. If the price did not change during the period, that will give you an earnings yield of over 11 percent (5.95/53.87). In ten years, if the growth rate sustains, the company will be generating about $9.59 per year and, at current prices, the earnings yield would be almost 18 percent.

That is, for a company that keeps growing the earnings at a steady rate, if the price does not change, the earnings yield would keep rising. But such rise in earnings yield can go on only up to a point, after which prices have to rise to bring the earnings yield down to a level that is comparable with the interest rates and corporate bond yields prevailing at that time.

This logic of rising prices is valid, however, only if the company can continue delivering the growth that it has delivered in the past. Further judgments need to be made, therefore, about the stability and sustainability of the company's earnings and its earning power. Some such additional judgments we will make in the next chapter.

Caveat: Not All Companies Can Be Valued

The discussion thus far must be understood with an important caveat about valuation: not all companies or stocks can be adequately valued. That is, if the earnings are wildly unstable and you cannot get a good fix on the discount rate, then the discount model formulation becomes very difficult to implement. If the company under question does not have much of a history and track record, for example, then even implied growth rate has no suitable benchmark to measure up against.

As such, valuations obtained by discounting expected future flows are most applicable to fairly stable companies with long history—those that have a steady track record and those that have a sustainable business model that would allow them to continue delivering or bettering their historical performance. Even though estimates of the discount rate are moderately difficult for such companies, they are virtually impossible for more complex companies with a short history or volatile track record.

So, investing is really about deciding which companies can be set up for refutation. Of the nearly 45,000 companies on the stock exchanges around the world, only a few hundred are likely at any given time to qualify as candidates for such evaluation. For some companies, as in the case of Wal-Mart, it may be possible to set up an investment thesis that can be refuted and disconfirmed. Such companies are suitable investment prospects.

For the vast number of companies that have a checkered history or no history at all, you may have little or no basis for making subjective judgments that are necessary to estimate the discount rates. That is, when you cannot set up a refutable investment thesis, you risk getting into situations where the intrinsic economic worth cannot be estimated with any degree of confidence. You then rely, instead, on hope. You speculate.

The best way to avoid getting caught up in speculative activities is to limit the search to companies that you can evaluate because you have access to sufficient and credible information of good quality.

15

Yield–Stability–Strength[82]

————

So far, we have reviewed how to think about economic worth using capitalization ratios, such as price-to-earnings, and discounted future flows. Given the ease with which a wide range of prices can be justified by using convenient assumptions, we have argued that the correct approach to valuation requires that we use the principle of negation.

That is, confidence in our investment thesis is best accomplished when we try to refute rather than prove it. The key to using refutation, moreover, is the proper setting up of the thesis so that it can be appropriately put to clear tests; the thesis *must* risk rejection.

Applying the principle of negation, in the previous chapter we evaluated the hunch that Wal-Mart was a potentially good investment at just under $54 per share in November 2010. As a first step, we set up the investment thesis in terms of the growth rate implied in the price at which the company was trading. Then we tried to refute that thesis by comparing the implied growth with the company's historical rate of growth. We found that the historical growth was greater than the implied growth—much above the threshold of two. As such, we were not able to refute the investment thesis and, therefore, have somewhat greater confidence in it.

Yet, the inability to refute provides grounds for further, more rigorous, attempts at refutation. Remember, the inability to refute does not mean that Wal-Mart is certain to produce profits. It only means that, pending more information, it does not yet appear to be a poor investment. We update the thesis tentatively and cautiously, with a degree of confidence—but never with certainty—in its correctness, and remain open to uncovering other evidence that may be able to help refute it. In this sense, as discussed, investing is a negative art.

The effectiveness with which a thesis is tested depends, of course, on the clarity of the data. Quantitative data are generally preferable for the initial serious attempts to refute. In this chapter, we will rely on additional quantitative data that are generally widely available in the public domain. Of course, the credibility and reliability of the data are both very important; how to ensure the integrity of the data is a whole different issue and requires a treatise in its own right. For the time being, we will simply assume that the available data that we use in our analysis are correct for the most part.

Updating the Investment Thesis

Remember that our baseline assumption is that all stocks are being appropriately priced by the market. That is, even though markets can sometimes grossly misprice assets, we begin our analysis with the thought that the collective wisdom of the market is likely correct and, therefore, we assume that prices have not deviated significantly from the true underlying economic worth of a particular stock. So, our null or general expectation is that price equals value, more or less. That is, we write the null as: No: Price = Value

Now, based on our inability to refute on the basis of implied growth rate, our investment thesis for Wal-Mart still stands as:

T: Price ≠ Value

or, more specifically, in this case as:

T: Price << Value

That is, we tentatively accept our original hunch that the stock may be an attractive opportunity, and now need to look for additional information with which to update the evolving thesis. Yet, in order to guard against our deep bias to try to confirm our priors, we seek data that may help us refute the expectation that this company represents a good opportunity at the given price. As such, we subject our thesis to further disconfirmation analysis based on additional financial data.

Note that we are using a non-statistical variant of Popper's method here. Usually, in the scientific method, we first develop a null hypothesis based on whatever theory (or belief) we may be testing and then go about trying to reject the null using the available data. In investment analysis of the sort we are doing here, repeat observations are usually not available when evaluating a single investment at a point of time. Instead of using formal statistical analysis, therefore, we use the spirit of Popper to make judgments against specific quantitative markers. Note also that that, technically, we are supposed to try to reject the null because it embodies the belief we have about what the truth is in a given situation. Since the alternate thesis is a belief about the appropriateness of an investment in question, it acquires the character of a null and that is, therefore, what we try to refute.

Beyond the general thesis as above, therefore, the next stage in trying to refute the investment thesis is comprised of three parts. To that end, we formalize three corresponding sub-theses before trying to refute each with additional batteries of empirical tests. Note that we examine these sub-theses *after* we have already been unable to refute the main investment thesis using the implied growth rates. If any of the tests succeed in refuting one or more sub-thesis discussed below, then we will have cast doubt on our original hunch about the appropriateness of the investment in question. If we are unable to refute any of the three sub-theses, however, then we gain greater confidence in the thesis—and go on to a series of qualitative or narrative tests that we will discuss in later chapters.

First, with the *Yield Tests* we question the notion that the company in which we are thinking about investing is generating sufficient earnings. That is, we want to *refute* that, based on how much of the company's earnings each dollar of our investment will buy, the shares are a better place to invest than putting our money in the bank or in corporate or treasury bonds or perhaps in another stock. The tests require that we compute earnings, cash flow, and dividend yields.

Second, with the *Stability Tests* we try to refute the notion that the past performance of the company was stable, so that we may have grounds for questioning its ability to continue delivering the expected results through our investment time horizon. We assess stability using patterns in the historical financial and operating ratios.

Finally, with the *Strength Tests* we try to refute the notion that the company is financially strong. The financial strength of the company is indicated in the quality of its balance sheet and it is evaluated using a series of leverage and liquidity ratios.

In the three sections that follow, let's take each test in turn.

1. Yield Tests

After having estimated the range of future perpetual growth rates implied in the prevailing prices, the next step in trying to refute the thesis [T: Price ≠ Value] is related to the attractiveness of the stock in comparison with competing investment opportunities. In particular, the competing opportunities are those where you can obtain comparable or better returns on your investment. Formally, therefore, the first sub-thesis that needs to be refuted using a variety of yields.

S-T$_a$: The stock offers attractive yields.

Now, you can invest in U.S. Treasuries and get a return prevailing at a given time. Let us say that you want to invest $100,000 and have a time horizon of ten years for which you'd like to invest that amount. Suppose that the 10-year T-Notes are yielding 2.89 percent, as they were as of this writing on November 26, 2010. This means that if you chose to invest in these treasuries, you would get an interest payment (coupon) of $2,890 for each of the next ten years and then get the full refund of the $100,000 you had invested originally. You will get the coupons usually in two payments a year.

The T-Notes provide a good benchmark for evaluating the sub-thesis because they do not have default risk. That is, if you hold the T-Notes until maturity, then you expect to get back all your money along with the owed interest. Default is highly unlikely because the government of the United States stands behind the Treasury notes.

The risk that you do have when investing in the Treasuries is the interest rate risk. Suppose, for example, that while you are holding the T-Notes at 2.89 percent rate, inflation picks up and the interest rates in the economy rise to, say, 5 percent. Now you are still stuck with $2,890 payment per year, whereas if you were to invest $100,000 in T-Notes in the new environment of 5 percent rate, your payment would be $5,000 per year. But you have already made the commitment at 2.89 percent for ten years, so you are out of luck.

Seeing this, you may think you would like to sell the Treasuries you hold and reinvest in new Treasuries at the new and higher interest rate of 5 percent. But the market value of your old Treasuries in the new interest rate environment will be lower than what you had paid for them. Let us see how the market value of your old Treasuries will be affected by the increase in the interest rates from 2.89 percent to, say, 5 percent.

Bond Yields

How much will the price of your T-Notes need to be to yield the prevailing interest rate of 5 percent? We know that once you purchased the T-Notes as above, the coupon became fixed at $2,890 per year until maturity, of ten years in this case. Knowing the fixed coupon, any buyer in the market will demand a price that yields the same return as the prevailing interest rates at the time you may want to sell the T-Notes. To yield 5 percent, the price of the T-Notes you hold will clearly have to drop in order to match the interest rates that potential buyers can get elsewhere (e.g., by buying the new T-Notes that the U.S. government may be issuing at the time).

So, we have to solve for Price (X) in (2,890 / X) = 5 percent. This gives us X as (2,890 / 0.05) or $57,800. That is, because of the increase in interest rates in the new environment, the value of your T-Notes dropped from $100,000 to $57,800. If you sell at this point, you will be taking a massive loss on your original investment. So, you may decide to keep the Treasury notes, sadly accepting a coupon of $2,890 (2.89 percent) per year and then getting your investment back in full at the time of maturity.

The T-Notes, then, have no default risk but they do expose you to the risk of changes in the interest rates. If you are comfortable making a 10-year commitment to the Treasuries and not worrying about what happens in the interim, then the interest rate risk would not be of much concern to you. Just hold on to the Notes until maturity, accepting the rate you got at the time of making the investment, and be secure in the virtual guarantee that you will get all your money back.

It is for this reason of no default risk that the 10-year T-Notes make a good benchmark against which to measure the attractiveness of the stock you may be considering. Lately, however, since the financial troubles post-2007, the safety (default-free) feature of Treasuries is attracting a good deal of capital and their pricing may have some speculation built into them, as highly risk-averse investors flock to them for the guarantee they offer.

Ironically, therefore, the default-risk-free nature of the Treasuries can create distortions in their prices and yields. For instance, in periods of intense fear, the Treasuries become very attractive and demand for them rises sharply, quickly inflating their prices and pushing down their yields. Similarly, during strong bull markets, risk-seeking investors abandon the safety of the Treasuries in favor of fast rising stocks, demand drops and the yields increase rapidly. Interventions by the Federal Reserve can make the story a bit more complex, but the possibility of speculation in the Treasuries can dilute somewhat their effectiveness as a good benchmark for stock analysis.

A possibly more stable benchmark to use is the composite index of 10-year corporate bonds with AAA or AA rating. This is the yield on a basket of high-grade corporate bonds that have a very low risk of default. These bonds do not have the backing of the U.S. government but that of issuing corporations that are typically large and financially among the healthiest. These companies are deemed by the rating agencies[83] to have a very small likelihood of defaulting on any of their bonds. Moreover, the basket comprises bonds of not just one but several companies and, therefore, may represent the broader economy.

On November 26, 2010, the yield on a composite index of AAA rated 10-year corporate bonds was 3.14 percent, just a little higher than the 2.89 percent yield available on the 10-year T-Notes. At that time, this yield spread of 0.25 percent (or 25 basis points) accounted for some unknown but small default risk for a basket of high-grade corporate bonds.

Earnings Yields

When applying the bond yield benchmark to evaluate stocks, it is best where possible to find the bonds of the company itself. So, take Wal-Mart for instance. As of November 26, 2010, Wal-Mart had two 10-year bonds outstanding. One of these, maturing in October 2020, was yielding 3.353 percent and the other, maturing in July 2020, was yielding 3.355 percent. Fitch rating agency classi-fied these bonds as AA, one notch below the top rating of AAA. On the same date, the 10-year composite index of AA bonds was 3.97 percent.

It turns out that Wal-Mart 10-year bonds did not get the top billing; still, they were considered to have lower yield (3.35 percent) or lower default risk than the composite of AA bonds (3.97 percent). So, let's use this information to begin evaluating the common shares of Wal-Mart, and to see if we may be able to refute our sub-thesis about yields.

As of the morning of November 26, Wal-Mart common was trading at $53.87 per share. For the previous full year (as of January 2010), the company had reported diluted earnings per share (EPS) of about $3.70 per share. As shown in the previous chapter, if the company's earnings power was safely reflected in this EPS, the earnings yield (EY) was:

$$EY = (EPS \ / \ Price) = (3.70 \ / \ 53.87) = 0.069 \qquad (15.1)$$

That is, for each dollar invested in the common shares of Wal-Mart at the current price, the company generated 6.9 percent earnings yield. Compare this with the 3.35 percent yield that the bondholders of the company were getting for the AA-rated bond maturing in ten years.

The difference, or the equity premium, is based in the supposition that the company's AA-rated 10-year bonds had a very low risk of default, whereas the earnings of the company could decrease over that time period. Moreover, since companies typically do not distribute all their earnings to shareholders, earnings yields are not directly comparable to bond yields. Bondholders get their yields in cash whereas shareholders do not unless, of course, the company pays out regular dividends.

Dividend Yields

Let's compute dividend yields for the ongoing example of Wal-Mart. In the full year reported in January 2010, Wal-Mart paid out four quarterly divi-dends adding up to $1.11 in total cash dividends per diluted share (DPS). So, we compute the trailing dividend yield (DY) as:

$$DY = (DPS / Price) = (1.11 / 53.87) = 0.0206 \qquad (15.2)$$

At $53.87 per share, if Wal-Mart continued paying the annual dividend of $1.11 per share, then for your investment of $100,000 you will get about $2,061 in cash every year until you sell your stake in the company. This is cash in hand and, therefore, directly comparable with the yields that the bond-holders get. While bondholders would receive $3,355 in interest every year for the next ten years, the shareholders would get $2,061 in dividend payments. By contract, unless the company gets in trouble in the interim, the bond-holders get the full principle back at maturity in ten years; the shareholders are not assured that they will get their principle back, and the company has the option of raising or cutting the dividends, or stopping them altogether. As a shareholder, you do have the option of continuing to hold the shares of Wal-Mart or selling them at any time.

We now have bond yields to be compared to earnings and dividend yields. The earnings yield is useful in assessing how much in earnings the company is able to generate from each dollar of your purchase price or your original investment in it. The dividend yield is useful because it indicates the approximate annual cash return you can expect from your investment in the company at current prices. But what happens if the company does not issue any dividends? After all, a good many companies issue no dividend at all.

Understand that when you own common shares in a publicly traded company, you own the right to the earnings for your share of ownership. So, if you own one share in Wal-Mart, then you have the right to total earnings divided by the number of diluted shares outstanding, or about $3.70 per share.

Cash Flow Yields

Yet, the above are not cash earnings but only on paper. By some accounting convention, the $3.70 earnings per share (EPS) are the company's best estimate after it has deducted all expenses and taxes from the revenues. These earnings need to be translated using additional accounting conventions to see how much earnings in actual cash the company generated. From those cash earnings then, the company puts some back into the business so as to maintain the quality of assets and its ability to continue generating earnings.

The remaining cash earnings, the free cash flow, then rightfully belong to the shareholders even if the company decides not to distribute them out. The cash that the company retains may be used for other purposes such as retiring debt, repurchasing shares in the open market, or for making investments in new growth opportunities. These *free* cash flows are the theoretically correct basis for evaluating the real cash yields available to you as a shareholder. As such, we compute the Free Cash Yield (FCY) for Wal-Mart as follows. Even though the company had accounting earnings of $3.70 per share, their cash earnings from operations were $6.93 per share. First, we compute their Operating Cash Yield (OCY) as follows:

$$OCY = (OCPS / Price) = (6.93 / 53.87) = 0.129 \qquad (15.3)$$

Of the cash generated from operations, Wal-Mart reinvested a portion back into the company, as capital expenditures of $3.22 per share and, as a result, generated $3.72 in free cash flow per share (FCFPS).

$$FCFY = (FCFPS / Price) = (3.72 / 53.87) = 0.069 \qquad (15.4)$$

The yield calculations are summarized in table 15.1. The numbers suggest that investing in the common stock of Wal-Mart would likely result in a much higher (more than double) free cash yield than investment in either T-Notes or in a basket of AAA corporate bonds. In fact, investment in Wal-Mart, at $53.87 per share, yields a premium of 106 percent over the company's AA-rated long-term bonds.

Table 15.1

10-Year Treasury	2.89%	Earnings Yield	7.02%
10-Year Corporate AAA	3.14%	Dividend Yield	2.06%
10-Year Corporate AA	3.97%	Operating Cash Yield	12.86%
10-Year Wal-Mart AA	3.35%	Free Cash Flow Yield	6.91%

How much premium over the 10-Year Corporate AAA is acceptable remains a question, however. Unfortunately, that question cannot be answered conclusively in the abstract. Every investor needs to understand her or his own risk tolerance and demand equity premium that is acceptable given their own financial situation. For some, more than 100 percent premium over yields from good quality bonds would be sufficient; for others, strong risk-averse nature may demand even more premium, and in the illustration above they may choose to invest in the Treasuries instead or look for other companies where the yield premium may be even higher.

For a risk-neutral stock investor, however, Wal-Mart's yield premium suggests that the sub-thesis S-Ta cannot as yet be clearly refuted. For another attempt at refutation, therefore, we go to the next test in the sequence and evaluate the company on the stability of its performance.

2. Stability Tests

Unable to refute the investment thesis based on valuation and yield, the next step in the process is to try to refute that the company has a long record of good operating performance. That is, you need to be careful not to make a decision based on performance in a single year but see if the company has exhibited steady performance over several years. The objective here is to look for indications that the company has sufficient earning power so that it can continue delivering the earnings reflected in the yield tests and that the discrepancy between the historical and implied growth rates is justified. You must look at the past to assess the potential for the future but, again, in the spirit of refutation. Formally, therefore, the next refutable sub-thesis is as follows:

S-T_b: The Company has a track record of steady performance.

There are two broad ways of assessing the steadiness of the company's historical performance. One, yields as computed in the previous section can be redone but as average earnings, free cash flows, and dividends for the previous several years. Two, key margins and other ratios are evaluated both numerically and visually for patterns over the preceding five to ten years—or, ideally, over an entire business cycle, from peak to trough back to peak again. The assessments then indicate whether or not S-T_b can be clearly refuted.

Average Yields

In order to examine stability using average yields, let's stay with the example of Wal-Mart selling at $53.87 per share. Table 15.2 shows the average historical per share earnings (EPS), dividends (DPS), and free cash flow (FCFPS).

We can make several observations from these data. For starters, the company does indeed have performance data available for at least ten years. We cannot make estimates of stability unless the company has a history of reasonably long duration. Different investors will have different levels of comfort with the length of historical data, but brand new companies or those with only a few years of operating history are not amenable to this kind of analysis.

The absence of historical data creates a great deal of unresolvable uncertainty and increases the chances of making Type I errors. For those with a cautious temperament, therefore, it may be prudent to work only with companies that have been publicly traded for at least ten full years.

Table 15.2

	Averages			2010
	10-Year	5-Year	3-Year	1-Year
EPS	2.48	3.12	3.41	3.70
DPS	0.59	0.84	0.97	1.09
FCFPS	0.086	1.94	2.64	3.63
	Averages			2010
	10-Year	5-Year	3-Year	1-Year
EY	4.60%	5.79%	6.32%	6.86%
DY	1.09%	1.55%	1.80%	2.02%
FCFY	1.59%	3.61%	4.89%	6.73%

Using the share price of $53.87 and the historical track record as shown above, the various yields are also shown in table 15.2.

It is evident from table 15.2 that the company has steadily increased both earnings and dividends during the previous ten years. The free cash, computed as operating cash less capital expenditures, has also increased for the most part, from

$-1.11 in 2001 to $3.63 in 2010. The negative free cash flow in the earlier years was because of large capital expenditures, perhaps as investments for growth.

Using the share price of $53.87 and the historical track record as shown above, the various yields are also shown in table 15.2.

A good deal of steadiness is evident in the operating track record of Wal-Mart; the current year performance is clearly not an aberration, and it fits in quite well with the pattern of performance over the previous ten years.

Given the steadiness of past performance, let's assume for the moment that the earning power of the company is correctly reflected in the averages. The above yields then reveal whether or not Wal-Mart shares are attractive at $53.87. So, for instance, if Wal-Mart were to continue delivering performance as it had done on average over the previous three years, it would then be a company that has EPS= $3.41, DPS=$0.97, and FCFPS=$2.64. The corresponding yields would be EY= 6.32 percent, DY=1.80 percent, and FCFY=4.89 percent for an investor purchasing the shares at the price of $53.87 per share.

Both 3-year EY (6.32 percent) and FCFY (4.89 percent) are higher than the yield of 3.97 percent available for AA corporate bond composite. The dividend yield of 1.80 percent is, however, 45.3 percent of AA bond yield (see table 15.2).

The yields for Wal-Mart show a decreasing trend as we go from current year to three-year average to 10-year average. This is because the company's performance has been improving over time, so the older numbers show lower yields. If there was reason to believe that Wal-Mart's performance will revert to, say, its 10-year average numbers, even then the earnings yield of 4.60 percent would be above comparable yield on the AA bond composite yield; but it would not be as attractive as that based on the 2010 numbers which show EPS=$3.70 and EY=6.86 percent. For a company on a steady growth trajectory, the yields based on historical averages provide a conservative estimate of past performance—and potential future performance.

Clearly, Wal-Mart cannot as yet be refuted with regards to stability in its operating record and financial results. So, let's next look at patterns in past performance.

Patterns in Historical Data

Of particular note are the margins of the company. Again, using Wal-Mart as an example, table 15.3 shows the 10-year history of operating (OpM) and net margins (NM) for the company. Our objective is to try to refute the subthesis that the company is stable.

Clearly, the company has steadily increased its margins over the years, indicating a gradual improvement in its performance with 2005 the peak year. The margins stay within a fairly narrow band during the ten years on view in this table.

Table 15.3

($mm where applicable)									
Year	OpM	NM	ROE	ROC	A T/O	Inv T/O	Op Inc	Int Exp	Int Cov
2010	5.87%	3.51%	20.26%	12.79%	2.39	8.97	23,950	2,065	11.60
2009	4.59%	3.34%	20.53%	12.46%	2.46	8.68	18,435	2,184	8.44
2008	4.73%	3.40%	19.70%	11.65%	2.29	7.96	17,723	2,103	8.43
2007	4.88%	3.27%	18.33%	11.22%	2.28	7.68	16,839	1,809	9.31
2006	4.90%	3.59%	21.12%	12.21%	2.26	7.32	15,303	1,420	10.78
2005	5.02%	3.60%	20.79%	12.70%	2.37	7.31	14,324	1,187	12.07
2004	4.94%	3.53%	20.76%	12.92%	2.44	7.32	12,673	996	12.72
2003	4.76%	3.29%	20.44%	12.42%	2.58	7.57	11,643	1,063	10.95
2002	4.62%	3.06%	19.00%	11.71%	2.61	7.44	10,064	1,326	7.59
2001	4.98%	3.29%	20.08%	11.73%	2.45	6.87	9,524	1,374	6.93

Similar evaluation of the historical data can be made for performance metrics such as Return on Equity (ROE) and Return on Capital (ROC), and for operating performance metrics, Asset Turnover (A T/O) and Inventory Turnover (Inv T/O).

All the above tables reflect fairly stable historical performance, and suggest that the earning power of the company is fairly robust. We cannot, therefore, refute the investment sub-thesis S-T$_b$ that the company has a track record of stable performance. Combined with the results of implied growth rate analysis and the yield tests reported earlier, the results of the stability tests suggest that we cannot yet refute the primary investment thesis that Wal-Mart is an attractive—potentially profitable—investment opportunity. The thesis gains strength yet again.

Note that the focus in the stability tests is on historical performance so as to avoid ungrounded optimism about the future. Yes, the main idea here is to assess whether the company can continue delivering performance into the future. So, the intent behind stability tests is to strongly anchor expectations about the future in the experiences from recent history. Such anchoring is conservative, certainly, and it is based on the need to control unbounded optimism that periodically infects investors at large.

The conservative nature of stability tests based in historical analysis has some costs, of course. Sure, by emphasizing the importance of the historical track record, we are displaying caution against the seductions of hope. Yet, we are also becoming vulnerable to letting go of opportunities that may come about from uncharacteristically rapid growth in the future. That is, by insisting on reasonableness grounded in historical performance, we are liable to make Type II errors; we accept this trade-off in order to reduce the chances of making the Type I error of investing in a company that does not live up to its promise.

Unable to refute the investment thesis thus far, let's next try to refute the sub-thesis that the company is financially sound.

3. Strength Tests

Next, in trying to refute the investment thesis [T: Price << Value], we perform a series of tests related to the financial strength of the company. These tests are designed to evaluate the ease with which the company would be able to meet the obligations to those from whom it has borrowed money. Financially strong companies have the resources to weather economic storms and to make investments in their operations to deliver future performance. Financially weak companies are vulnerable to serious setback or even collapse should internal or external business conditions take a turn for the worse; they also have limited resources to invest in future growth.

Formally, therefore, the next testable sub-thesis to be refuted is:

S-T$_c$: The Company is financially strong.

A series of ratios can provide an indication about the financial health of a company, and the flexibility it has in terms of access to internal or external financial resources. This focus on financial health is particularly important, as it helps reduce the accidents of investing in a company that may be vulnerable to sudden change in fortunes.

Broadly, three sets of tests indicate the financial health of companies: Coverage, Leverage, and Liquidity. These tests indicate the difficulty a company may have in bearing the costs of borrowed money, the degree to which the assets exceed liabilities, and the extent to which the company may lack cash funds to be able to comfortably service its debt obligations. As such, we first consider below the interest coverage ratio and then the various ways of estimating the interest bearing debt in relation to equity and cash flows.

Interest Coverage

The starting point for strength tests is the interest coverage ratio, computed as:

Interest Coverage Ratio = Operating Income / Interest Expense   (15.5)

For Wal-Mart, for the full year ending January 2010, this ratio comes out as follows (all data except ratio in $mm):

Interest Coverage Ratio = (23, 950 / 2,065) = 11.60   (15.5 Sol.)

That is, in 2010, Wal-Mart generated $23.95 billion in operating earnings whereas the interest expense it incurred was $2.065 billion. As such, the company had plentiful resources to cover interest expenses. Interest coverage ratios for the previous ten years are as shown in the last column of table 15.3.

The ability of the company to make regular interest payments is a key test, mainly because being residual owners, stockholders stand to lose a great deal if the company gets in trouble with the lenders.

In addition to evaluating the history with regards to interest coverage, it is also helpful to compute the ratio using current year interest expense and the average operating income from the previous three years ($20,036 million). The three-year average is a more conservative estimate of the resources that the company is able to generate internally. As such, the re-computed interest coverage ratio is (all data except ratio in $mm):

Interest Coverage Ratio = (20,036 / 2,065) = 9.70   (15.5 Sol.)

It is apparent that Wal-Mart can easily make the interest payments equivalent to those incurred in the past year. The risk of non-payment or default appears to be rather small, as for that to happen the operating income would have to drop rather dramatically from the current levels of over $20 billion per year.

The acceptable coverage ratio varies, of course, depending on the company. Typically, larger companies are deemed safer than smaller companies and, therefore, the acceptable coverage ratio is lower for them. It is generally understood, for instance, that large companies with market capitalization of over $5 billion are considered in excellent health if their coverage ratio is anything greater than about eight; for smaller companies, interest coverage upwards of ten is desirable. As of this writing, the market of capitalization of Wal-Mart equity was a little under $200 billion. As such, the ratio of 9.70 shows excellent financial health.

In addition to size, acceptable coverage ratios also vary by industry. For industries with inherently volatile earnings and where companies are vulnerable to rapid technological or market changes, coverage ratio requirements are generally higher. Technology and fashion clothing, for instance, are vulnerable to swift changes; well-established industrial companies, on the other hand, are relatively less vulnerable to sudden changes. The nature of the industry is an important factor in determining the threshold for acceptable coverage ratios. Generally, as a rule of thumb, companies in most industries other than utilities, perhaps, are deemed to be vulnerable to default as their interest coverage begins to fall below to about two.

So, both high coverage ratio and stability of earnings, in combination, are important indicators of the company's ability to weather economic storms and meet the obligations to its debt. These factors are highly influential in how the company's bonds get rated by rating agencies such as Moody's, and they influence as well the cost of borrowing from external sources.

In the case of Wal-Mart as of the end of 2010 reporting year, we have so far not yet been able to refute the sub-thesis S-Tc that it is a financially strong company. Both stability of operating earnings and the high coverage ratios are indicative of good financial strength. So, we make further efforts to refute sub-thesis S-Tc by going from the income statement to the balance sheet of the company.

Financial Leverage

The next step in trying to refute S-Tc is to understand how much financial flexibility the company has to weather economic storms as and when they come. The idea here is not so much the company's ability to make annual interest payments but to evaluate its overall debt burden.

Refuting financial strength requires that the company have very high debt in relation to its resources. Too much debt or rapid increases in debt are often, although not always, indicative of potential problems on the operating side of the business. The exception to rapidly growing debt is when the company has borrowed, within reason, to pursue legitimate opportunities that could not be adequately funded from resources already at hand.

So, the first check is to see the total debt the company has in relation to its common equity on the books. Also sometimes called "net assets" or "common shareholders' equity," common equity is the difference between all the assets of the company (what it owns) minus all its liabilities (what it owes).

Debt-to-Equity = Total Debt / Common Equity   (15.6)

For the year ending January 2010, Wal-Mart had total debt of $41,320 million and common shareholder equity of $70,749 million. The debt-to-equity ratio for the company was therefore (data except ratio in $mm):

Debt-to-Equity = 41,320 / 70,749 = 0.58   (15.6 Sol.)

That is, for every dollar of equity belonging to common shareholders, Wal-Mart had 58 cents in debt. So, in addition to being able to comfortably cover annual interest payments from operating income, the company also had net assets comfortably in excess of total debt.

Let us now understand what this debt ratio implies for the company.

Assume for the moment that the company could borrow more up to the point where debt equals its equity. That is, let's assume that the target debt-to-equity ratio for the company equals one, which usually is a comfortable ratio for most well-established large companies. Since Wal-Mart had $70,749 million in equity and its total debt was $41,320 million, all else equal, the company had the capacity to take on an additional $29.429 ($70,749–$41,320) million in debt.

Now, if the company were to take on this additional debt, its interest payments would increase. Assuming that the interest rate on the new debt is the same as the average interest rate on the current debt, for Wal-Mart at the end of 2010 it would be (all data except ratio in $mm):

Interest Rate = Current Interest Expense / Total Current Debt   (15.7)

Interest Rate = 2,065 / 41,320 = 0.05   (15.8)

If the company can borrow the additional money at its current average cost of 5 percent, then the new $29,429 million in debt will cost it $1,471 more in interest payments per year. That is, for the target debt-to-equity ratio of one, the company will have total debt of $70,749 million and its annual interest expenses will rise to $3,536 million. These interest expenses need to be covered by the annual operating income of $23,950 million, resulting in a revised interest coverage ratio as follows (all data except ratio in $mm):

Interest Coverage Ratio = 23,950 / 3,536 = 6.77   (15.9)

That is, if the company were to maintain earnings but increase debt-to-equity ratio from 0.58 to 1.0, its interest coverage would drop from 11.60 to 6.77, a significant decrease but still high enough to maintain a debt rating of investment grade. These data show that the company has enough capacity to take on substantially more debt to the tune of up to $29 billion. The additional debt would hurt its financial position somewhat but still would likely keep it financially robust.

So, a financially strong company has the capacity to borrow more money in times of need and thereby weather economic storms (when the interest rates or cost of borrowing usually go down) better than companies that are financially weak and have little or no debt capacity.

From the above, we can see that we are still unable to refute the sub-thesis S-Tc that Wal-Mart is a financially strong company. Let us, therefore, make one more attempt to refute this sub-thesis about financial strength.

Debt Coverage

While the capital structure provides a sense of how much the company common shareholders own net of all liabilities, it does not fully indicate the company's ability to manage all the debt. That is because equity is simply a residual derived from subtracting all liabilities from all assets. It is not cash with which to pay off debt. Even the interest coverage ratio is simply the paper ability to pay interest expenses, and not necessarily an indication that the company has cash resources to service its debts.

As such, the third set of ratios with which to evaluate financial strength is related to the strength of cash flows in relation to the total debt the company has on the books.

Free cash flow is simply the cash from operations *less* the capital expenditures and other investments necessary to keep the company a going concern. As such, the company's ability to handle its debt load is reflected in the ratio as follows:

Debt Coverage Ratio = (Total Debt / Free Cash Flow)   (15.10)

For Wal-Mart, this ratio comes out as follows for the full year ending January 2010 (all data except ratio in $mm):

Debt Coverage Ratio = (41,320 / 14,065) = 2.94   (15.10 Sol.)

That is, Wal-Mart generated enough free cash flow during the past year to be able to pay off all its debt in fewer than three years if it chooses to do so. Once again, since a single-year performance could be an aberration, its best to use free cash flow average over three years and re-compute the above ratio. The three-year average of free cash flow from Wal-Mart operations was $10,377 million. As such, the recomputed debt coverage ratio for the company is:

Debt Coverage Ratio = (41,320 / 10,377) = 3.98   (15.10 Sol.)

So, using the average annual free cash flows over the previous three years, Wal-Mart has the ability to pay off all its interest-bearing debts in fewer than four years. There is no obvious benchmark number for the debt coverage ratio, but the ability of the company to pay off all the debt in fewer than five years is generally a good sign. In practice, it does not normally make sense for financially strong companies to pay off their debt. In fact, as they grow their assets and equity, such companies only increase their debt capacity and take on more debt in order to fund ongoing operations and strategic activities.

In short, given that Wal-Mart has a high interest coverage, good debt ratio, sufficient debt capacity, and strong free cash flows in relation to total debt, we are so far unable to refute the sub-thesis S-Tc1 that it is a financially strong company.

Interim Assessment

In spite of several formal attempts, we have been unable thus far to cast serious doubt on the investment thesis that Wal-Mart is a good investment prospect at about $54 per share (in November 2010). We found that the company's historical growth rate was much higher than the future growth rate implied in its stock price as given. As such, we were unable to refute the thesis that the stock is attractively priced. Further efforts to refute the thesis were unsuccessful as well: at about $54 per share, the stock could not be refuted on the basis of implied growth, yield, stability, and financial strength.

Wal-Mart, of course, is used in the preceding pages simply as an illustration of the process whereby we try to negate the initial hunch about the company. The same process may be used for other companies as well. For investments other than stocks, however, alternate benchmarks may need to be established for refutation.

But, whatever the security, the basic principle of negation is at the heart of evaluating the investment thesis, whatever it may be. The specific criteria for refutation would depend on the context, however, and would most likely be different from the criteria we are using here to evaluate stocks.

Since we have been unable to refute the thesis about Wal-Mart stock being a good investment prospect at about $54 per share, by now we should have a fair degree of confidence in it.

Alas, we are still not quite done. Since the previous tests were based on quantitative data from financial statements filed by the company, there is still a concern that we may be missing important qualitative information that is reported elsewhere in the filings. We still do not have very high confidence in the thesis, as there is still a chance that some unnoticed but important information may undermine the thesis in spite of our inability to refute it thus far.

Hence, starting in the next chapter, we develop a systematic process for further trying to refute or disconfirm the thesis using additional quantitative and qualitative information. Of particular importance in the next few chapters, you will see, is the ability to make sound subjective judgments about the defining narratives of the companies under scrutiny.

Book IV

Diligence

Chapters

———

16. Depth Analysis

17. Dive for Strength

18. Define Good Business

19. Meet the Managers

20. Watch the Game

———

16

Depth Analysis

The refutation analysis we have done thus far is based solely on the quantitative data visible from the financial statements, from the surface, so to speak. Additional scrutiny of the company is necessary with qualitative data and narrative analysis. So, in the chapters that follow, we'll see how to highlight and evaluate information that is often dispersed through the company literature. We continue to try to refute the investment thesis, strenghtened though it may be because of our inability to refute it using tests as shown in the previous chapters.

Perhaps the most important easily accessible sources of qualitative information about public companies in the United States are their reports to the Securities and Exchange Commission (SEC); companies listed on foreign exchanges have similar filing requirements in the corresponding countries. For now, to illustrate how to incorporate qualitative information into the process of refutation, let us focus on the regulatory filings of companies on the U.S. exchanges.

Of the many reports filed by the companies in the United States, perhaps the most immediately useful are the Annual Reports (10-K), Quarterly Reports (10-Q), Current Reports (8-K), and the Proxy filing (Def 14A). The annual report filed by foreign companies listed on the U.S. stock exchanges is 20-F. In fact, the list of filings required by the SEC is very long,[84] and any investor wanting to fully explore those will have a great deal to read.

A word of caution for those planning to dig into the company filings: the amount of information you will encounter is likely to be overwhelming. You will quickly learn that the big problem in analysis is not the lack of information but too much of it, and it is unstructured for the most part. It is easy to get lost, therefore, in the mass of data that the companies are required to report, with reporting itself sometimes becoming convoluted and confusing.

Part of such complexity arises because the public companies vary in size from tens of millions in sales to hundreds of billions, and employ thousands of people across the world. Wal-Mart, for instance, has over two million[85] employees globally, not to mention the hundreds of thousands of others who are indirectly connected to it as suppliers, vendors, and contractors.

Public companies are complex entities, in other words, and the mandatory reporting is to ensure that they take the time to explain to investors and other interested parties as to what is going on with them. Yet, the regulatory requirements can be so cumbersome that even simple facts can on occasion become befuddling and opaque to the uninitiated.

Perhaps the best way to navigate through these filings, therefore, is to know exactly what you are looking for and then cut through the noise and go straight to the information that is relevant for the analytical objectives at hand. Not everything in the filings is equally important; the key to being a wise investor is to have or develop the skills to quickly locate important facts about the company, and then make analytical judgments about the key uncertainties that characterize your investment thesis.

So, just as we have so far tried to refute the investment thesis on the basis of valuation, yield, stability, and strength, we are now ready to dive deep inside the company, so to speak, to look for traps and pitfalls that may be awaiting unsuspecting investors. These potential vulnerabilities are mostly qualitative and, even though we may use some quantitative markers, evaluating them requires considerable subjective judgment.

As is true with most professions that rely on a body of experiential knowledge, such as law and medicine, only with experience will an investor be able to make such judgments with confidence. But the basic elements of qualitative inquiry can be learned fairly quickly and that is what I will emphasize in the following chapters.

The principle of negation with which to approach the deep dive is the same as the one we have been using thus far but with one major difference.

Instead of quantitatively refuting a clearly articulated investment thesis, we are looking for qualitative or narrative data that may help disconfirm the investment thesis. Because the judgments made in doing so are based on personal interpretations of qualitative data, you may not be able to clearly "hard" refute the thesis. The intent here is still to cast doubt to such an extent that disconfirmation is all but obvious.

That is, our approach still is to interpret conservatively and to try to disconfirm the emerging beliefs based (by this time) in the previously executed but unsuccessful quantitative tests designed to refute the investment thesis. Yet, the skills necessary for the next stage of analysis favor journalists over mathematicians, poets over quants. The objective of the qualitative analysis is to try to cast clear doubt on the defining narratives of the company.

To that end, we will try to disconfirm the investment thesis by trying to cast doubt on the narratives on three broad fronts.

First, if we have thus far been unable to refute the thesis on financial strength, we now want to use qualitative data to disconfirm that the company has few or no obligations other than interest-bearing debt that is visible in the balance sheet. That is, we want to check that not just debt but the overall financial burdens of the company are manageable and that their assets are in good order.

Second, if we have thus far been unable to clearly refute the thesis using the stability tests, we now want to try to disconfirm the ability of the company to continue on its historical trajectory. As such, we try to discredit the business model of the company and question its ability to deliver consistent performance and growth in the near future.

Finally, if we have thus far been unable to refute the company using the yield tests, we now want to disconfirm the proposition that the company is in an opportunity-rich environment, and that it has suitable leadership in place to sustain the business and navigate through the uncertainties that inevitably lie ahead.

Let us take each in turn.

17

Dive for Strength

——

Perhaps the most to fear when investing in a company are the hidden but big problems, those that are not visible from the surface but which could create implosions and destroy your investment. While there are all varieties of hidden problems that could be plaguing a company at any given time, it is advisable to watch out for at least the most notable ones. Often the best place to start the search for potential trouble spots is the balance sheet.

Even though we were unable to refute the investment thesis based on the strength tests, and the company's balance sheet looks healthy based on certain debt ratios, we know that reported liabilities and assets can mask trouble.

We need to look deeper, therefore, to refute the by-now much-strengthened sub-thesis that the company is financially strong and able to withstand economic shocks. For this, we look specifically for obligations or potential obligations that may not be fully reflected in the reported liabilities on the balance sheet. Similarly, we scrutinize the assets side of the ledger to see if they are indeed what they seem to be.

The reason such diligence is necessary is that companies can stay within the reporting rules and still be able to hide obligations or *faux* assets in the thicket of their mandatory SEC filings. Regulators often simply play catch-up with companies, some of which find ever clever ways to navigate their troubles around complicated reporting requirements; sometimes those clever ways are benign but at other times such shenanigans become dangerous for investors because they hide the true economic condition of the company.

So, in order to try to disconfirm the investment thesis, here are a few potentially big problem items to look for when digging into the regulatory filings, especially the annual report (10-K): (1) operating leases, (2) pension and post-retirement obligations, (3) loan guarantees and other off-balance-sheet arrangements, (4) lawsuits and legal claims, and (5) quality of assets. Let us take each in turn.

1. Operating Lease[86]

If a retail clothing company wanted to open another store, it has a couple of options on how to do so. It can purchase a building or space in the desired location, in which case it will have to put the full cost of the assets on the balance sheet and take depreciation charges as periodic expenses. If the financing of the purchase was done with debt, then debt shows up as the liability corresponding to the new assets on the balance sheet. If cash were to be used, then the cash account would deplete and fixed asset account would rise by the same amount.

Alternatively, the company could simply lease the space from another party which actually owns the property. In this case, the space does not show up at all on either side of the balance sheet and the lease payments are reported as periodic operating expenses on the income statement.

Now, even though the leased assets do not get reported on the balance sheet, they are in fact contractual obligations of the company. Periodic lease payments are usually required by contract for the duration of the lease, no matter how poorly the company may be doing operations-wise. The company can, of course, break the lease but typically only after paying a substantial penalty for doing so.

Because of this contractual obligation, operating leases ought to in reality be seen as equivalent to interest payment on debt the company would have taken if it had bought the properties rather than leasing them. By leasing property and keeping the assets/debts off the books, the company's obligations to outside parties may appear understated and give the impression of better financial health than may be justified.

Let us take Wal-Mart again for illustration. At the end of fiscal year 2010, the company reported that it owned only thirty-four of the 132 distribution

facilities tied to its international operations. Third parties owned and operated sixty-one, whereas the company leased and operated an additional thirty-
seven distribution facilities. In the domestic operations, the company owned
and operated 113 of the 146 distribution facilities. In addition, quite a few of
other buildings were also under operating leases.

Clearly, then, a substantial proportion of the distribution facilities did not
show up on the company's balance sheet. Overall, as of the end of fiscal 2010,
the company reported that it had a total of more than $13 billion in non-
cancellable operating leases, representing rental payments of about $1 billion
over each of the next five years.

As such, the true periodic obligations of the company are not simply the
interest expense of $2 billion as reported in 2010, but an additional periodic
payment of $1 billion in operating leases. This $3 billion is then the correct
figure with which to re-compute the coverage ratio of the company, which
drops, as a result, from 11.60 to 7.81:

Fixed Charge Coverage = Op. Income / Fixed Charges   (17.1)

Fixed Charge Coverage = (23,950 / 3,065) = 7.81   (17.1 Sol.)

Moreover, the $1 billion in annual operating lease payments, if taken to
persist well into the future and discounted with a rate of, say, 5 percent yield a debt
equivalent of $20 billion that are not visible on the balance sheet. That is, if the
company were to actually own the assets that it was leasing, the cost to the company
would be roughly $20 billion, which would need to be financed somehow. So, if
this amount were to be added to the debt reported by the company, the true debt
equivalent obligations of the company would be not $41,320 million as shown on
the books at the end of fiscal 2010 but $61,320 million. Re-computing with the
new obligations, the debt ratio increases from 58 percent to 87 percent.

How does this new information and analysis update your judgment about
the company as a potentially good investment? Can you now refute the investment thesis?

From the revised debt ratio now incorporating operating leases, Wal-Mart
still seems like a financially healthy company, although somewhat less so than
it appeared before the operating leases were taken into account. We cannot,

therefore, refute the thesis and are, again, more confident about our original hunch.

Note that for many companies, such as some airlines or retailers or manufacturers who rely heavily on leases so that they do not have to own the corresponding assets, incorporating operating leases into the analysis can change the evaluations of financial strength quite drastically.

Operating leases are, therefore, a kind of hidden problem. So long as the company does well operationally and each location generates enough cash to comfortably meet lease obligations, there is no problem. But, if and when the company begins to get in trouble financially, then the burden of contractual lease payments can add to the company's woes and make your investment vulnerable.

2. Pension Obligations

Many companies manage their pension plans so as to be able to provide for employees once they retire. These are moral and legal obligations, contractually obligating the company to make future payments in return for service the employees provide while they are working.

Two kinds of plans are common among publicly traded companies in the United States: 1) defined benefit plans or DBP, and 2) defined contribution plans or DCP. The essential difference between the two is that the former can create significant liabilities for the company, while the latter limits or eliminates the financial obligations to retirees. Under DCP, not the company but only the employee is responsible for savings for his/her own retirement funds. As such, given that pension fund liability is one less thing to guard against, DCP is generally better news for investors.

Many companies such as Wal-Mart and others (e.g., Microsoft) offer only Defined Contribution Plans and are, therefore, off the hook for managing the pension assets for their employees and retirees. As such, the investment thesis about Wal-Mart cannot be refuted on the basis of financial obligations that may have been generated from pension fund deficits.

The trend for several years has been for companies to limit their exposure by eliminating benefit plans and encouraging employees to take control of their own savings by offering such things as company matches. Even so, many long enduring companies sometimes have significant pension fund obligations and they are exposed to risks that arise from managing billions of dollars in the retirement plans.

Let us briefly discuss the financial impact of the defined benefit plans. For those interested in more detail, most accounting textbooks will be a good place to start, although good discussions can also be found on some public websites as well. See in particular the Pension Benefit Guarantee Corporation, a U.S. Government agency tasked with providing oversight and assistance to private-sector pension plans.

In DBP or defined benefit plans, the company makes contributions into and then manages a pool of pension funds, which are typically kept not in some cash account but conservatively invested in a mix of asset classes such as stocks, bonds, real estate, and other. That is so as to get a decent return on the pension assets. These invested funds, or assets of the pension plan, are then drawn upon to pay the retirees in accordance with some formula that is based on factors such as age and salary at retirement, numbers of years of service, etc. How well these pension assets are invested influences how secure they are and how fast they grow to cover future contractual obligations to the retirees.

So, in managing the pool of pension assets, the company assumes the liability for any current and future deficits. If the funds are invested poorly or happen to show significant investment losses, the pension plan shows a large deficit and creates what are called unfunded pension liabilities for the company.

The unfunded liabilities are required by law to be covered periodically, forcing the company to put up cash to reduce or eliminate the deficit in a reasonable amount of time. Naturally, this obligation creates a problem since the cash for pension plan deficit reduction (to fund the unfunded liabilities) comes from the company's coffers and takes money away from operating or financing activities required for conducting business; they also threaten dividends and share repurchases. For investors, therefore, the key is to understand how much the company has by way of pension assets and obligations. This knowledge is important for updating your subjective judgment about the company's vulnerabilities.

Let us take the example of ConAgra (CAG) to get some traction on how pension obligations can impact the numbers. For the year 2010, the company reported that it had a shortfall in the pension plan in part because of the downturn in the equity markets. As such, the company contributed $123 million to the pension plans and another $55 million to cover post-retirement healthcare obligations. In all, in order to make up for the shortfall, the company took a charge of $178 million that year. The previous year, in 2009, the company had taken a charge of $319 million because of similar shortfalls from downturn in the equity markets.

These contributions to the pension plan are, of course, quite substantial for ConAgra. The company had reported net earnings of $978 million and $726 million in 2009 and 2010, respectively. The pension and retirement related charges amounted to 33 percent and 25 percent of the total reported income during those two years—and took monies away, in effect, from important value-creating and shareholder-friendly activities.

It is clear, therefore, that pension and post-retirement obligations can create substantial risks and liabilities to investors of companies that manage their defined benefit plans. A quick check on those obligations is an important part of the process for trying to refute the investment thesis.

Yet, the story of pensions does not really end here. A particularly careful investor will dig a little deeper to see how the company is estimating pension assets and obligations, for the deficit or surplus of pension funds is determined by how such estimates are made. Let us consider below both assets and obligations related to pension funds.

Fair value of plan assets is relatively easy to pin down and is typically reported by companies in their annual (10-K) filings: Start with the fair value of plan assets at the beginning of the year and then make additions and subtractions of things like returns during the year on those assets, contributions by employees and employer, payments to retirees, and sundry items. All these adjustments yield the fair value of plan assets at the end of the reported year.

Estimates of plan liabilities, also called projected benefit obligations (PBO), require some actuarial assumptions but the idea is still the same as for assets: start with the PBO beginning of the year, make adjustments as necessary to accommodate changes during the year, and come up with PBO end of the year.

The difference between the end of year plan assets and obligations then indicates whether the pension fund has a surplus or a deficit. If the pension fund has a deficit at the end of a fiscal year, then it creates unfunded liabilities and the company is obligated to fund those in short order. The cash for covering such unfunded liabilities has to come from the company's coffers and is a drain on resources that would have otherwise been put back into the operations or retained in the equity account or simply been returned to shareholders via dividends or share buybacks.

Note in particular that since the estimates of projected future benefit obligations (PBO) require assumptions, they are subject to error or manipulation. Unjustifiably rosy assumptions can lead to low estimates of future obligations, implying that the company is financially healthier than it actually may be. If the obligations turn out to be much higher than anticipated and the plan assets do not generate the expected returns, then the company is on the hook to plug the deficit. Investors need to pay attention, therefore, to what assumptions the company is using in making estimates of fund assets and liabilities. These estimates need to be reasonable and in line with the historical investment performance of pension assets.

Unfunded pension liabilities are reported as long-term liabilities in the consolidated balance sheet, but the assumptions embedded in the estimates of obligations and assets are not quite visible there. The assumptions and the actual historical performance of plan assets need to be dug out from the 10-k filing where the details are usually reported. In this sense, therefore, unfunded pensions are an invisible but potentially significant source of loss for shareholders.

So, checking the facts about pensions and other obligations to retirees is an important step in trying to refute the investment thesis.

3.   Litigation and Lawsuits

For most publicly traded companies, lawsuits of various kinds are usually part of doing business. Often these lawsuits are settled out of court because of the very high costs of litigation and uncertainty about outcomes for both sides. For investors, such routine lawsuits are usually of little concern, as their costs are absorbed in the course of running the business.

Investors should look more closely at lawsuits that have the potential to put the company under or perhaps cost several years' worth of cash flows. Issues such as conflict with other parties regarding key patents or large-scale fraud can be quite detrimental to investors, as the resulting losses can divert massive amounts of cash away from operations and shareholder-friendly activities. Such large and sometimes potentially fatal lawsuits have another cost in that they distract the management from the business of running the company and creating value for investors.

Take, for example, Armstrong World Industries back in the late 1990s. This was a blue chip company with sales of about $3 billion and a history going back to the late nineteenth century. The company was well-entrenched in the building products industry, making floor and ceiling systems as well as cabinets and selling into the residential and commercial markets. It was a profitable company that had done well by the investors for a long time.

Then, on December 6, 2000, Armstrong World Industries filed for bankruptcy protection. The company had for some time been under pressure from lawsuits related to asbestos, which it had used in its products at one time for such uses as fireproofing and electrical insulation. For those historical wrongs, the claims against it had been building for a while and the company had begun to set up reserves against those claims. But the weight of the lawsuits became unbearable, and in the year 2000 the company reported that it was facing 173,000 personal injury claims that would cost about $1 billion over the next several years. A good deal of uncertainty remained as to how much it would actually end up costing, but there was little doubt that the eventual number would be very large in proportion to the company's resources.

For investors, the challenge is to know when the lawsuits are significant in terms of cost and when they are routine. This takes some digging around, of course, but some of the signs to look for are the reserves being set aside and some educated estimates about the total potential cost in relation to the size and strength of the annual cash flows.

It is sometimes possible that the market punishes the company for lawsuits even when the potential costs are a small fraction of the company's annual free cash flows. Careful digging may reveal that, even in the worst case scenario, a company under the pressure of lawsuits may be able to handle the costs relatively easily. Excessive fear about minor issues may in some situations offer attractive opportunities.

On the whole, though, investors with a defensive stance are generally best served by staying out of potentially disastrous situations. Avoiding trouble is half the battle won.

4. Off-Balance-Sheet Liabilities

Liabilities that are not disclosed in the balance sheet are akin to hidden bombs that can destroy a company and your investment in it. This problem is perhaps best illustrated by the infamous case of Enron, which had set up special purpose entities (SPE) so as to control assets without owning up to the debt that was necessary to finance the purchase of those assets. In essence, a typical transaction involved selling assets to a newly set up SPE or having it buy assets from third parties, co-signing a bank loan to the SPE to finance the purchase of those assets, and then guaranteeing those loans with the company's own stock or some other company assets.

Because of limitations of the accounting rules at the time the SPEs were set up, the loan guarantees were not visible in Enron's balance sheet, as apparently was the company's intent. As a result, the debt ratios monitored by the rating agencies, banks, and investors appeared to remain within proscribed limits—allowing the company to continue doing business without undue scrutiny.

It turned out that some of the SPEs did not, in fact, qualify for non-consolidation and they had to be brought back into Enron's books. The result was a massive decrease in reported income for 1999 and 2000, and also a substantial increase in the outstanding debt of the company. Thus began the rapid unwinding of the SPEs and the demise of the Enron. Investors who did not understand the deception and hung on to the stock too long ended up losing all their investment in the company.

You would think that Enron would have made investors wiser. But even as Enron was collapsing under the weight of the SPEs and related fraud, another kind of off-balance-sheet chicanery was taking off.

As far back as 1988, Citi Group had invented and others had quickly followed suit with what came to be called structured investment vehicles (SIV). An SIV is an operating finance company, usually set up by a large bank as a separate entity that functions in many ways like a traditional bank but with some major differences. Taking advantage of the (usually) upward sloping yield curve, the SIV borrowed short-to-medium-term money at low interest rates by issuing commercial paper and medium-term notes. It then used the proceeds to make higher-yielding long-term investments. The spread between the interest earned on long-term investments and the cost of short-term borrowed funds created the profits that were then shared among the principals. This is no different, in principle, from your local bank taking demand deposits from you in exchange for very low-interest rates and then turning around to loan out monies for autos and mortgages at much higher-interest rates.

The advantage for sponsoring banks was that SIVs were off-the-books and, for the most part, fell outside the purview of bank regulation. As such, through the SIVs the bank could benefit without having to raise additional monies to bulk up its capital base. Without the SIV, such financing and lending activity would have to be put on the balance sheet and the bank would have needed to raise more equity capital to meet the reserve requirements. The SIVs allowed the banks to do off-the-books business.

Now, the trouble for SIVs, and for their sponsoring organizations, was built into their design. First, unlike traditional banks where the demand deposits are guaranteed by the government, the commercial paper issued by the SIVs had no such guarantees. Safety for those who bought the commercial paper from an SIV was in the backing of the parent banks that sponsored the particular SIV. At the time, if the parent bank appeared to be of high quality, the SIV was able to issue commercial paper and medium notes at very attractive (low) rates.

Second, the long-term assets in which the SIVs invested were usually in investment grade corporate bonds and asset-backed securities of long maturity, those built by securitizing such things as student loans, car loans, and, of course, commercial and residential mortgages. The supposed high quality of these long-term investments was also a signal that the short-term money that the SIVs had borrowed was quite safe.

The financial crisis of 2007–2008 changed all that. The SIVs got in trouble when the home prices started declining in the summer of 2007. Many of the mortgage backed securities (MBS) that the SIVs had bought because of their high-interest yields dropped sharply in value because of increasing homeowner defaults. That is, the bonds and securities that the SIVs had bought as investments had to be written down to their now lower market value, thus shrinking the banks' assets and sharply reducing or even wiping out their equity. This created a panic, of course, among those who had loaned short-term money to the SIVs by buying their low-interest, short-maturity, commercial paper with the assumption that they were lending, in essence, to parent banks with strong balance sheets. This is just as if you lent me money thinking that I was financially sound but then discovered that my only house was in foreclosure. You'd panic if you were sane.

The market for mortgage-backed securities had already begun to dry up because of troubles in the wider economy, and the fear that the SIVs were now too risky was like adding fuel to the fire. With their assets shrinking and unable anymore to borrow freely in the commercial paper market, the SIVs tried to sell the assets, partly to pay back the commercial paper coming due and partly to get what they could for the long-term investments they had on the books. But with everyone trying to unload those assets at whatever prices they could get, the market for asset-backed securities was already in deep trouble. This, of course, depressed the asset prices even further.

Since the assets were long-term and they had been financed by debt on a short-maturity cycle, the SIV troubles escalated. Because of deterioration of asset-backed securities and the larger liquidity crunch market-wide, it became difficult to refinance the commercial paper, the short-maturity debt as it became due. With a shrinking pool of monies with which to finance long-term investments, the SIV were even more pressured to try to sell the assets in their loan portfolio. But such selling in a fast falling market became problematic, as there was a rush to sell such assets by a large number of parties. The viscous downward spiral was gaining momentum and a full-blown panic quickly set in.

Soon enough, unable to sell the assets to generate liquidity, some SIVs started defaulting on the commercial paper. Such defaults set the panic even deeper. In just a few months, for instance, Victoria Finance, a $6 billion SIV managed by Ceres Capital Partners, had their credit rating slashed from AAA to below investment grade. The SIV defaulted later in the year. Many other SIVs based in the United States and Europe began winding down or going out of business.

Under pressure from the U.S. Treasury, large banks such as Bank of America, Citigroup, JP Morgan Chase, and HSBC started rescuing their own SIVs and, as a result, had to absorb very large losses. In January 2008, Bloomberg reported that financial companies had written down $100 billion from the value of assets linked to mortgages.[87] On October 2, 2008, Financial Times reported that Sigma Finance, the last surviving and the oldest of the SIVs, dissolved when JP Morgan pulled funding from it.[88] By the end of that month, the once $400 billion SIV sector was there no more.

Now, the SIV story is instructive for many reasons. The idea of borrowing for less and lending for more has been around for a very long time and the SIVs were playing a version of it that allowed them to do so outside the purview of banking regulations. It was a good idea so long as it worked. And it could have continued working if the rating agencies had been up to correctly evaluating the complex securities that the SIVs were putting on their balance sheet. But in the end, the SIVs relied too much on the rating agencies and appear not to have done their own due diligence on the long-term assets in which they were investing. In a sense, they were investing massive amounts of monies on blind faith in the ratings and, as such, were doing so at great risk to their capital.

More important, the lesson from both SPEs and SIVs is that there is a great deal of pressure on companies to do things off the balance sheet. The demand for consistently high returns on invested capital and the incentives used to reward managers are such that opportunities to generate new returns are hard to pass by. Smart people induced by career advancement opportunities and by the chance to make more money come up with interesting and creative products that look good on the face of it but may be full of hidden risks that are not visible to the uninitiated. Often, as John Kenneth Galbraith once noted, these innovations are creative ways of taking on more debt where the returns are visibly attractive and immediate but risks and uncertainties are underplayed and for the most part invisible.

Given the potential for outsized risks that may be hidden from view, we are well-served by looking closely at the fine print in the mandatory filings. Of particular benefit would be a special search for complex financial arrangements that might create significant liabilities for the company. If such arrangements existed to a substantial degree, they may be grounds for refuting the thesis.

5.   Quality of Assets

Liabilities are only one side of the equation, however. The other important consideration when trying to refute an investment thesis is the quality of assets that the company has on its balance sheet. After all, what you as an investor own is not only future cash flows but the very assets that enable companies to deliver those future flows. That is, as an owner of common shares, you own part of the common equity or net assets of the company.

Common Equity = (Total Assets − Total Liabilities)   (17.2)

So, common equity is the residual (also called book value) or assets net of all liabilities. If for any reason the liabilities turn out to be different than what is shown on the books, then your ownership stake would reduce accordingly. Similarly, for a given level of liabilities, errors on the assets side of the balance sheet get carried over to the equity account. If assets are inflated or shown to be much larger than they actually are or have a great amount of risk built into them, then the equity account would reflect that inflation, misleading investors into thinking that they own more in net assets than they actually do.

Perhaps the most common problems on the assets side of the balance sheet are the errors in measurement. It is, in fact, not easy for companies to go out and count each line item on their books; some physical assets such as inventories and property are spread all over the map and not readily available for easy in-person count. As such, each line item on the asset side is an aggregation of estimates that the accountants make using appropriate estimation procedures; they are subject to errors.

The likelihood of measurement errors increases for certain kinds of assets, such as plant and property, which are usually recorded at historical cost or, when acquired in a merger, at estimated fair value at the time of the transaction. In some cases, the estimates can be so out of line with the actual market value of the assets that the measurement errors become quite severe.

So, for instance, imagine that a company has a building worth, say, $50 million on historical cost basis but it has appreciated to $100 million. The balance sheet will show the building at historical cost of $50 million and the undervaluation would result in a measurement error that translates into a depressed common equity account.

Along the same lines, assume that the asset in question is not actually a building but a portfolio of high-risk subprime bonds worth $100 million at a given time. Rules require that these and other financial assets be recorded or marked to whatever their market value might be about the time the books are closed every quarter. Even if the bonds are marked on the books at par, however, that does not mean that their true value is what is shown on the books. A sudden drop in the market value of the bonds would reduce the assets side of the equation and translate into lower equity. In fact, many banks had subprime mortgage-backed securities on their books just before the housing market crash in 2007; as the value of these securities plummeted during the crisis, the asset base of these banks shrunk and wiped out the minimal equity they had on the books.

Banks and financial institutions also often have loans and complex financial instruments on the asset side of their balance sheet. If investors are not able to correctly assess the quality of the loans and the risks embedded in the financial products, such assets pose serious risks to them. Investing in the financial sector companies is often hazardous, therefore, for most investors who do not have the expertise and the resources to make a thorough evaluation of the asset portfolio.

In fact, the risks embedded in the assets sometimes become so great that some managers, under pressure to deliver on expectations, may begin to contort data and use deceptions that are virtually impossible for an average investor to catch.

Consider, for example, the case of Lehman Brothers and their accounting gimmick that has become notorious as Repo 105.

It appears that, as the financial crisis of 2007–2008 picked up steam, Lehman like many others had a strong urge to unload some of its risky assets (bonds) and pay down their massive debt. But the markets were already seizing up and bond prices were plummeting. In such an environment of rapidly falling prices, selling their own inventory of bonds would have immediately generated massive reported losses for Lehman. So, with the bonds on the balance sheet virtually illiquid, the company devised an imaginative scheme through which it got both risky assets and debt off-the-books.

According to the Chapter 11 bankruptcy examiner,[89] here is what Lehman appears to have done. Just before it closed the books for a quarter, the company went to the repo market for overnight lending and swapped some of its risky bonds for cash (thus moving bonds off the balance sheet). It then used the cash from bond sales to pay down the debt and reported a healthy looking balance sheet at the close of the quarter. Then, as soon as the quarter closed, it borrowed back the money and bought back the bonds it had swapped earlier. It's suspected that Lehman didn't really sell the bonds but in fact used them as collateral to borrow money for the short-term, with the agreement that it would buy them back (at cost plus interest) shortly thereafter. Yet, the company classified the swaps as sale so that it could get the risky bonds off the balance sheet.

The trick came to be known as Repo 105 because Lehman swapped $105 worth of bonds in order to borrow $100 in cash, giving the impression that it was actually selling the risky assets at a discount. According to the examiner's report, the company moved tens of billions of dollars off the balance sheet using this trick and $50 billion in just the second quarter of 2008. Moreover, the company never disclosed these transactions in any of its filings or even to its own board, so no one was the wiser until after the company had collapsed under the weight of large quantities of highly toxic bonds on its balance sheet.

For all but the most sophisticated and well-resourced investors, manipulations like Repo 105 are difficult to catch. Many variations to the theme exist and smart professionals are often paid handsomely to think up new ways of pushing at the edges and finding creative solutions to difficult problems. Repo 105 appears to be a case of creativity applied to the wrong cause.

Investors must know that toxic assets on the balance sheet are both the cause and consequence of risky behaviors that sometimes cross the line and become fraud.

In summary, then, for investors practicing the fine art of investing wisely, a careful scrutiny of the balance sheet and the associated risks is an indispensable part of due diligence.

18

Define Good Business

———

For the investment thesis that still stands after all the previous attempts to refute it, the next step is to make judgments about the manner in which businesses create economic worth. A business blessed with good economics, when purchased at good prices, improves the likelihood of good-to-great returns over time. Shares of companies in businesses with poor economics may sometimes offer good opportunities when prices are especially depressed, but they do so at considerable hazards and limited upside potential. As investors, then, our task is to try to uncover and disconfirm the narrative that the investment under scrutiny has sound economics intrinsic to it—or that the company underlying the stock is fundamentally a good business.

So, what is a good business? While there may be many ways to define it, in perhaps the simplest of terms, a good business is one that, on average and over time, consumes a dollar to produce an amount that is sufficiently larger than one dollar, adjusted for risk, in cash. Such ability to make more from less is a fundamental characteristic common to all good businesses. In this chapter, therefore, our purpose is to learn to evaluate companies on how well they deploy capital.

Measuring Economic Performance

Before we delve into some basic math to try to quantify economic characteristics of companies, note that measuring performance is not always an easy endeavor. Most companies are complex, multi-faceted entities so, depending on our objectives, we can try to measure their performance in a number of different ways. For instance, if we were to define performance as the degree to which a company dominates the markets it serves, then we must try to clearly define those markets and know that such definitions can be difficult because markets are often not well delineated. Similarly, if we were to think of performance as corporate social responsibility, then we must be clear about what social responsibility means and what specific measures best proxy that aspect of the company's performance? Or, if our focus was on financial performance, then we must decide what specific measures we ought to use and why? Do we measure financial performance as returns to shareholders or as returns on the capital deployed in the company; market returns or accounting measures?

As if finding good measures is not complex enough, fixing the time horizon over which to measure performance is not straightforward either. The quarter and year are arbitrary periods commonly used because of convenience and convention. In reality, some businesses (e.g., day trading) may require daily measures of trading performance whereas some others (e.g., large-scale construction projects) may need to be evaluated over the life of the projects or over a whole business cycle.

Moreover, any one dimension of performance may not be sufficient given the different stakeholders often associated with an organization. Different types of equity holders, different classes of bondholders, the executive team, mid-level managers, rank-and-file, suppliers, customers, and others, all bring different perspectives to the table and demand that the company use measures that best reflect their particular interests.

Sometimes, because of power differentials among the parties involved, one stakeholder may dominate the debate and force a single perspective—on financial or social or market power measures. For instance, during bankruptcy proceedings, the creditors of a company have a disproportionate say in how the residual assets are to be distributed. When a company is about to go public, the institutions and other equity investors may have a great deal more say than the other parties involved, including the founders who built the company. But even in such cases when one stakeholder dominates the debate, the other perspectives don't necessarily go away—they just recede into the shadows for the time being, biding their time to reassert themselves as conditions change and opportunities arise.

Much of the conflict in and around organization arises, in fact, because of differences in opinion about what to measure and how to measure it. A classic case is that of conflict between shareholders and bondholders as the two categories of capital that have different objectives. Bondholders typically want preservation of capital so that they can be assured of getting their money back along with the financing charges owed to them. Shareholders, on the other hand, want to leverage fully the limited liability bestowed upon them and they want managers to take on more risk, even if the greater risk may endanger the survival of the company and increases the chances of bondholders not getting their money back. Conflicts can also arise among bondholders themselves when different maturities and different levels of seniority are involved in the capital structure of the company.

It is important, therefore, for equity investors to understand the political dynamics inside the company and make judgments regarding the degree to which the performance evaluation metrics used by the management support their interests. As we will see in chapter 19, some managers will clearly articulate their shareholders friendliness and follow through with actions such as share repurchases and dividends. Some managers may argue that other aspects of performance are more important because of the multiple stakeholders they must satisfy or because the long run performance is only possible if non-economic considerations are given their due. But, investors should be careful with such rhetoric and actions because, ultimately, valuation is driven by economic performance that the company is able to deliver on a consistent basis.

Equity investors should, in other words, cut through the complexities that surround performance measurement and keep their focus on economic performance—the efficiency with which the company deploys the capital entrusted to it. Moreover, following convention, they can use annual figures provided in the filings of the company in question, but do so with the knowledge that the time horizon over which to measure economic performance depends on the nature of the businesses under consideration. Finally, investors who invest in common equity should evaluate the efficiency with which the company uses not only equity capital, but also the efficiency with which the company deploys all capital at their disposal, including the debt capital. Since equity is junior to debt, poor use of debt capital is likely to reflect poorly on equity capital as well.

In sum, remember that measuring performance is not as straightforward as it may seem at first glance. While we should be aware of the complexities inherent in such an endeavor, however, it is okay to use relatively simple approaches that focus attention on the company's use of equity and debt capital. So, let's review below what investors should look for in the companies in which they invest.

Capital Efficiency

As equity investors, we can measure capital efficiency in a number of different ways, but the most common way is to compute a handful of simple ratios and understand the key factors that drive those ratios. In essence, we want to understand how companies generate returns on capital, and which key areas to monitor to assess its ability to continue creating economic worth.

To that end, we use three specific measures that indicate capital efficiency:

1. Return on Equity (ROE)

2. Return on Assets (ROA)

3. Return on Capital (ROC)

That is, we measure economic performance as efficiency with which the company deploys capital. We measure efficiency as the returns on: 1) equity capital on the books (ROE), 2) total assets used (ROA), and 3) total capital deployed in the company (ROC).

In order to understand why ROE is a good measure for understanding the economics of a business, it is best to break it down using the DuPont formula, which spotlights the three useful aspects of a company's operating and financial performance. So, by definition, ROE is the ratio of Net Income (NI) and Common Shareholders' Equity (CEQ).

$$ROE = NI / CEQ \qquad (18.1)$$

Equation 18.1 may be re-written by incorporating the Total Assets (TA),

$$ROE = (NI / TA) \cdot (TA / CEQ) \qquad (18.2)$$

Note that, in equation 18.2, Total Assets is in both the numerator and the denominator and, therefore, it can cancel out to yield equation 18.1.

Since, NI/TA is simply Return on Assets (ROA) and the second term is Financial Leverage (Lev), we can re-write equation 18.2 as,

$$ROE = ROA \cdot Lev \tag{18.2a}$$

Note that financial leverage, as defined above, is the dollar value of total assets for each dollar of common equity on the books. Also note that ROE is the product of 1) efficiency with which the company uses its total assets to produce profits (ROA), and 2) the financial leverage (Lev) it has on the books. In this sense, ROE is leverage-adjusted ROA. Since financial leverage is usually greater than one (or, total assets are usually greater than common equity), ROE must be greater than ROA.

We can further re-write equation 18.1 by also incorporating Total Revenues (TR).

$$ROE = (NI / TR) \cdot (TR / TA) \cdot (TA / CEQ) \tag{18.3}$$

Again, note that Total Revenues (TR) and Total Assets (TA) are in both the numerator and the denominator and, therefore, they cancel out to yield equation 18.1.

Since the first term (NI/TR) in equation 18.3 is Return on Sales (ROS), the second (TR/TA) term is Asset Efficiency, and the third term is Financial Leverage, we can simplify equation 18.2 as,

$$ROE = ROS \cdot AE \cdot Lev \tag{18.3b}$$

Note that the term ROS reflects the amount that flows to the bottom line for every dollar of sales; AE is the dollar sales that the company generates for every dollar it has in total assets; and, Lev is the dollar value of total assets for each dollar of common equity on the books. So, Return on Equity is mathematically equivalent to the product of profitability, asset efficiency, and financial leverage.

Furthermore, from equation 18.3, we can see that

$$ROA = (NI / TR) \cdot (TR / TA) \tag{18.4}$$

$$ROA = ROS \cdot AE \tag{18.4a}$$

As such, ROA is simply a product of profitability and efficiency.

Finally, let's break down ROC, or the Return on Capital, in three similar components. We define the Total Capital (TC) deployed in a company as the Total Equity (TE) and the total interest-bearing debt (TD).

$$TC = TE + TD \tag{18.5}$$

$$ROC = NI / TC \tag{18.6}$$

As we did above, we can disaggregate equation 18.6 to yield ROC as a product of Return on Assets (ROA) and Total Capital Leverage (CapLev).

$$ROC = (NI / TA) \cdot (TA / TC) \tag{18.7}$$

$$ROC = ROA \cdot CapLev \tag{18.7a}$$

Note that CapLev is similar to Lev except that it indicates the full financial leverage and incorporates the debt capital along with the total equity capital that includes both common and preferred shareholders' equity. Furthermore, as in equation 18.3, we can write ROC as below.

$$ROC = ROS \cdot AE \cdot CapLev \tag{18.8}$$

From the above equation, it is evident that Return on Capital, which indicates the efficiency with which the company deploys the total capital entrusted to it is, once again, a simple mathematical equivalent of its profitability, asset efficiency, and full financial leverage.

The three capital efficiency ratios, ROE, ROA, and ROC, together reflect the operating and financial performance of the company, and they relate to each other mathematically. The higher these ratios are, the higher is the efficiency with which the company deploys the financial resources (equity, debt, and assets) available to it. Additionally, high efficiency reflects efficiencies in operations and wise choices in the financial structure of the company. Hence, companies that deliver high efficiencies create a great deal of economic value.

In order to understand the practical application of the above, see table 18.1 below. The data in the table are three-year averages for five well-known companies, and they highlight the different economic characteristics of companies within and across a few different industries. The five companies in the table are Wal-Mart (WMT), Target (TGT), Coach (COH), Microsoft (MSFT), and Caterpillar (CAT).

Table 18.1

	Three Year Averages Ending Fiscal Year 2012				
	WMT	**TGT**	**COH**	**MSFT**	**CAT**
ROE	21.63%	17.86%	51.86%	35.59%	31.87%
ROA	8.36%	6.18%	32.23%	19.03%	5.54%
ROC	13.27%	9.08%	51.33%	30.52%	10.22%
ROS	3.59%	4.11%	21.12%	28.72%	7.72%
AE	2.33	1.50	1.52	0.66	0.71
Lev	2.59	2.89	1.61	1.87	5.78
CapLev	1.59	1.47	1.59	1.60	1.84

Note from the first two columns that, for the three years ending in the 2012 fiscal year, Wal-Mart had used its capital more productively than did Target. For instance, the ROE for Wal-Mart was 21.63 percent to Target's 17.86 percent. Note how the two companies accomplished those numbers. As indicated by ROS, Target was more profitable than Wal-Mart because each dollar of sales at Target flowed to 4.11 cents in bottom line profits, whereas that number was lower at 3.59 cents for Wal-Mart. That is, Target was 14 percent more profitable than its bigger competitor. Target also had higher financial leverage at 2.89 to Wal-Mart's 2.59.

Even so, Wal-Mart more than made up for the deficiencies in these two areas by delivering a much higher asset efficiency. Wal-Mart generated, on average, $2.33 in sales for every dollar of assets, whereas Target delivered only 1.50 by way of the Revenues-to-Assets ratio. That is, the operating efficiency of Wal-Mart rewarded the shareholders with better utilization of the equity capital.

For these two companies, also note that ROC (Wal-Mart, 13.27 percent; Target 9.08 percent) was much lower than ROE—indicating that both companies had substantial debt. This reliance on debt is also visible in much lower full financial leverage (CapLev) than the equity-based financial leverage (Lev): 1.59 versus 2.59 for Wal-Mart; 1.47 versus 2.89 for Target.

Moving on to the next two columns in table 18.1, we see that both Coach (COH) and Microsoft (MSFT) had strong average ROE performance, even though Coach was by far a much stronger performer. Let's see how the two companies accomplished such high returns. Microsoft had very high bottom line performance with the three-year average ROS at 28.72 percent to 21.12 percent for Coach. Microsoft also had a somewhat higher financial leverage at 1.87 to 1.61 for Coach. But, Coach far outperformed on asset efficiency with 1.52 versus 0.66 for Microsoft. This difference in asset efficiency produced a much higher ROE of 51.86 percent for Coach, as compared with 35.59 percent for Microsoft.

Note, however, that Microsoft's asset efficiency was depressed somewhat because of a very large amount of cash on its balance sheet. At the end of fiscal year 2012, the company had more than $60 billion in cash and investments, which accounted for more than 60 percent of total assets. Coach, in contrast, had under $1 billion in cash and investments, which made up 28.2 percent of total assets. Computing three-year average asset efficiency net of cash, Microsoft's number changed from 0.66 to 1.53 and the asset efficiency of Coach increased from 1.52 to 2.12. As a result, the non-cash ROE for Microsoft and Coach re-compute as 82 percent and 72.24 percent, respectively. In essence, both companies made highly efficient use of equity capital, and the efficiency was driven largely by the very high profitability of their businesses. The cash was an unproductive drag on the ROE.

Furthermore, both companies delivered high ROE in spite of very little debt. As such, ROC for both companies (COH 51.33 percent; MSFT 30.52 percent) was close to their respective ROE numbers.

Finally, examine the last column in table 18.1 and note the performance of Caterpillar (CAT). The healthy three-year average ROE of 31.87 percent suggests that the company made very good use of the equity capital entrusted to it. But look at how they accomplish the high ROE in spite of modest profitability. At 7.72 percent, their three-year profitability (ROS) was about twice that of Wal-Mart or Target but it was much lower than that of Coach or Microsoft. At 0.71 percent, their asset efficiency was also very low. But the financial leverage of Caterpillar was very high at 5.78 and that is what drove their ROE to a seemingly-healthy 31.87 percent. Substantially lower ROC, ROA, and CapLev numbers betray the high amount of interest-bearing debt the company had on the books.

Clearly, companies can legitimately increase their ROE numbers by taking on a great deal of debt. But at some point, debt can create substantial obligations that may endanger the financial health of the company. As discussed in chapter 15, therefore, investors should not take ROE at face value but examine closely how it is accomplished and what it might imply about the company's profitability and operating efficiency, and especially about its debt burden. Hence, even if the company cannot be refuted based on its overall capital efficiency, it may be possible to refute it on the basis of strength tests as discussed in the case of Caterpillar above.

Efficient use of equity capital (ROE) is particularly important for stockholders because it relates directly to the intrinsic valuation of the company.[90] In fact, following the discount flow model as discussed in chapter 14, we can show that intrinsic value (IV) of a company relates directly to ROE along with Book Value (BV), Growth Rate (g) and the Discount Rate (r) as follows:

$$IV = [ROE \cdot BV \cdot (1 + g) / (r - g)] \tag{18.9}$$

That is, higher the ROE, higher is likely to be the intrinsic valuation of the company, provided we hold constant the other terms in the equation. Understanding ROE is, in other words, imperative for investors to be able to invest wisely.

Cash Economics

The above discussion about ROE presumes innocence about the many meaningful differences between accrual and cash accounting. Usually, we have to make assessments about the economics of a company from afar and mostly through the financial statements and other mandatory filings. It is necessary, therefore, to understand the many thorny issues that surround the reporting of performance through company filings. Reading the company literature is itself a bit of a skill, in fact, as the various rules and vast discretion that managers and accountants apply in the preparation of the filings can sometimes distort and mislead rather than clarify and reveal.

Financial statements are difficult to understand because they are prepared under the guidance of complex rules encoded in the generally accepted accounting principles (GAAP); such rules give the managers and accountants wide discretion in how they report financial information. Sometimes the accounting is so complex, in fact, that it can be difficult for an average investor to ascertain the true economics of a company. This is especially true for the income statement and the balance sheet because they use the complex rules of accrual accounting. The measures of capital efficiency that we have used above are constructed using variables from the income statement and the balance sheet and, therefore, they are subject to quite a bit of managerial discretion and possible manipulation.

One way to overcome this problem is to penetrate the statement of cash flows, which uses cash accounting and is relatively (although not completely) a better representation of the company's true economics. Moreover, understanding how cash flows in and out of a business provides important insights into its enduring power to produce cash. Hence, in order to be able to disconfirm the investment thesis on the criteria of good economics, we must also examine how the company gets the cash to finance its operations, how much cash those operations generate, and what the company chooses to do with the cash so generated.

In the remainder of this chapter, therefore, we go beyond the above-discussed capital efficiency issues to outline concepts for understanding the overall financial picture of the company in terms of the sources and uses of cash. Our objective here is to understand the overall financial story of the company.

Financial Statements in Brief

In the main, investors have three financial statements to interpret. First, the Statement of Financial Condition (SFC—or the Balance Sheet) presents the overall financial health of the company at a point in time. SFC is a snap shot of the assets and liabilities, and presents accountants' estimates of how much the company owes to outside suppliers, creditors, and various other third parties in relation to what it owns as current and long-term assets.

Next up is the Statement of Income (SOI—also called the Income Statement) that presents the revenues the company generated during a fixed period (quarter or year), and in broad strokes outlines the expenses and taxes incurred during the period. The income account provides basic insights into how the revenues flow through to the bottom line.

The Statement of Cash Flows (SCF—or Cash Flow Statement) reports the sources and uses of cash from operating, investing, and financing activities of the company. SCF provides an overview of how much cash the company's operations produce and how the management chooses to allocate cash to the various purposes.

A fourth table, the Statement of Shareholders' Equity (SSE), reports changes in the ownership structure of the company. Although very important at times, we will not discuss SSE here, as it is not directly related to the usual operating functions and, as such, has more to do with the ownership than with the economics of the business.

In combination, the three financial statements (SFC, SOI, SCF) provide the overall operating and financial picture of the company. In order to be able to challenge an investment thesis on the basis of its fundamental economics, it is important for us to understand each statement in broad outline and also in interaction with the others.

Take a look at the schematic in figure 18.1. Take particular note of the cash flows from operations (CFFO) in the circle at the bottom of the figure. Watch CFFO especially closely, as the financial health of a company is often tied to the strength of the operating cash flows it is able to generate over the long-term. A great deal about the economic character of a company can be grasped, in fact, by understanding how the operating cash flows are generated and to what various purposes they are allocated.

So, as shown in the schematic in figure 18.1, the income statement reflects the basic economics based on accrual accounting methods. The sales filter down through the cost structure of the company to produce operating income or earnings from operations. Subtract the financing cost of debt (interest expense), and we get the operating earnings before taxes (EBT). Pay the various taxes, and the bottom line is the net income. Occasionally, there are non-recurring charges as well, for things such as loss/gain on sales of assets of the company or for restructuring of operations. Usually, these appear before the tax line.

More thorough analysis can also reveal the breakdown of revenues from different segments or lines of business; preliminary insights into the company's cost structure are also evident in the main line items in the statement. The bottom line (or the net income or net earnings) is then divided by the total number of shares outstanding to get net earnings per share.

Remember that the income statement is prepared using *accrual* accounting, and the rules dictate that revenues should match with corresponding expenses in the same reporting period. So, if we make a sale at the very end of this fiscal year but don't get paid until the next year, we book the revenues even though the cash did not flow from the customer to us. That is, we book *non-cash* revenues for the year. Similarly, if we incurred expenses purchasing supplies but did not pay the supplier before the books closed, then the income statement will reflect those as non-cash expenses.

As such, while the accrual accounting numbers are important, they do not capture the inflows and outflows of actual cash. The adjustments for non-cash revenues and non-cash expenses are reported in the Statement of the Cash Flows, which shows the cash flows in and out of the company.

The first thing shown in the statement of cash flows is the net income, which is then adjusted by adding back all the non-cash expenses and subtracting from it all the non-cash revenues. The biggest add back is usually the depreciation and amortization expense. Next up are any changes to the working capital, which shed light on how efficiently the company is running its operations. Changes in accounts receivable, changes in accounts payable, and changes in inventories are the chief working capital adjustments. These show how much cash the key operating activities and transactions are consuming or generating.

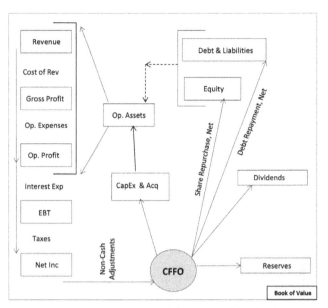

Figure 18.1: Financials-at-a-Glance. Accrual and cash flow economics of a hypothetical business

All the above adjustments convert accrual net income into an item called cash flow from operations (CFFO) or, simply, operating cash flow. This is the crucial number, because it indicates the amount of cash generated by the operations in the given fiscal year. For a company in steady state, the CFFO is usually the primary source of cash and it strongly influences what opportunities the company can pursue without having to go to outside investors to raise more money. Companies with strong economics usually generate strong operating cash flows, usually much more than those needed for the routine maintenance and growth; weak companies need to supplement operating cash flows with external sources of financing.

What does the company do with the operating cash? Skillful uses of the operating cash can make a company strong over time; poor uses of this cash can break a good company fairly quickly.

So, from the CFFO circle in the figure, follow the flows of cash to its various uses. First and foremost, the company has to put money back into operations so that it can sustain itself by replacing depreciating assets. That is, it needs to refresh the assets and strengthen the operating capabilities. Cash is also needed to invest in future growth opportunities, for most healthy companies want to grow even if it is to simply keep up with inflation in their cost structure. So, the capital expenditures, or the monies reinvested in the operations is especially important to ensure future competitiveness.

Depending on their strategic objectives, companies can also legitimately use operating cash to make frequent or periodic acquisitions or asset purchases. Either way, capital expenditures and acquisitions together reflect reinvestments in the company to ensure its future health. These reinvestments become part of the company's asset base that is necessary for the ongoing operations. In this manner, some of the cash flows into the fixed assets that are reported on the balance sheet.

The remaining cash after subtracting capital expenditures (CapEx) and routine acquisitions from CFFO is the free cash flow (FCF) with which the company can satisfy other, perhaps discretionary, obligations. For instance, part of the free cash flow can be used to pay dividends to shareholders. Most companies with a long record of paying dividends have strong incentives to continue doing so; long-term shareholders depend on the dividends and would be at a loss if the dividend were to be cut. For such dividend paying companies, the discretionary cash flow is actually the surplus free cash flow after dividends have been paid.

The discretionary cash flows are the enablers of a variety of other purposes such as share buybacks and debt repayments. Many American companies producing surplus cash buy back their shares periodically. This is partly a way to reward shareholders by increasing their share of future earnings, but sometimes it may also be done simply to manage per share metrics.

The discretionary cash is also often used to retire outstanding debt so as to maintain a healthy balance sheet. Then there may be other minor uses of cash, but the remainder, if any is left, usually goes into the reserves and show up as cash on the balance sheet.

Note that if the company does not generate sufficient operating cash, the various operating and financing activities that depend on it get jeopardized. The company can borrow money to make up the shortfall or issue additional equity that dilutes the existing shareholders. When unable to generate enough cash from operations, external financing becomes unavoidable and the company has to go the debt and/or equity markets to raise costly money.

Note, however, that even financially healthy companies often go to the debt markets opportunistically when interest rates are low—and use those funds to repurchase shares or, occasionally, pay special dividends. All in all, operating and free cash flows are key numbers.

The business of a company that generates strong cash flows cannot usually be refuted on economics alone; a company that has trouble producing cash from its operations may, in contrast, be refuted on the basis of poor economics. So, let's evaluate Wal-Mart as in figure 18.2.

Wal-Mart had revenues of $421 billion in the fiscal year ending January 2011. After the revenues passed through the operating cost structure, interest expense and taxes, the company reported $16.4 billion in net income. When adjusted for cash accounting, this net income was converted to $23.7 billion in operating cash flow. Note that the operating cash was 40 percent larger than the reported net income. The CFFO is usually larger than the net income because most companies add back the non-cash depreciation expense to net income during the process of converting accrual to cash accounting.

Of the $23.7 billion CFFO, $12.7 billion (54 percent) were invested back into the company through capital expenditures. Note that the CapEx figure is much higher than the $7.6 billion the company depreciated during the year. This difference between CapEx and depreciation charge is usually the sign that the company may be investing more than just to keep up—possibly to expand the asset base, perhaps to pursue growth opportunities. The company did not report using cash for acquisitions during the year.

The next item of note is the dividend payment of $4.4 billion or 19 percent of the operating cash flow. Since Wal-Mart has a long record of paying dividends, both CapEx and dividends figure in computing the free discretionary cash flows as $6.5 billion.

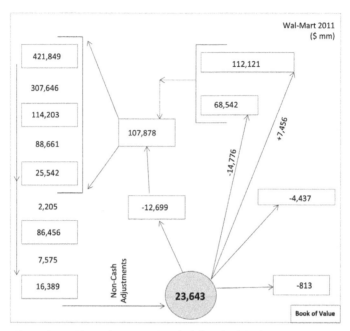

Figure 18.2: Financials-at-a-Glance. Economics and cash flows of Wal-Mart for FY 2011

The company also bought back $14.7 billion worth of its own shares, spending about $8.3 billion more than the surplus free cash generated during the year. To account for the difference, Wal-Mart borrowed a net amount of $7.5 billion. The remainder, $813 million for the year, was made up by dipping into the cash on hand—or that available as of the end of the previous fiscal year.

Note that the new debt issue changed the capital base of the company: the borrowed money raised the debt level and share repurchase reduced the equity account. Borrowing to repurchase shares can be a red flag sometimes, although in this case it seems that the additional debt does no harm to the balance sheet as the company had sufficient debt capacity. Moreover, the borrowing appears to have been strategic as the interest rates during the year were at all-time lows.

All in all, from the above outline of its financials, Wal-Mart appears to have had a good year. They generated more than $23 billion in operating cash and then allocated substantial amounts to build for the future; they also returned a significant amount of money ($19.3 billion) to shareholders through share repurchases and cash dividends.

Typically, such an analysis should be done with three or five year averages so as to avoid basing decisions on performance over just one year. Averages over a longer time horizon are more likely to reveal the true cash flows the company is able to generate over time.

Even so, based on the analysis as above and the preceding analysis pertaining to capital efficiency, we are unable to refute the sub-thesis that Wal-Mart has good economics. Our original investment thesis stands as is, therefore, and is stronger still because of our inability to credibly challenge it in spite of several attempts to do so.

Hence, we next check on the people in charge of the company.

19

Meet the Managers

———

At the helm of every company is a group of people who make most if not all the key decisions, and they get handsomely rewarded for doing so. This group, call it the top management team (TMT), is responsible for the performance and financial health of the company and, therefore, for the safety and growth of your investment in it.

Inside the company, the TMT wields a great deal of power; they exercise a good amount of discretion as to what gets prioritized, what gets the money and, ultimately, what gets done. In the modern corporation, small or large, power is highly centralized in the hands of a few people.

Partly because of the power they have, good manager can create tremendous value for shareholders. Steve Jobs, to take a well-known example, transformed the music industry by imagining what could be done with an external hard drive, a commodity which was then widely available in the civilized world. Upon recognizing the potential in the hard drive, he boldly allocated company resources to build a global business that changed the way we listen to music. Moreover, even as he built the iPod, Jobs also developed a powerful platform for innovations that has given us the iPhone and the iPad. One good insight of one good manager created billions of dollars in value for Apple shareholders.

There are many other examples of good managers creating economic value either by building new companies or transforming existing ones. Sam Walton built Wal-Mart, Ray Kroc built McDonald's, Thomas Watson, Jr. revived International Business Machines, Jack Welch transformed General Electric,

Larry Ellison built Oracle, Phil Knight built Nike, Louis Gerstner revived International Business Machines yet again, Bill Gates built Microsoft, Jeff Bezos built Amazon, Howard Shultz built up Starbucks, and the list goes on endlessly.

It is hardly an exaggeration to say that all successful companies are a reflection of the quality of people who build them and those who lead them. After all, the performance of a company and of your investment in it depends a great deal on the skill with which the leaders seek opportunities and allocate capital among the various projects.

Good managers are, in essence, good stewards of the resources entrusted to them; they create value by competently and creatively managing the resources of the company. More importantly, they also understand their fiduciary responsibility to the suppliers of capital at risk, the shareholders. As such, they manage the company with the goal of creating shareholder returns through strong operating performance over time. In many ways, the perks of their jobs are rewards for the returns that shareholders get for entrusting them with the money.

Yet, there is also another side to this story.

Many managers are not particularly keen on anyone's interests but their own. For shareholders, generally too dispersed and often too small, not having managers who look after their interests bodes trouble, sooner or later. This is because managers have all the power and, as eons of social history teaches us, with power comes the potential for corruption in its many forms: hubris, entrenchment, nepotism, negligence, incompetence, and downright fraud.

With the likes of Ken Lay and Jeffrey Skilling of Enron, Bernie Ebbers of WorldCom, Dennis Kozlowski of Tyco, John Rigas of Adelphia Communications, Conrad Black of Hollinger International, and, of course, the one-and-only Bernie Madoff, we are reminded that capitalism produces its share of misfits and crooks in high places, and that unwitting shareholders are easily duped.

Clearly, there are many instances where the top managers have systematically looted the wealth that was at their disposal, using company resources as if they were monies in a personal account. For shareholders, there is perhaps no more important an issue than the competence, integrity and the character of managers running the companies.

Take Christopher Finazzo, for example, the former executive vice president and chief merchandizing officer of teen clothes retailer, Aéropostale. In June 2010, about four years after he was terminated following an internal investigation by the company, the United States Attorney and the Federal Bureau of Investigation (FBI) charged him with surreptitiously channeling more than $350 million in business to a major supplier in return for about 50 percent of the supplier's profits.

The FBI alleged that the vendor, South Bay Apparel, paid Finazzo more than $14 million and invested the rest in a joint venture that he shared with the vendor. Finazzo was also charged with lying and being the cause of a misstatement in the regulatory filings to the effect that the company did not engage in related party transactions.[91]

The many high-profile cases notwithstanding, investors can lose even when executives do not engage in criminal action or outright fraud. Managers can enrich themselves in any number of ways, for the simple reason that they are in control of resources and close to the action; they have a great deal of discretion on what goes on and what gets reported.

While most managers do their jobs honestly and well-run companies usually have considerable internal controls to prevent misdeeds, investors trying to disconfirm their investment thesis need to keep a lookout for what may be amiss in the character of the people who run the companies in which they invest.

So, it is important for investors to learn to make judgments about the competence and trustworthiness of the managers running the company. Also important is to assess the degree to which the words and actions of the managers demonstrate respect for the rights of the shareholders. An investment thesis that appears to be sound on the basis of other criteria should be disconfirmed if the people leading the company fall short on competence, integrity, or shareholder-friendliness.

Yet, evaluating managers is hard to do, especially if you do not have direct contact with them. Information about the managers is often spotty and business issues can be complicated; you may also not have sufficient access or resources with which to uncover major fraud, especially when those committing the fraud could be actively camouflaging their actions. Big investors and institutions with large amounts of capital at stake may be able to hire specialists, such as forensic accountants and private investigators, to evaluate the background and character of the top managers. For small investors, however, digging deep into every company out there is simply impractical.

As such, for both small and large investors, a quick run-through some of the basics could be useful, especially to the extent that doing so helps keep your money out of at least the most obvious trouble spots. No guarantees, but a checkup can be helpful nevertheless.

Let's discuss below the key issues that we must examine in order to make preliminary judgments about the quality of the managers. To do so, we make assessments in three broad areas: 1) Demographics—to understand the people and the dynamics in the executive suites, 2) Track Record—to evaluate past accomplishments by way of tangible results, and 3) Oversight—to comprehend the incentives and monitoring mechanisms in place. Significant doubts about managers arising from such scrutiny may be grounds for rejecting the investment thesis.

Demographics

The first set of issues in the evaluation concerns the managers themselves. Our objective is to understand the demographic profile of the group at the top of the organization. Here we are concerned with the background and tenure of the top managers, the dynamics and stability of the top management team, and issues related to turnover in the management ranks, along with leadership succession.

Background and Tenure

Where the key managers have cut their teeth is important to understand as well. Previous experiences are no doubt brought into current assignments and it is useful to know the breadth and depth of experiences managers bring to their jobs. It is difficult to know for sure the competence and integrity of the person from his or her demographic data, but these data can be useful, nevertheless, for gaining insights into the quality of the people running your company.

Also useful for such insights are the age and tenure of the key people on the management team. Are they young, say, in their 40s and 50s, building careers and wealth, or are they older, more experienced people looking to sew together an institution to which they may have devoted their careers? How long have they been with the company? Such questions provide no clear answers but they can give helpful clues to the motivations that may be driving the actions of managers.

Investors would do well by understanding how the stewards of their capital think and what their aspirations might be. To be able to see the company as the managers do and understand their game plan for creating economic value allows investors to better monitor their investment over time.

More than demographic information, the quality of thinking of the managers is the key to understanding how good they are likely to be as stewards of your capital. A peek into the thinking of managers is usually available from what they say in interviews, in the letters to shareholders, and in the earnings calls with analysts. Although not quantifiable, particularly important is the clarity with which the managers articulate what strategic objectives they are trying to accomplish, why those objectives are important for creating economic value, and how they are going about doing so.

Evaluating managers in this way takes some maturity and experience, of course, but doing so is essential for being able to closely monitor the investment in the company. So, in combination with quantitative markers such as past performance, subjective judgments can give a fairly good sense of the quality of the people leading an organization. If your judgment casts doubts about the integrity or quality of people at the top of a company, then it may be wise to reject the investment thesis even if other, more objective criteria do not allow you to refute it.

Team Dynamics and Stability

Typically, while all members of the top management team are professionally at the top of their game, the drivers of key decisions are usually the chief executive office and the chief financial officer: one has the overall responsibility and sets the tone and the other keeps an eye on the money. One cannot do the job well without full cooperation of and in full coordination with the other. Sometimes, other functions such as design, or merchandising, or logistics or, information technology are absolutely the key for long-term success of the company. Even so, in most cases the CEO and CFO are usually the people to watch closely.

Yet, it's not just the CEO and the CFO but the whole management team that ultimately executes the game plan; getting a good sense of the whole team is, therefore, an important part of due diligence. As such, some of the questions to ask are: How much does the CEO dominate the team? How stable has the team been over the past several years?

The CEO dominating the team is not necessarily a bad thing. It is quite common for good companies to be driven by strong chiefs. Jack Welch at GE, Bill Gates at Microsoft, Steve Jobs at Apple, Larry Ellison at Oracle, Howard Schultz at Starbucks; the list is very long of strong individuals who built wonderful companies and rewarded the shareholders incredibly well. So, strong CEOs may be desirable as long as they have a consistent record of delivering strong operating performance over time. They have figured out how to hit the sweet spots, and it is okay to let the company be under their watchful eye.

The trouble comes when dominant CEOs are entrenched in the face of persistent anemic performance, yet they are not replaced because of the personal power they have built. It is, in fact, very difficult to displace a poorly performing but powerful CEO and it takes Herculean effort on the part of shareholders to do so. Investors should watch out for entrenched CEOs in poorly performing companies.

The other extreme of entrenched CEO is, of course, a revolving door to the corner office. Companies that cannot retain a chief and need to go out every few years to look for a new one are likely to suffer from the lack of stable leadership. In recent years, for example, the shareholders of Hewlett Packard appear to have suffered from the revolving door in the corner office and, as a result, instability at the top.

The happy medium is the CEO tenure of somewhere around ten years: long enough to take control of the company and shape it but not so long that it makes the company stale or stifles the ambitions of talented professionals in the waiting.

As goes with the CEOs, so it goes with the rest of the management team. While entrenchment of loyalists is a concern in poorly performing companies, stability of the team is important for good companies to continue delivering performance. It takes time for people working together to get in sync with each other, to work as a cohesive team; it does little good if the CEO is not able to retain skilled team members. Revolving doors not just in but also around the corner office can be highly unsettling by getting in the way of good team dynamics that are essential to developing and executing good game plans.

Turnover and Succession

Even good CEOs have to eventually retire. When that time comes, the transition to new leadership can be disruptive unless the company has a succession plan in place. Such planning also comes in handy if the CEO departs suddenly for any number of reasons, as was the case at Hewlett Packard, where the talented CEO Michael Hurd was forced out in August 2010 because of a scandal. Death, illness, or allure of better opportunities can be among any number of other reasons why the CEO may suddenly leave.

Succession planning is not natural to most companies, as the current CEOs don't often want to think about the end of their own careers. It may also raise all kinds of personal issues inside the company, such as power struggle and other unsettling dynamics among internal candidates. Perhaps for these reasons, many charismatic CEOs hold the top spot for a long time.

Still, leadership succession is an important issue and some large companies such as Wal-Mart, GE, Johnson & Johnson, and Intel do a fairly good job of it. These companies have the luxury of size, of course, as their many divisions are often the breeding and testing grounds for future leaders. Some of these companies, such as GE and J&J, are leadership factories of sorts, and many of their alumni often go on to lead other companies.

For smaller companies with fewer resources, planning for future leadership is often not on the agenda. Even so, the depth of executive talent on the bench and policies about succession planning are important investor considerations.

In this regard too, we are not able to challenge the investment thesis for Wal-Mart. The company has a long history of stability at the top and smooth leadership transitions about every ten or so years.

Performance Track Record

The second set of issues in the evaluation of managers concerns their ability to deliver results. Here we are concerned with the financial performance during the recent past, the quality of the financial statements through which the managers present their accomplishments, and the tangible evidence of their shareholder-friendliness.

Financial Performance

Clearly, the first thing to check is if the management team has delivered satisfactory operating performance over time. If you have been unable to refute the company on valuation, yield, stability, strength, and liquidity, and the deep dive into the company literature has not yet revealed fatal flaws, then the chances are that you will find past performance to reveal competent management.

Even so, the key here is to understand how efficiently the company has been run in terms of some key operating ratios. Inventory turnover, asset turnover, operating cycle, and cash management are particularly important. These ratios show the guts of the operations and help assess the competence with which the management has been running the company.

Also important to see over time is the efficiency with which the managers have deployed capital in the past; return on equity (ROE) and return on capital (ROC) are both useful indicators. High and steady returns, when compared with those of direct competitors or other similar companies, usually mean that the managers are making good use of the resources entrusted to them. It is prudent to do such checks to see if the company is being/has been well run over at least the preceding three-to-five years.

Returning to the ongoing example of Wal-Mart: as of the end of fiscal 2011, the company showed good financial performance over the preceding decade—with expanding margins as well as strong operating and performance numbers. As such, Wal-Mart's management appears to be sound on these criteria and the company still cannot be refuted.

Accounting with Honesty

Some insights into the temperament and trustworthiness of the management can also be obtained from the quality of the financial statements.

Remember that managers and accountants have a good deal of discretion in how they report the economic activities of the company. In the end, accountants can do little by way of shading the numbers if the managers are also not complicit in that. Hence, the quality of the financial statements reflects the integrity of the management team.

What accountants can do is help fraudulent managers accomplish fraudulent reporting that hides the troubles in the operations or in the economic structure of the enterprise. This is because even the rulebooks leave considerable leeway in how data are interpreted and what assumptions are used to make the various estimates that go into pulling together the many line items in the financial statements. So, with the help of their accountants, managers can stay within the rules and still be able to stretch the truth to paint a picture that is rosier than it ought to be.

Aggressive accounting practices reflect the eagerness of managers to meet and deliver the expectations often already built into the stock prices. Especially in fast growing companies where expectations of future growth are very high, pressure on managers to deliver the numbers is often quite intense; some managers can respond to such pressure by insisting or facilitating aggressive choices in reporting. Moreover, once managers cross the line and get fancy with their reporting, it is likely that they would do so again, and little by little the seemingly innocuous evasions or exaggerations will turn into shades of falsehoods and then outright lies.

Aggressive accounting can be accomplished in any number of ways, and at least a passing acquaintance with some of the most common forms of stretching the truth is important for investors know. Many books exist on the subject, and investors are well-advised to acquire a working knowledge of the most common forms of deceptions. It is not possible to cover in these pages the full range of accounting shenanigans, so we will consider just a brief framework to understand the kinds of tricks that usually distort the true economics and financial condition of a company.

Essentially, investors should look for four things when scrutinizing a company for aggressive accounting practices: revenues, expenses, assets, and liabilities. Misstating any of these gives distorted impressions of how well the company is performing and how strong it is financially.

So, for instance, one way to keep tabs on the accounting practices of companies is to see how often and how significantly they restate earnings or revenues. To the extent the company cuts corner in reporting, over time, the seemingly minor choices often add up to create substantial pressure in the reporting regime and, eventually, the company is forced to restate.

Similarly, if a company takes large restructuring charges every few years, such action could be a reflection of possible aggressive reporting over the years followed by what in the profession is sometimes called "Big Bath" accounting. Hence, paying attention to the reporting history is a useful way to monitor accounting practices and the quality of the management.

In some cases, companies may also be able to alter the top line and give a wrong impression of how well they are selling their products. Computer Associates, for example, misstated over $3 billion in revenues during the late 1990s, largely to meet analyst expectations and, arguably, to keep the stock price at high levels. The top executives had lots of stock options and their bonuses were tied to delivering performance, so they likely had the motivation to stretch the truth.

In particular, the company executives appeared to have recorded revenues prematurely–by keeping the reporting quarter open for several more days beyond the official closing date, so that the new contracts could be reported as sales in the desired reporting period. The falsehood became too difficult to continue after a few years, and the company finally reported earnings below expectations in the first quarter of 2001. Investors paid dearly for this subterfuge; the CEO went to jail for conspiring to file materially false financial statements and for obstructing justice by lying during the investigation.

More brazenly, Quest Communications recorded fictitious revenues when they did asset swaps with other companies and then posted their side of the swap as revenues. This and some other tricks enabled the company to fraudulently book over $3 billion between 1999 and 2002. According to the charges filed by the Securities and Exchange Commission, the company also understated expenses by $231 million over the same period. Once again, the scheme was to meet the optimistic revenue and earnings projections perhaps already built into the high stock price.

As is evident from Computer Associates and Quest Communications, in short, it is especially important for investors to understand the revenue line. Reporting problems on the expense side can sometimes be overcome with strong revenue growth, but misstating the actual sales can be devastating for investors and have the potential to destroy their entire investment.

Accounting shenanigans also often involve shifting items between the income statement and the balance sheet. For instance, a company may be able to make aggressive sales targets by incentivizing customers to build up their inventories or sign multi-year contracts before the end of the reporting period. These non-cash revenues are then booked aggressively on the income statement and show up as inflated accounts receivables in the balance sheet.

Similarly, companies may be able to defer some current period expenses to future periods and thereby inflate current operating earnings. Those expenses then show up on the balance sheet as inflated current liabilities accounts, only to be brought back on the income statement another year or during a Big Bath. Companies may also be able to pre-pay some future expenses and hold them in current assets, only to bring them back as expenses on the income statement in some future period when the operating performance turns out to be healthier than expected.

Because the Generally Accepted Accounting Principles (GAAP) that govern financial reporting provide only broad guidance, in effect, companies can stay within the rules and still make choices that overstate revenues and understate expenses in any given period. The integrity and honesty of managers is crucial in how the reporting choices are made, and their trustworthiness is usually directly related to how conservative they are in making those choices.

Managers who repeatedly inflate reported performance can be trouble for investors. Keeping an eye out for aggressive accounting can go a long way in avoiding potentially debilitating losses; aggressive accounting is a usually a negative signal about those at the top.

Once again, coming back to Wal-Mart, a quick review of the financial statements does not reveal obvious shenanigans. Their revenues are essentially cash payments by customers for the goods they buy in stores. The expenses do not seem to be swapped between the income statement and the balance sheet.

So, unless a deep analysis reveals otherwise, we are still unable to cast serious doubt on the thesis that Wal-Mart is an attractive investment at about $54 per share.

Shareholder-Friendly Orientation

Another key for investors is whether the managers are shareholder friendly, not only in words but more so in deeds, as reflected in dividends payments and share repurchase programs.[92] These two forms of returning money have slightly different motivations but they have the same effect of shareholders getting tangible reward in return for risking their capital. Dividends put cash in the hands of shareholders; repurchases support the market for the company's shares and give shareholders marginally greater ownership of the company.

As cash in hand, dividends give shareholders the flexibility to do what they want with their money, although they do have to pay taxes on the distributions they receive. Dividends constrain the companies, however, as they are not easily reduced or eliminated; they commit the companies to future cash outflows. Once they start receiving them, shareholders generally expect their dividends to be steady, predictable, and growing. Frequently raising and then cutting dividends and raising again sends mixed signals and is generally a bad practice that most good companies try to avoid.

Even so, it's not uncommon for companies to declare special dividends now and then. In the summer of 2004, for instance, Microsoft declared a one-time special dividend of $3 per share, putting to good use $36 billion of the $56 billion cash hoard it had piled up over the years. Similarly, the clothing retailer Buckle paid a special divided of about $2 per share for three years starting in 2009. It so happens that in both cases a few insiders were also very large shareholders who benefitted handsomely from the windfall. Whatever the motivation, sharing the wealth with shareholders is the right thing for companies to do, provided, of course, that they can afford both current and future cash outlays. Investors should beware and ensure that, in order to pay dividends, the company does not dip into the funds needed for necessary business expenditures or for future growth.

Share buybacks, on the other hand, are more of an indirect benefit, as they reduce the number of shares outstanding and, therefore, increase the proportion of earnings and ownership of the remaining shareholders. Over time, this increased ownership can yield significant rewards. Share buybacks also allow a good deal of flexibility as the companies can be opportunistic as to when to do the buying; they can regulate their purchases depending on the conditions, internal and external.

Investors should know, however, that share buyback programs are beneficial if the company is also not simultaneously issuing significant numbers of shares through stock options and warrants. Many companies make liberal use of stock options in their compensation packages, for instance, and dilute the ownership share of outside equity investors. Then, when they repurchase shares, these companies are in effect buying back those additional shares exercised by the options and warrants holders, severely diluting any gains to the other shareholders. This is sometimes a way for managers to enrich themselves while giving the impression that they are returning money to shareholders, which they are not actually doing to the extent that share buyback numbers may imply.

Consider, for instance, Proctor & Gamble. At the end of fiscal 2010, the company had about 2,843,500,000 common shares outstanding, but the average diluted share count during the year was 8.82 percent higher at about 3,099,300,000. The overhang of diluted shares was in a large part a result of the payment terms used in the company's acquisition of Gillette in 2005.

During the first three quarters of fiscal 2011, the company spent more than $4.5 billion buying back shares. Given that the average price during the period was about $61 per share, the actual number of shares purchased during the $4.5 billion buyback was about 74,361,000. Yet, the actual share count decreased by only 52,207,000 to 2,791,293,000 at the end of the third quarter. This implies that the company in effect bought 22,154,000 of the diluted shares and spent over $1.35 billion to do so.

What the above means is that Proctor & Gamble actually bought back a lot more than reflected in the reduction in basic share count. Of the $4.5 billion spend in the buyback, more than $1.35 billion provided no immediate benefit to the existing shareholders. In essence, if the dilution is a result of stock options given to managers, share buybacks can be a roundabout way of using shareholders' money to benefit managers.

Dilution can be costly for shareholders, and investors must to keep a close eye on it. Unfortunately, share dilution appears to be a common practice across corporate America, and it is particularly rampant in some areas of the economy, such as the technology sector and fast-growing startups. Investors would be well-served to watch out for companies that issue a great deal of options to executives and then buy back those shares at possibly inflated market prices. Such subterfuge can severely undermine the returns to shareholders.

Share buybacks are also not helpful if they are done for the wrong reasons: to manage earnings per share. If the earnings are flat or declining, a company can buy back shares to show growth in earnings per share and, ironically, take resources away from projects that may in fact help renew top-line growth.

Such actions are especially hurtful if the shares being repurchased are overvalued, as repurchases are then not only poor use of resources but also bad investment decisions. Netflix, for example, authorized $400 million share buyback at a time when its share price was rising rapidly—and then spent nearly $260 million buying the shares at speculatively high average price of $222 per share. Soon after the buybacks, the company's market valuations dropped sharply and, by the summer of 2012, the share price was under 30 percent of what it was at the time of the purchases.

Then there are companies that will simply not do dividends or repurchase programs at all, arguing that doing so is a poor use of monies that need to be retained and reinvested. This is indeed true if they can deploy the retained earnings or cash at very good rates of return, or significantly better than what shareholders might be able to get elsewhere.

The arguments for not paying dividends or repurchasing shares have some merit in specific cases where the company has a track record of attaining far above normal returns and they have a well-articulated, rich set of opportunities for future growth. This is especially true for fast growing companies, those that need the resources to continue growing and/or establish competitive market positions.

Many companies also seem to preserve cash as a cushion against unexpected liquidity crunches or for investing opportunistically. Apple, for instance, rarely bought back shares over the last decade and, in fact, its share count has steadily gone up from 710 million in 2002 to 909 million at the end of fiscal year 2010. Share dilution as of the end of 2010 was at 1.32 percent. The 10-year average Return on Capital for Apple stood at just under 19 percent as of the end of fiscal 2010.

For most steadily growing established companies, it's reasonable for investors to expect a share of the spoils. For investors to not receive either dividends or share buybacks should raise questions. In the case of companies that generate sufficient cash but do not issue dividends or repurchase shares, two things are possible. Either they are holding on to cash and generating poor or risky returns on it, or they will do something really questionable with it. If they are hoarding too much cash, then it is important to try to understand why they may be doing so.

It is sometimes possible that the managers are skilled and have a track record of using the cash wisely. Berkshire Hathaway, for instance, does not give dividends nor does it buy back its shares; the company uses the operating cash, instead, for acquisitions and investments that have historically produced good returns for shareholders.

The other possibility with the hoarded cash is that the managers will misuse it, either spending on non-productive things such as lavish corporate offices or frittering it away on hubris-driven, empire-building acquisitions. The better course of action from the point of view of investors is that the companies not keep for long any unproductive cash on the balance sheet but, instead, raise monies as needed for out-of-the-ordinary acquisitions and strategic initiatives. Piles of cash can do little good and much harm.

Overall, sharing the spoils of genuinely good performance, when prudently done, reflects a healthy shareholder orientation and should be welcomed. Wal-Mart demonstrated shareholder-friendliness by having consistently bought back its own shares and having steadily issued and raised dividends since 1974. We are, therefore, still unable to cast doubt on the thesis that the company is an attractive investment at under $54 per share as of late November 2010.

Oversight of Managers

Finally, the third set of issues in the evaluation of managers concerns the incentives they have to deliver performance and the extent to which they are answerable to the representatives of the shareholders, the Board of Directors. Here we are concerned with the compensation structure and the relationship the managers have with the people who are supposed to monitor their activities.

Executive Compensation

How much should the executives make? This has been one of the most controversial issues in recent years and strong voices argue both sides of the issue. Some say corporate executives are paid too much while others say they are, and deservedly so. There is no winning, as both arguments are valid to a small or large extent.

Irrespective of how much the executives are paid, compensation packages can be good or bad depending on how they motivate and incentivize desirable behaviors—both in terms of encouraging good long-term performance and in terms of encouraging shareholder-friendly actions.

Compensation data on publicly traded companies in the United States are available in the mandatory *Proxy* (DEF 14A) reports that companies file with the SEC in preparation for the shareholder meeting every year. Investors have access to broad compensation data for the top earners who meet certain criteria as required by regulation. The different components making up the total compensation are also usually disclosed in the report.

In the April 2011 *Proxy* filing, for instance, by Wal-Mart reports the compensation data for six Named Executive Officers (NEOs). Several things are evident in those data: The total compensation for all six NEOs for 2011 was just over $62 million or 0.38 percent of the total net income that year of over $16 billion.

The ratio of compensation-to-income, or compensation ratio, is a useful metric to see how much the executives are paid in relation to the profits generated. This ratio will vary by the size of the company, of course, but can suggest how reasonable the compensation is in relation to what the managers are doing for the shareholders.

As shown in the second column of table 19.1, Wal-Mart's compensation ratio of 0.38 percent is in line with those of other similarly large companies. For Exxon Mobil, the compensation ratio for 2011 was 0.24 percent and for Johnson & Johnson 0.44 percent, Proctor & Gamble 0.30 percent, and Coca-Cola 0.47 percent. So, it appears that the total compensation for Wal-Mart top earners was generally in line with what other large companies were paying in relation to the annual net income. Among large technology companies, Intel had a compensation ratio of 0.37 percent, Microsoft 0.18 percent, and Apple 1.06 percent.

The compensation ratio increases as the size of the company decreases. Target, which is about one-sixth the size of Wal-Mart, had a compensation ratio of 1.24 percent for the year ending January 2011. Costco, larger than Target, had a compensation ratio of 1.42 percent.

The ratio gets troubling for smaller companies, however, as compensation in relation to net earnings can often be quite large. Abercrombie & Fitch filings, for instance, showed the compensation ratio of 25.29 percent, with 61 percent of the reported NEO compensation going to its chief, Michael Jeffries. This number is obviously out of the ballpark and ought to be of concern to shareholders, especially when compared with competitors such as American Eagle (15.85 percent) and Aéropostale (7.59 percent).

Table 19.1

Company	CompRat[1]	SalaryComp[2]
Wal-Mart	0.38%	8.72%
Johnson & Johnson	0.44%	8.68%
Exxon Mobil	0.24%	8.43%
Microsoft	0.18%	10.26%
Target	1.24%	12.28%
Proctor & Gamble	0.30%	15.10%
Abercrombie & Fitch	25.29%	13.29%
American Eagle	15.85%	21.94%
Aéropostale	7.59%	22.64%
Costco	1.42%	19.74%
Intel	0.37%	7.39%
Coca Cola	0.47%	6.88%
Apple	1.06%	1.92%

1. CompRat is Total Compensation as a percent of the Total Net Income

2. SalaryComp is salary as a percent of Total Compensation

Unjustifiably high compensation must raise questions, especially when what a few top managers make in a given year is a large proportion of the earnings of the company during that same year.

While keeping an eye on the total compensation is helpful, even more important is the actual breakdown of the compensation structure. For most well-known public companies, as shown in the third column of table 19.1, fixed salary is usually a small proportion of the total compensation; the rest is variable tied to some measures of performance.

For the year ending January 2011, for instance, Wal-Mart reports NEO salary as only 8.72 percent of the total compensation. The salary as a proportion of total compensation is similarly low for other large companies: Johnson & Johnson 8.68 percent, Exxon Mobil 8.43 percent, Microsoft 10.26 percent, Target 12.28 percent. Others are similarly weighted low on salary vis-à-vis total compensation: Proctor & Gamble 15.1 percent, Abercrombie & Fitch 13.29 percent, American Eagle 21.94 percent, Aéropostale 22.64 percent, and Costco 19.74 percent. Some, such as Intel (7.39 percent), Coca-Cola (6.88 percent), and Apple (1.92 percent), are even more strongly driven by variable, non-salary compensation that is tied to performance outcomes.

Levels of compensation aside, for investors, the low proportion of fixed salary is usually a plus, as it indicates that most of the compensation is tied to performance measures. How the variable compensation is structured indicates, moreover, whether the managers are turned toward the short-term or the long-term and, more importantly, whether they are oriented toward strengthening the core operations or directed toward maximizing immediate performance in the stock market.

With the salary usually being much under 25 percent of total compensation, investors should try to understand the nature of incentives that are built into the variable compensation: what sorts of behaviors do the compensation packages encourage among the top managers?

In essence, then, the compensation structure reveals a great deal about the motives and behaviors of top management teams.

The ideal compensation structures are those that have a healthy mix of all the elements as discussed, but which still favor actions that steadily build up the intrinsic value of the firm. To this end, compensation structures should (1) orient managers toward the long-term and, at the same time, (2) encourage them to strengthen the core operations and deliver high returns on the total invested capital. Once again, Wal-Mart could not be disconfirmed as an investment at the price of just under $54 in late 2010.

Board of Directors

Last but not the least, members of the board are elected directly by the shareholders to safeguard their interests against possible misdirection or misappropriation of funds by the managers. In most companies, the governance structures are such that the managers make day-to-day decisions, the board weighs in on important decisions such as the hiring of the CEO and big strategic initiatives, and the shareholders have a say in game-changing decisions such as mergers and acquisitions. In theory, the board provides the oversight to ensure that the managers are acting in the interests of the shareholders—who are usually dispersed and, in most cases, do not have the skills or access to monitor the goings-on in the company. The top managers report directly to the board, which has the authority to hire and fire and authorize important actions, such as mergers and acquisitions.

In practice, it does not always work that way. In many companies, in fact, managers have a great deal of say in who gets on the board of directors. In some cases, strong CEOs fill the board with people they like and those who are favorably inclined towards them. In a well-known story from some years ago, the board of Walt Disney was stacked with managers, outside professionals doing business with the company, and close associates of the very long-time CEO, Michael Eisner. News media reported that Mr. Eisner refused to discuss succession even after nearly twenty years at the helm. It was only after Roy Disney, the company founder's nephew, resigned from the board and started a long and costly campaign that Eisner was finally persuaded to step down.

Even when the CEO and the top management team are not strongly entrenched, the board is often not as free as theory would have us believe. Members of the board do not have the same immersion in day-to-day operations as do managers running the company, and they don't have access to information other than what is channeled towards them. They are elected for a term that lasts only a few years and, a particular board membership being only one of the many commitments, they are usually not able to devote fully to the job. As such, the role of a typical board member is merely advisory and their oversight cursory.

Moreover, board members don't usually rock the boat too much lest the managers don't nominate them for the next round of elections. Asking too many difficult questions and putting the managers on the defensive is a socially difficult thing to do anyway, but board members often have to tread cautiously because a miffed CEO can recommend replacing a member for any number of reasons or no reason at all. This is usually a meaningful threat to board members because not only is it prestigious to be on a board, but the remuneration can run into several hundred thousand dollars per year. The prospect of losing money and privileges can undermine the independence of the board members and hinder proper oversight of the managers.

In practice, therefore, the board of directors is often an instrument of strong-willed managers and only occasionally does it serve the purpose of safeguarding the interests of the shareholders.

Governance structures do require board members to serve on audit committees and compensation committees so that they can provide oversight in a more formal manner. These committees do useful routine work but rarely do they take an activist position, especially if the CEO and the managers are deeply entrenched and powerful. Members of the board only have so much time, after all, to devote to what in many cases is essentially a part-time sinecure. In fact, board members are the social elites who serve on the boards of multiple companies at the same time, and, therefore, may have even less devotion than what a single part-time job would demand.

Where the boards often do play an active and useful role is when the company has large shareholders, such as active investors and family trusts. Such strong interests on the board can exert direct pressure and, therefore, resist the power of managers and provide good oversight.

Boards also play a useful role in critical periods such as hiring of a new CEO and when evaluating significant, potentially transformative events such as mergers or acquisitions. And the boards play a particularly crucial role in times of crisis, such as discovery of fraud or outright violations of clearly articulated codes of conduct. Moments of crisis allow board members to overcome their trepidations about crossing the managers, partly because of clear justness of their actions but also because of social support they may be able to get from each other.

Although mostly deferential to the CEO Conrad Black, for example, the star-studded board of Hollinger International did eventually come together to force him out in response to an emerging scandal about misuse of company funds. Similarly, upon discovering that the CEO, Brian Dunn, was having a relationship with a female employee, the board of Best Buy reacted quickly to oust him. A few months later, when it became evident that the founder, Richard Schulze, had known about the affair but had not disclosed it at the time, the board forced him out as well.

But such instances of a board playing a proactive and activist role are few and far between, and they come rather late to do much good for the shareholders, who have by then already suffered for too long.

All in all, there is no substitute for you as an investor to do your own due diligence and rely on your own judgments about the competence and integrity of the top management teams. Good managers are worth their weight in gold; bad managers can be a whole lot of trouble. Boards of directors are limited in their ability to control bad behavior by managers. Investing wisely requires that you be aware of the character of those to whom you entrust your money.

Ultimately, evaluation of the top management team is a crucial part of investment analysis. Based on a range of quantitative and qualitative information, as discussed above, investors should make judgments about the competence and integrity of the managers. If it turns out that your analysis reveals grave doubts about the managers, then you must refute the investment thesis.

20

Watch the Game

————

A well-defined business model, competently executed, is essential for a company to deliver consistently strong operating performance and, therefore, to its intrinsic valuation. As part of the due diligence, therefore, we must understand the quality of the company's business model and assess the ability of the management team to monetize it.

A business model should be thought of as the economic narrative or the "story" of the company, articulating the overall game plan that managers execute for the company. It articulates in a broad outline the mechanisms through which a company generates revenues and controls costs to deliver operating performance. It reveals, in other words, what game the company is playing and how its various activities are structured to prevail in that game— by generating profits and cash flows.

In order to be able to refute the investment thesis, investors must try to understand the business model and make judgments about its ability to generate profits. If the model is not clear or it is clear but reveals fundamental weaknesses in how the company makes money, then the investment thesis must be refuted.

In essence, investors must be able to see clearly that the company has significant and durable strategic strengths that will enable it to continue generating at least the historical returns well into the future.

A Business Story

Consider Best Buy, for instance. Founded in 1966 as a single-store audio specialty retailer, by the early 1990s the company had grown to be a significant player in electronics retail. Part of the reason for its success was that the management had shrewdly committed the company to the emerging big-box store format. Growing fast throughout the 1990s, by the end of the decade, Best Buy was the largest specialty electronics retailer in the country. It competed with Circuit City (which filed for bankruptcy in 2008); the West Coast firm Fry's Electronics; an Indiana company Gregg Appliances; and general retailers such as Wal-Mart and Target. Electronics retail was the game, and Best Buy chose to play it by aggressively rolling out big-box specialty stores.

Now, the power of retail stores like Best Buy usually derives from their ability to attract and build traffic that flows through the stores. But traffic itself is a function of the range and mix of products the retailer sells. So, retailers are often caught in a double bind, as they need to please both manufacturers and customers: If you do not have in-demand products to display, the customers don't show up; if you do not have enough shoppers coming in the door, you lose the access and volume discounts reserved for bigger retailers. This is the retailers' dilemma.

This dilemma can be solved in several different ways. For instance, many retailers reach back and integrate manufacturing in their operations. Branded clothing companies such as Gap, American Eagle, and Ann Taylor manage stores that carry only their own products. In such cases, retail gives companies control over their brand and manufacturing is simply a point in the supply chain that is aligned with the needs of the brand. With manufacturing so integrated in the operations, these companies can focus their attention on strengthening connections with their customers.

Retailers such as Best Buy do not have such an option; they carry too many different kinds of products to be able to effectively integrate backwards into manufacturing. They do not own the brands that they stock, and manufacturers can harden their terms if business starts lagging; similarly, customers are notoriously quick to drive elsewhere for a better deal or sharply curtail spending during tough economic times.

Retailers like Best Buy are, therefore, strategically vulnerable; they experience a consistent squeeze from both ends but have limited options for relieving those pressures.

One option that retailers do have is to solve the traffic problem first by building big stores that offer a full range of products. Large size of individual stores helps build traffic because of availability of a full range of products; large number of stores dispersed geographically helps control costs by enabling scale economies in advertising, vendor contracts, and administrative overhead.

So, the decision of Best Buy to grow aggressively had the above logic embedded in it. The company built up a network of big-box stores spread across the country, filled those stores with a wide array of electronics products, and successfully took advantage of scale economies to build a strong national brand. They took the risk and it worked.

With the store infrastructure in place, Best Buy turned its attention to executing the model. Capabilities in logistics and distribution were critically important to keep inventory under control and costs down, and heavy promotion as well as in-store service were necessary to keep the traffic flowing. Over time, Best Buy built the capabilities to execute the model and it began delivering strong operating performance. The company's ability to execute the well-defined and fundamentally sound model was a key to their success throughout the 1990s and into the first decade of the twenty-first century.

On the strength of building and executing their well-defined business model, Best Buy's revenues rose 46-fold from $665 million at the 1990 fiscal year-end to over $30 billion at the end of fiscal 2005; during the same period, market value of the company's common equity rose 376-fold from $69 million to over $26 billion.

Investors who understood the basic storyline and recognized early the manner in which Best Buy was trying to solve the problem of retailing electronics goods benefited handsomely for their insight. Ten thousand dollars invested in the common equity of the company in 1990, if held for the duration, would have grown to more than $3.76 million by the end of fiscal year 2005.

A Changing Story

Yet, the story of Best Buy doesn't quite end in 2005. A successful business model is built on certain underlying assumptions about how the world works and needs to evolve as the world changes. An essential assumption of the big-box store model is that shoppers would be attracted to the wide selection of competitively priced products on display, and the traffic thus built would create sales that justify the high costs of running such stores. Dimly visible at first, the changes taking place in the large economic landscape were about to seriously challenge that assumption.

In spite of the enormous successes, as evident in its spectacular growth, the fundamental risk for Best Buy was that large brick-and-mortar stores have high fixed costs and are, therefore, vulnerable to substantial drops in traffic. The company remained exposed to economic downturns or other reasons for people to not shop in the stores. If the inventory became stale or consumption patterns changed, big-boxes were likely to suffer heavy losses as they tried to lure the customers back by more promotion and aggressive markdowns.

Since the basic business model was a spectacular success for more than a decade, perhaps because of it, Best Buy was slow to respond to an emerging threat that would greatly undermine the logic of big-box stores. The emergence of Amazon and other online retailers offered customers a viable and in some ways superior alternative for shopping electronic goods. Since Best Buy sold the same branded goods that could be found on the Internet, customers could simply turn to the websites that offered a better deal and shop from their laptops and, increasingly, from their smartphones. Internet stores, moreover, did not need the expensive inventory or floor space to display products and they could operate with a much more competitive cost structure.

Ironically, what was once the strength of the big-box model became a big liability. Instead of shopping at the Best Buy stores, customers began to use them as showrooms to get educated by the service staff on the floor, make up their minds, and then go to the Internet for best deals. So, the stores continued attracting traffic but it was traffic without sales.

The company did belatedly respond with Best Buy Online, but the tide had already turned and masses of customers were ditching the brick-and-mortar stores to go shopping on their web browsers. Perhaps impressed with past successes, Best Buy was slow in seeing the changes threatening the core of its business model. Incredibly, in fact, even as online commerce was gaining momentum and threatening the foundations of their business model, the company continued to emphasize the traditional way of doing business, going aggressively into other countries such as England and China.

When they did finally recognize the inevitable, Best Buy tried to integrate the physical stores with the Internet by offering free store pickup for products purchased at Best Buy Online. But it was too little too late. Online commerce had continued unabated in the meantime and the Internet retailers had sharpened their own models as well.

All this was not lost on the financial markets. Missed opportunities, a failing business model, and dimmed future prospects for the company were visible in its market valuation. While the annual revenues climbed to more than $50 billion at the end of fiscal 2011, the market value of the company had shrunk two-thirds from its peak to under $9 billion.

As of this writing in April 2012, Best Buy had announced that it was closing 50 of the 1,400 domestic big-box stores. The company was beginning an overhaul of its business model, lowering the number of big-box stores and increasing the number of mobile stores in the mix. Clearly, these changes were long overdue. But with most of the stores still in big-box format, it was not clear what revised business model the belated transformation would reveal.

Lessons from Best Buy

The story of Best Buy illustrates the importance of outlining the business models of companies in which you invest. It shows that good investment prospects are not just about profit and loss in the short run, in this year and the next quarter. Strong investment performance comes from investing in businesses that have honed in on the fundamental problems to be solved and that then assemble, align, and concentrate resources to address those problems in a systematic way. Durable and meaningful rewards for investors come from selectively investing in companies that solve significant problems at a sufficiently large scale to make the effort worthwhile. A business model is a means for doing all that.

As early as 2007, it was clear that Best Buy had a weakened business model and was, therefore, less attractive as an investment than it had been in the 1990s. In spite of historical successes, emerging vulnerabilities in the company's business model were increasingly good grounds on which to question Best Buy as an investment prospect.

So, for example, even though Best Buy looked good based on historical growth rates and performance record up to about 2007, alert investors would have paused and paid heed to emerging headwinds to the company's business model. Clearly, Best Buy had been successful because of the success of its big-box store format. But the rapid rise of the Internet had posed significant challenges to its way of doing business. To these challenges the company seemed to have no good answer.

Instead of fretting about stock price fluctuations in the short run, in other words, investors are better served when they step back and evaluate the larger story; they should try to outline the mechanisms by which the companies in which they invest navigate the larger economic forces and create value for their customers.

Business models are, in fact, a crucial due diligence check for investing wisely. They can help sort out companies that are genuinely good investment bets from value traps—or those companies that suffer low market valuations because of truly dim prospects. That is, a clear understanding of the business model of a company can help refute its stock even if it looks attractive on the basis of the quantitative tests and qualitative analysis as shown in the preceding chapters.

Intrinsic valuation, after all, is derived by discounting the projected but uncertain future cash flows. The projected cash flows depend in large part on the company continuing to maintain its competitive position and operating strength. So, it stands to reason that the intrinsic valuation of a company is directly related to the quality of its business model and the finesse with which it is executed.

Naturally, business models need to evolve as technologies and consumption patterns change. The reasons that had made a company a success in the past may no longer apply as things change. As we see in the history of Best Buy, past strengths can become liabilities in a new world.

Yet, the need for change is not easily visible. Although clear in hindsight, it was not easy for Best Buy to comprehend the huge impact that the Internet would have on its business. Perhaps the managers thought that changes at the margin, such as Best Buy Online, would be adequate and the network of big-box stores would not have to be dismantled. Unfortunately for the company, the Internet induced an accelerating pace of change in consumption patterns—and changed the destination of millions of people who had previously shopped at Best Buy.

Changing a once successful business model is difficult, as past successes are built on existing assets and organizational routines that are difficult to undo. Past successes also harden a way of thinking and make companies resistant to disruptions that any overhaul of an existing model would require. Plus, there is usually a great deal of uncertainty about what effect new initiatives would have on the short-term profits and long-term possibilities for the company. The certainties of the known model and the uncertainties inevitable in new directions both create strong incentives for managers to continue with a failing course of action.

Just because it is hard for companies to change their business models does not mean, however, that investors cannot spot the need for such change. Uninhibited by the constraints and incentive structures that limits action by managers, investors can take independent action if convinced that the story of the company is changing for the worse.

Still, investors must know that no one mechanism for wealth creation fits all companies. What made Best Buy successful between 1990 and 2005 is very different from how Dell changed the personal computing industry in the 1980s and 1990s. Why Home Depot succeeded differed a great deal from how Monster Beverage achieved stunning success as a leading energy drinks company. Panera Bread had a different model than Starbucks or McDonald's. Priceline and Expedia, although in the same general business, go about attaining success in very different ways. Similarly, Nike and Under Armour do things very differently even though they compete in footwear and athletic apparel.

There is wide diversity of business models out there, in other words, both within and across industries. More so, new models emerge frequently as businesses leverage emerging technologies and changing consumption patterns to exploit new opportunities. Your ability to grasp the details of a particular business model depends to a great degree on who you are and what you bring to the table in terms of previous experiences.

Given your skills and knowledge about particular types of businesses, you may be able to clearly understand certain business models and pick up on nuances about how particular companies function and make money. Yet, other business models may be opaque to you because of your lack of familiarity with the business and/or the complexities inherent in it.

In some cases, you may understand the business model clearly but also see enough instability and risk that you want to stay away from the company in question. In still other cases, the business model may be clearly articulated by the management but you don't quite see much evidence that the company can successfully and profitably execute the model.

So, for instance, you may find the business model of Expedia is too complex because of your lack of familiarity with the travel industry. Yet, you may have the skills to read much into how the energy drink company Monster Beverages or online jeweler Blue Nile goes about generating revenues and profits. Understanding the business model allows you to be able to set up the investment thesis for disconfirmation and, therefore, improves the quality of your investment decision.

In essence, it is advisable for investors to use a check of the business model to try to refute the investment thesis. As such, it is also advisable that investors limit themselves to those companies whose business models they can understand and evaluate. By so narrowing the focus of inquiry, investors can be well prepared to refute companies on the grounds that they are too complex, opaque, risky, defenseless, or poorly suited to the changing competitive conditions. Limiting investment decisions to such zones of comfort is essential for investing wisely.

Essentials of a Business Model

So, what is a good business model? The simplest way to understand a business model is to view it as a mechanism whereby the company consumes a dollar of investment to produce cash flows greater than the original investment. From the cash flows thus produced, a portion is reinvested in the company to sustain and strengthen the business model, with the rest either returned to the investors or placed in a reserve fund for pursuing additional opportunities.

As such, at least in hindsight, the strength of a business model is evident from the average historical returns on invested capital. Future such returns depend on the resilience of the model to sustain its core elements even as it evolves in response to changing circumstances.

So, essential to the definition of a business model are: 1) the markets where the products are sold, and 2) operating capabilities that are necessary for creating, marketing, and distributing those products. To the extent that the company has a sharply defined and well-executed business model in an opportunity rich environment, it is likely to generate high cash return on capital and create substantial intrinsic value for investors.

The schematic in figure 20.1 shows what a business model for a manufacturing company may look like. It tells the story that has a logical narrative about how the company produces and sells products in order to deliver profits. The story is usually about who buys the products or services of the company and why they do so when similar products from elsewhere may exist. The model tells the story about how big the product markets are and the various channels used to get products to those markets. The model also clarifies the arrangement of production assets and the ability of the company to innovate and control costs in the procurement, manufacturing, distribution, and sales processes.

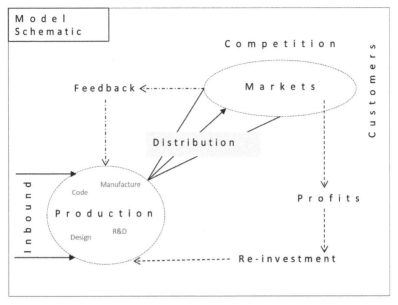

Figure 20.1: Full view business schematic of a hypothetical manufacturing company.

To illustrate, let's consider Coach, the maker of accessories and gifts, although it is mostly known for handbags for women. As of early 2012, the key elements of the company's business model were:

1. Coach is positioned as an affordable luxury, selling handbags mostly under $300 but going to price points above $1,000, yet well below Gucci and Prada bags that sell for thousands or tens of thousands of dollars apiece. As such, the company is positioned to appeal to a very large market that comprises style-seeking women looking for affordable options.

2. Nearly 70 percent of the company's sales come from United States, about 18 percent from Japan, and the rest from other parts of the world with China the new growth target.

3. Product positioning in the market is facilitated by a strong design team that actively incorporates feedback from customers via ongoing surveys and research studies.

4. The company does not have its own manufacturing plants and outsources all production to a network of independent manufacturers, but it tightly controls the supply chain from design through manufacture and then distribution thereafter.

5. Coach brings its products to customers through company owned stores, by placing products in department stores and specialty stores that can support the brand, and via the Internet.

6. During the period 2009–2011, Coach re-invested about $470 million or nearly 17 percent of the operating cash flows back into the business. Of this amount, $375 million was to refresh the assets and the remaining for future growth.

7. The average return on capital for the five years ending in July 2011 was 45 percent.

The model clarifies, in essence, the key elements that come together to make the business work. It shows the mechanisms through which the company conducts business, gets feedback from the markets, and re-invests in operations, so that it could continue the profitable cycle of design, production, and sales over time. More broadly, it shows how the company is positioned in the business ecosystem, how it generates market power, how it solves which fundamental problems for which customers, how it controls costs, and how it makes money. The return on capital shows how productively the company has used the debt and equity capital on the books.

As we saw in the case of Best Buy, however, the business model of any company always is—needs to be—in flux because the external environment is forever changing. While the past performance of Coach has been strong, for example, alert investors will want to understand how their model is evolving and what potential the company has to continue generating their historical numbers. Among other things, they will need to assess the long-term economic impact of the company's bold initiatives in Asia and their increasing efforts to develop accessories for men.

There are many nuances to any business, of course, but the key for investors is to try to cast doubt on the dominant narratives either from logical holes in it or by discovering problems in the ability of the mechanisms so revealed to make profits.

Book V

Policy

Chapters

———

21. Diversification

22. Another Way to Portfolio

23. Core Holdings

24. Growth

25. The Buffett Portfolio

———

21

Diversification

———

Consider two likely events, X and Y, that you think can happen with probabilities $p(X)$ and $p(Y)$, respectively. What is the probability that both events will happen at the same time?

The answer to the above question depends upon what the relationship is between X and Y. The simplest case is when the two events are independent of each other. So, for instance, let's assume that X represents heavy rain in Seattle on a particular day and Y represents a train accident in New York on the same day. The two events are so far apart in distance and in their nature, that for all practical purposes we can assume they are unrelated and independent; the probability that both would occur on the same day is the product of individual probabilities, or $p(X\&Y) = p(X) \cdot p(Y)$.

So, if $p(X) = 20$ percent and $p(Y) = 1$ percent then $p(X\&Y) = 0.2$ percent. That is, the independence of the two events makes the chances of them happening together very small, much smaller than the chances of either of them happening individually.

If, on the other hand, another event Z were to represent flooding in Seattle on the same day as heavy rain occurred, then we know intuitively that X and Z are not independent, as the likelihood of Z increases when X happens. In this case, we have $p(X\&Z) = p(X) \cdot p(Z|X)$. That is, the probability that both X and Z would happen is probability of rain multiplied by the probability of flooding *conditional upon* the probability of rain.[93]

So, if $p(X) = 20$ percent and $p(Z|X) = 50$ percent then $p(X\&Z) = 10$ percent. Even though the two events are not independent, the chances of them happening together remain small. But the higher the conditional probability of Z given X, or p(Z|X), the higher is their joint probability. The limiting cases: 1) p(Z|X) = 1, which says that it always floods when it rains heavily, and 2) p(Z|X) = 0, which says that it never floods when it rains.

The above way of thinking is, in essence, the foundation for the modern portfolio theory. The greater the independence between the returns of two stocks, or smaller the conditional probabilities of the two, the lower is the likelihood that the returns of the two stocks will move together in the same direction. The theory is that if you hold a diversified portfolio of, say, two stocks, where the performance of one is unrelated to that of the other, then the probability is small that both the stocks in your portfolio will go bust at the same time.

"Modern" Portfolio Theory

It had been known since at least the beginning of the twentieth century that investors could reduce risk by diversifying their holdings, just as a prudent measure to guard against mishaps in one of their investments or the other. But the assessment of risk to each investment was based on intuition, as no objective measures of risk existed. There was also no way to think about the risk of the diversified portfolio as a whole. That is, investors did not quite know how to think formally of the joint risk of all the investments they owned. Portfolio-level thinking had not yet been developed.

So, as discussed in the prologue, Harry Markowitz comes along around 1950 and sees that the above problem of portfolio risk could be solved by using the ideas and the math of conditional probability. He takes it up as a topic for his doctoral dissertation in economics, and then, using concepts from the statistics texts of the time, he develops and formalizes the concept of portfolio risk. In particular, he defines risk of a stock as the standard deviation of its returns, and then formulates portfolio or joint risk using covariance of past returns of all the stocks in the portfolio.

In order to understand how he computed portfolio risk by weighting the risk of individual stocks in the portfolio, some basic math is necessary. So, follow along as I work through it below:

Assume you own two stocks A and B equally in a portfolio (weights $w_A = w_B = 0.5$; $w_A + w_B = 1$) and assume that you can compute the variance of past returns for each. Let us say that the variance of each stock is 4 percent ($\sigma_A^2 = \sigma_B^2 = 4$ percent), so the standard deviation of each is 20 percent ($\sigma_A = \sigma_B = 20$ percent). Then, the variance of the portfolio comprising those two stocks is computed as:

$$\text{Portfolio Variance } \sigma_p^2 = w_A^2\,\sigma_A^2 + w_B^2\sigma_B^2 + 2w_Aw_B\sigma_A\sigma_B\rho_{AB} \qquad (21.1)$$

The term ρ_{AB} in the above equation is the correlation between the returns of A and B, or the extent to which the returns move in the same or opposite directions. Markowitz defined portfolio risk simply as the standard deviation or square root of the variance, σ_p^2, as computed above. By this definition, portfolio risk depends on variance of the two stocks and the covariance between them. The third term, covariance, is of particular interest because as the number of stocks in the portfolio increases, the number of covariance terms increases much faster and the equation (risk) becomes dominated by the covariance terms.

This, in essence, is the portfolio theory as conceived by Harry Markowitz in the 1950s. He figured that if he defined risk as the standard deviation of returns, then he could compute not only the risk of individual stocks but also the risk of the portfolio comprising those stocks. Then, applying this concept to a diversified portfolio, he showed how to compute the individual and group standard deviations (risk) using historical data.

It had been known for several decades that diversification was a key to managing risk because the returns of different stocks, especially those in different economic sectors, often moved in different directions. It was not until Markowitz, however, that the risk of the portfolio as a whole could be quantified. This was a breakthrough.

If the idea of equating risk with standard deviation of past returns makes you uncomfortable, you are not alone. But hold on to that thought and follow along for the time being. I will come back to your objection later.

Of special note in the equation of portfolio variance, Markowitz observed, was the third term (ρ_{AB}), which indicates the correlation between the returns of the two stocks.[94] So, if the returns of the two correlate perfectly, $\rho_{AB} = 1$, then portfolio variance computes as 4 percent and portfolio risk is 0.2, the same as the risk of either stock on its own. That is simple enough.

But what got Markowitz excited was the fact that most stocks did not move in perfect unison. Subject to the same systemic factors, such as the economy and political environment, returns of different stocks were usually only partially related; they were neither correlated perfectly nor were they completely independent of each other. It was in such imperfect correlations that the true power of statistics became apparent.

So, in order to understand Markowitz, consider three scenarios: when the correlation (ρ_{AB}) is zero, positive, and negative.

If the two stocks happen to be independent of each other ($\rho_{AB} = 0$), the variance of the portfolio is simply the sum of the first two terms. In this example, when there is full independence between the returns of A and B, the portfolio variance computes to 2 percent and portfolio risk (standard deviation) is 14.14 percent.

If, on the other hand, the two stocks are not independent ($\rho_{AB} \neq 0$), then portfolio variance depends on the covariance being positive or negative. So, for instance, if $\rho_{AB} = 30$ percent then portfolio variance computes as 2.6 percent and portfolio risk as 16.12 percent; if $\rho_{AB} = -30$ percent then portfolio variance computes as 1.4 percent and portfolio risk as 11.81 percent.

That is, even when the two stocks making up the above portfolio are not perfectly correlated with each other, portfolio risk is lower than the risk of either stock taken individually. So, forming a portfolio with unrelated stocks can actually reduce the risk to the investor.

The practical implications of this insight were powerful. The problem that investors now had to solve was to find stocks that did not co-vary perfectly and group them together so as to minimize their joint risk while not sacrificing their expected joint returns. Markowitz then went a step further to define *efficient* portfolios as those where the proportion of each stock is such that the standard deviation or portfolio risk is minimized for a given expected return.

The same logic applies not only to two stock portfolios but to those with any number of stocks. The math remains the same even though the numbers of terms that need to be computed multiply fast and calculating portfolio variance and risk becomes computationally intense. Modern computers can handle the computations quite easily, however.

In essence, then, Markowitz's genius was in showing how investment risk could be lowered by pulling together unrelated stocks into a portfolio.

An important implication of all this was that investors should be thinking of investing not in terms of single stocks but in terms of portfolios of stocks. Since you can actually reduce risk by grouping stocks, you should try to build portfolios with best risk-reward trade-off, or efficient portfolios.

Particularly fascinating in the Markowitz's logic is the corollary that the risk of a single stock by itself means or should mean very little in large, well-diversified portfolios. The number of covariance terms increases as the size of the portfolio increases and they overshadow the effect of the weighted variance of any one stock.

See what happens to the portfolio variance equation when a single stock is added to an existing portfolio of, say, thirty stocks: the new stock will add one variance term but *thirty* covariance terms as the covariance of the new stock with each of the already existing stocks will need to be computed. The change in the total risk of an existing portfolio could then be impacted much more by the thirty additional covariance terms than by the single variance of the stock added to the portfolio.

Two implications are usually derived from the math of computing portfolio variance: 1) the risk of a single stock does not matter that much, and 2) each buy or sell decision must be made in light of whatever stocks you already have in the portfolio. As we will see later, the second implication is certainly very helpful, but the first implication that the risk of any one stock does not matter is patently misleading and, in our view, absurd.

Even so, this was breakthrough thinking at the time and Markowitz earned a Nobel Prize for conceiving risk in this way, and especially for delivering with the math to make it all possible. This way of thinking about investing revolutionized finance; the rest is history.

One of the early extensions to Markowitz was the idea of risk in relation to the overall market. To understand how he was extended, think of a fully diversified investor who owns a basket filled with all the stocks in the market. To that basket, you then want to add another stock and the issue is the degree to which that additional stock will increase or decrease the risk of the market portfolio.

This concept was captured by the idea of *Beta* (β), which is simply a mathematical formulation capturing the normalized covariance between the stock and the market index, which is usually approximated by the S&P 500 Index although other indexes are also possible. Doing so allowed each stock to be assigned a number, β, which captured its risk in relation to the overall market.

Other modifications followed, but the core ideas that took hold were that the risk of a stock could be approximated by a simple statistic (standard deviation) and that portfolio risk was also a statistic that could be computed using returns data for each stock in the portfolio.

The Trouble with Portfolio Theory

Now, the problem that you have with Markowitz's formulation is the assumption that the standard deviation of returns fully or even adequately captures risk to the invested principal. Using a statistic for risk certainly makes the math possible, but it stretches credulity to say that the way the prices moved in the past is a perfect or even a good indicator of the known and unknown future risks. This way of thinking does not give much by way of explicit consideration to the many operating, technological, and competitive challenges and uncertainties that a business may face; nor does it acknowledge that the price paid may be significantly higher than any reasonable estimates of the worth of the business. In order to get past these difficulties, portfolio theory assumes that markets are efficient and perfectly price all stocks, and that prices fully reflect all information about the company. Technically, the assumption of market efficiency translates into the assumption that price equals value, or that no systematic errors exist between market price and intrinsic economic worth.

These valiant assumptions gloss over the complexity inherent in companies and obviate careful consideration of the various hazards to which the company, and therefore the investment in it, are exposed. To his credit, Markowitz was well aware of this shortcoming. Perhaps, having read Graham and Dodd, he cautioned that risks be assessed using statistical analysis of returns *as well as* security analysis, so as to carefully evaluate the company and its financial statements.

Unfortunately for modern finance, Markowitz's suggestion to judge risk through the labors of analysis was ignored. Effective security analysis is labor intensive and, as we have seen, it requires subjective judgments based on careful study of the facts of the case, one company at a time. Large scale data analysis obviates such labor. Once each company is reduced to simply the average and standard deviation of returns, multiple companies comprising a portfolio are analyzed in the aggregate with nary a concern about the complexities that characterize each individual company in the portfolio. In fact, the nature of labor changes as, once the mathematical formulae are coded in software, portfolio analysis is amenable to being automated and delivered at an industrial scale.

By equating risk with standard deviation and posing investing as a problem of portfolios optimization, Markowitz defined investing as needing a mathematical solution and he devoted years laboring for the cause. But to a new breed of math-savvy professionals, he also gave permission to avoid judgment-heavy analysis of financial statements, the characteristics of the business and the management.

So, for sixty years and more, risk has been defined as standard deviation of returns and portfolio optimization has been at the core of investment research, teaching, and practice. This way of thinking has become stronger with time, even as concerns about the core assumptions have remained. The past few decades have seen many efforts to better define risk, but these have mostly all been mathematical in orientation, they continue to use past returns data by necessity, and for the most part they continue to ignore the fundamental business and management issues that are, in fact, the key to understanding the hazards of investing.

All this is unfortunate because the core idea of probabilistic thinking is good, and conceptualizing investing in terms of portfolio rather than individual stocks is very powerful indeed. Both probability and portfolio can be immensely helpful to investors but *only if* we could more realistically evaluate risk to accurately reflect the dangers that investors face.

22

Another Way to Portfolio

———

Clearly, modern portfolio theory is limited by its insistence on seemingly objective measures of risk. Yet, the core idea of grouping companies to temper the hazards of investing is sound and can be developed further—but only by first shedding the pretense of objectivity and incorporating subjective probabilities in the mix. That is, the power of portfolio-level thinking can be harnessed by using business judgment to assess risk subjectively and to then group well-selected companies into a carefully constructed portfolio. By understanding risk much more broadly as the uncertainties that surround an investment, it may be possible to leverage the benefits of both security analysis and grouping.

A good understanding of company history, business model, management team, and valuation in relation to price can provide a broader sense of hazards to the invested principal. From such a broader view, we may be able to assess, if subjectively, the chances that the fortunes of a company would worsen drastically or that the investment would deteriorate for other reasons. That is, rather than focusing on the variability of past returns, we must rely on well-informed judgments about the key sources of uncertainties and the hazards that the company may face.

Let us, therefore, *re*-conceptualize risk as *probability of loss*. Although not as precise as standard deviation of past returns, a subjective probability of loss can be assessed from the kind of analysis we have discussed at length in the book. Both quantitative and qualitative techniques of analysis, as shown in previous chapters, can help assess the probability of loss for each company in the portfolio. That is, we ignore the fluctuations in past prices and focus instead on the chances of meaningful deterioration in the worth of the company.

So, take again the two companies equally weighted in a portfolio. Assume that through quantitative refutation and qualitative disconfirmation exercises as described in previous chapters, we have carefully selected the two companies and think that they offer potentially attractive investment opportunities. Let us suppose that we come to the subjective judgment that there is a one-in-four chance of near term problems with the companies. The problems could arise from internal issues or because of macro environment that the company cannot control; say you assess that there is a 25 percent chance that the performance of either company could drop by 20 percent in the next year.

Instead of focusing on what price the market is attaching to a company at a given time, you are trying to understand the key uncertainties about the ability of the company to deliver economic performance. Let us assume in this example that the companies are very different and their future prospects are mostly independent of each other. Say one is a retail company in India and the other a defense company in the United States. That is, assume for the time being that the economic performance of the two companies is not related.

Making the assumption of independence greatly simplifies the math below and allows us to see the risk implications of pulling the two companies in one portfolio. Lack of independence would complicate the math, of course, but the basic story would not really change. This simplification allows us to illustrate how to construct portfolios using subjective probability of loss rather than the mathematical formulation of risk as standard deviation.

So, the subjective probability that the performance of this two-company portfolio will drop 20 percent can be written as follows:

$$p(\text{Portfolio} -20 \text{ percent}) = 0.25 \cdot 0.25 = 6.25 \text{ percent} \qquad (22.1)$$

The math works still the same as in Markowitz except that instead of deriving risk from the variance of past returns, the emphasis now is on assessments about potential problems with the underlying companies. By working diligently through the process of refutation and disconfirmation, and by selecting companies so as to reduce the chance of poor performance down to

25 percent, we have reduced to only 6.25 percent the chances of the portfolio dropping by 20 percent in the near term.

Now, let's see what happens when you add more companies, assuming that you have been careful in their selection and, again, that the expected performance of each is mostly independent from those of all the others. Assume also that the probabilities remain the same for all companies.

As evident from table 22.1, the chances of overall portfolio performance dropping 20 percent over the next year decrease rapidly from 25 percent in one company, to 6.25 percent in a two-company portfolio, to 0.1 percent in a five-company portfolio. Moreover, as in the chart, how sharply the probability of loss drops depends on the *initial* probability of loss that, in this case, we assumed to be 25 percent. This initial probability is the crux of the issue and is influenced to a great degree by the formal process of disconfirmation analysis.

Table 22.1

Portfolio Size & Risk

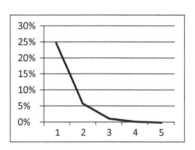

Companies	P(-20%)
1	25.00%
2	6.25%
3	1.56%
4	0.39%
5	0.10%

Clearly, diversification as discussed here substantially reduces the chances of loss. In order to reduce the probability of loss substantially, the example above shows that we need only a handful of well-selected companies with little or no correlation in their economic fundamentals.

The Downside of Diversification

The protection from diversification comes at a cost; just as it dampens the prospects of negative portfolio performance, so diversification also dampens the prospects of positive returns. To take the mirror image of the example above, if the probability of each company improving 20 percent in the next year was 25 percent, then the same logic would also rapidly reduce the potentially positive performance of the portfolio. Just five independent companies in such a portfolio would reduce to almost zero the probability that the portfolio as a whole would generate +20 percent return in the near term.

In effect, if probabilities were assumed to be symmetric, then portfolio diversification accomplishes not simply protection against the downside but it also dampens the variation on the up side. So, an inevitable cost comes along: diversification enables a defensive posture by limiting upside potential.

An additional problem faces those seeking to invest cautiously using the precepts of diversification as discussed above. In times of crises such as the recession following the technology-driven company market boom of the late 1990s, or the recession after the financial market meltdown in 2008, the economic performance of even relatively unrelated companies become highly correlated because they all become subject to the same systematic issues. Rising tides raise all boats and receding tides lower all.

So, when you need the protection during a systemic downturn, high correlations neutralize the protective effects of diversification. As correlations among companies increase because of systemic factors such as recessions or panics, the joint probabilities increase and the portfolio performance suffers. On the other hand, during economic recoveries or growth phases, whatever independence remains among the companies in the portfolio serves to undermine the overall portfolio performance and growth.

Ironically, diversification can be a problem for the hapless investor: it's not helpful when you most need it and it hinders performance when you don't.

Moreover, from a practical standpoint, constructing a perfectly diversified portfolio is not easy. The performance of companies is positively related in a vast majority of cases, and their performance is even more correlated when systemic events come along. Not only does diversification limit upside potential, in other words, effective diversification requires the kind of statistical analysis that diverts your attention away from the particulars of the companies in the portfolio. Statistical diversification as suggested by Markowitz makes it impossible to conduct a thorough company-centered disconfirmation analysis.

Putting Valuation in the Mix

Conventional wisdom has it that diversification ought not to be within one class of securities, such as domestic companies, but across asset classes and across geographies; well-diversified portfolios include a mix of companies, bonds, commodities, currencies, real estate, domestic, and international.

Yet, nowhere in the conventional theory is valuation of the component securities in the portfolio mentioned. Nor is much guidance given as to *how* the probabilities for future returns are to be determined. Instead, the usual tools for portfolio construction rely on measuring correlations and co-variances of past return and take on faith that the markets are efficient and everything is being correctly priced at all times.

The reliance solely on the past returns data to estimate expectations of future returns is problematic, however, especially in the absence of a clear understanding of how well a particular security is priced in relation to reasonable estimates of economic worth.

In practice, to know or even confidently estimate the probability with which the price of a particular company is going to go up or down is virtually impossible, let alone the magnitude of that change or the time horizon over which such a change would occur. Absent knowledge of such probabilities, the variance of a portfolio is indeterminate: in spite of vast quantities of data and the elegant math that may be used to compute statistics, the risk of a portfolio cannot be assessed with any precision.

For this reason, we have been discussing companies rather than stocks; our focus is on economic performance, with the assumption that the market pricing of the stock will eventually catch up to the performance of companies, sooner or later. We rely on subjective probabilities based on good judgments that come in part from a thorough use of the process of disconfirmation. The fundamental question that investors should persist in asking is simply this: is the price attractive in relation to reasonable estimates of value?

To this end, each company must be evaluated on its own merit, and included in the portfolio if deemed to be priced attractively in relation to reasonable estimates of its underlying worth. Considerations of the overall impact on the existing portfolio risk remain important but secondary to those of intrinsic worth or valuation of each company in the portfolio.

The focus stays on valuation and company selection is driven not by standard deviation of returns, not by what we think the prices may do in the near term, not by whether we like the products or the story or the earnings forecast. Personally important issues such as social responsibility, if relevant, may play a role in the decision process. But valuation is by far the single most important criteria in company selection and portfolio construction.

As such, to the extent that valuation drives investment portfolios, diversification by itself is fairly easily accomplished because it needs only a handful of lightly correlated but well-selected companies.

Having a concentrated portfolio has some downside, however, as in practice the economic performance of companies is correlated at least to some extent. Issues such as overall market sentiment or systematic prejudice against certain sectors can drive all the returns in the short run. As such, concentrated portfolios are usually quite volatile and novice investors can have trouble staying the course in the face of sudden and massive fluctuations. For those with rightfully earned confidence in their valuations, however, fluctuations in prices are not necessarily a bad thing, as they can provide opportunities for accumulating a position.

The confidence with which you construct a valuation-centered portfolio depends, therefore, on the confidence in the estimates of approximate value of each company in the portfolio. But, as we have discussed previously, not all companies can be valued with confidence: some don't have sufficient information to provide guidance about key assumptions, some have a checkered history that makes assumptions potentially unreliable, some are in in rapidly changing industries where the future can change abruptly and make the past less than meaningful, and some may be businesses whose fundamental dynamics of making money you may not be able to easily grasp.

In essence, a company must not be included in the portfolio just because the standard deviation of returns is low or the beta (β) is high. Whatever the past returns of a stock may be, the inability to value the corresponding company makes it speculative and raises the hazards for the investor.

Valuation and portfolio diversification are, in fact, two sides of the same coin. One without the other is incomplete.

As a corollary, the size of the diversified portfolio depends on the level of confidence you have in the valuation of each company in that portfolio. The greater the confidence, the lower is the number of companies you need in order to obtain the benefits of diversification.

As an illustration, consider again a portfolio of companies where the expected future performance of each is largely independent of those of all the others. Assume then that you have selected each company with care and the probability of 20 percent decline in the economic performance near-term has been reduced from 25 percent to, say, 10 percent.

That is, you now have sufficient margin of safety to feel that the chances of a significant decline is only about one in ten. In such a scenario, you will see a sharp reduction in the number of companies required for risk of the entire portfolio to decline by 20 percent. Just three companies reduce the risk to 0.10 percent and five independent companies provide almost full diversification.

Due diligence has its rewards. Effective refutation or disconfirmation analysis reduces the initial probability of loss and the result is a much tighter portfolio; that is, valuation well-done reduces the need to have a large portfolio of companies. In fact, for investors skilled in analyzing companies, the main benefit of diversification is in covering for irreducible uncertainties at the time the companies are purchased. Such irreducible uncertainties create a probability of loss that, when small, can be controlled by grouping a handful of well-researched companies.

Note that, based on the mathematical logic of grouping stocks, the math of diversification is relatively straightforward. The key to proper diversification is to assess realistically the probability of loss on individual commitments. Yet, in order to estimate such probabilities properly, you need confident insights about the underlying valuation, or economic worth, of each company in the portfolio. Once you have confident estimates of value at hand and provided you can make realistic assessments of the odds, as we will see in the next chapter, portfolios that are grounded in mathematical expectations can readily help produce strong upside with limited downside.

23

Core Holdings

———

Remember that traditional diversification dampens both the downside as well as the upside in future returns: with the good of protection during the down-swing comes the bad of hindrance on the upswing. That's the math.

In this chapter, let's discuss how this limitation of diversification can be mitigated with valuation-driven portfolios—which may be designed to limit the downside while still preserving much of the upside potential. We will see that portfolios constructed through company selection using the process of refutation and disconfirmation ought to be at the core of investment programs.

The disconfirmation approach seeks to ensure that the price paid is suffi-ciently below reasonable estimates of value and, therefore, that the chance of negative surprises is small. The valuation-driven process of selection, which also includes evaluation on other quantitative and qualitative company-specific criteria, truncates the distribution of future returns such that the losses are limited while the upside is not.

So, let's again work with the ongoing example. Suppose that company selection through the process of disconfirmation has reduced the probability of 20 percent drop in the valuation of each company from 25 percent to 10 percent; yet, the probability of 20 percent appreciation for each of those companies remains at 50 percent as in the original example. Assume, further-more, that the remaining 40 percent probability is for zero return for each company, and that the economic performance of the companies is more or less independent of that of the others. That is, each company so selected has a greater possibility of gain than the possibility of loss—you have found compa-nies that have asymmetric payoffs strongly in your favor.

As is evident from the table 23.1, if you had just three companies in the final portfolio, the probability of −20 percent portfolio performance is only 0.1 percent (1 in 1,000) whereas the upside chance of +20 percent portfolio return would still be 12.5 percent (1 in 8). That is, valuation-driven portfolios, where you purchase each company after thorough disconfirmation analysis, create a favorable asymmetry of future potential returns. Moreover, comprising only a handful of unrelated companies, they are relatively easy to monitor and can be easily followed over time.

Table 23.1a		Table 23.1b	
Value Portfolio with Truncated Distribution			
10% Chance of -20% Return		50% Chance of +20% Return	
# Stocks	P(-20%)	# Stocks	P(+20%)
1	10.00%	1	50.00%
2	1.00%	2	25.00%
3	0.10%	3	12.50%
4	0.01%	4	6.25%
5	0.00%	5	0.10%

In building investment portfolios, disconfirmation analysis is the key and diversification plays an important but secondary role.

Portfolio Theory and Investor Behavior

For investors not well-versed in statistical analysis, applying modern portfolio theory is difficult. Computing standard deviations, variances and co-variances requires a good deal of historical data and, with thousands of companies to sort through, the data crunching can easily get out of hand.

Furthermore, the theory is not much help with finer issues such as size of the portfolio and the historical time period over which analysis needs to be done; nor is there any way to know if the past data are meaningful for future performance or what the time horizon ought to be for measuring performance. That is, not only is the modern portfolio theory difficult to enact, grave doubts also persist about the very usefulness of the kind of statistical analysis it requires.

Modern portfolio theory may actually encourage investors to engage in self-defeating behaviors. By defining risk mathematically as standard deviation of returns and insisting that markets are efficient, the theory suggests that investors ignore thorough company analysis. Instead, the theory emphasizes using past data to find lightly-correlated companies, with little or no consideration to valuation or business risk. Since the objective of the theory is to minimize statistical risk for a given level of return, it encourages investors to simply purchase broadly diversified baskets of companies. That is, instead of encouraging diligence and valuation, the theory leads investors into broad (statistical) diversification and indexes.

Indexes exacerbate the problem, however. Unable to keep track of what companies comprise the index, investors no longer pay attention to the business fundamentals of the companies that make up the index. Indexing enables diversification, but provides no great insights into the economic worth of component companies. Instead, it shifts focus back to broad diversification in the hopes of spreading the odds and reducing statistical risk. Almost by definition, therefore, indexing inherits all the shortcomings of diversification as discussed previously. It is useful when you don't need it and not much good when you do.

As such, modern portfolio theory ignores the true value-creating potential of individual companies and companies. For those skeptical about indexing and wanting to make their own robust portfolio, the theory has no good advice. As a result, not quite knowing what to do, many investors end up trading excessively in hopes of quick gains and chasing performance that remains elusive for the most part.

Often driven to action by hype and hope of a quick gain, and with no credible theory as a guide, the average investor usually buys more on a whim than after thorough analysis, buys and sells too often to have the time to understand the fundamental drivers of value creation, and fails to make reliable estimates of intrinsic economic worth.

Skeptical of modern portfolio theory, moreover, investors ignore its most valuable insight that returns and hazards of investing should be portfolio level concerns. So, in spite of the fact that the benefits of group-level thinking have been strongly suggested by investment theory for almost six decades, investors appear to pay little or no heed to the benefits of systematic grouping as in a well-constructed portfolio.

Core Portfolios

A sensible way to think about investing is in terms of core portfolios comprising between five and ten companies. As we have seen, we can obtain the benefits of diversification through valuation-based selection of only a handful of unrelated companies. The limited number of companies in the core portfolios allows easy monitoring and in-depth understanding that together facilitate good investment decisions.

Each of the five or ten companies in a core portfolio must be bought at a discount to reasonable estimates of value, and each should be vetted through the process of disconfirmation. The chief emphasis in such a portfolio is on thorough and defensive valuation, and focus on the fundamental strength of operations that enable good economic performance to be delivered over the foreseeable future.

With such efforts to limit the downside of each company in the portfolio, selections are also spread wisely across different sectors. That is, the core portfolio is strengthened because the focus is on limiting the probability of loss for each selected company.

Unlike the modern portfolio theory that emphasizes portfolio-level risk to the virtual neglect of the many uncertainties that may surround each company, the emphasis is on minimizing the *initial* probability of loss for each company. As discussed previously, this initial probability is critical, as it directly influences the *rate of decline* in the overall probability of loss at the level of the full portfolio.

Secondary to the issue of valuation, and to the extent possible, the few companies in the core portfolio are in different sectors of the economy and, where possible, in different parts of the world. As such, our approach seeks as much independence as practically possible between the small number of companies in the group, such that the future economic performance of one is not strongly linked to the future performance of the others.

Little is to be gained from computing variance and co-variance among the past returns. No complicated math is necessary.

If it turns out that valuations are particularly attractive for several companies in one sector, then the concern over diversification need not get in the way of sensible investment decisions. Investors can rarely go wrong buying great companies at good prices.

Once investing is defined as the problem of making valuation-driven core portfolios, and investor behavior is aligned to this way of thinking, the approach to participating in the financial markets should change as well.

No longer do we need to search for variances and co-variances across the entire spectrum of companies listed on the various company exchanges. No longer must we constantly adjust the portfolio to keep up with the changing co-variances. No longer do we need to trade excessively, or buy and sell companies that we do not understand beyond the short-term statistical characteristics of their past prices and returns. No longer must we broadly diversify the portfolio, filling it with companies based simply on their co-variances but with no understanding of the companies. No longer, in short, do we need to fight noise with more noise.

What core portfolios do is economize on the most important resources that investors have: time and attention. Instead of being overwhelmed by the entire list of 6,000 companies on the U.S. company exchanges and nearly 45,000 worldwide, you need to simply locate a handful of companies that, bought at attractive prices, promise to give both downside protection and a steady upside over the medium-to-long term.

When bought at attractive prices and in sufficient quantities to make meaningful impact on portfolio performance, such companies also obviate the need for constant monitoring of the media; instead, through selective and periodic reading of the mandatory company filings, investor focus is maintained on the fundamental attributes that drive the ability of the company to create economic worth and to deliver steady performance.

Such focus on building and maintaining core portfolios also gives investors a simple way to deal with abundance of noise in the markets: simply ignore the hype and the cacophony. Since your objective is to locate just a few companies with good valuations and durability, most listed companies can simply be ignored; or, in our way of thinking, easily refuted. In fact, the 6,000 or so companies listed on NYSE and NASDAQ can be fairly quickly pared down to just a few hundred. Preliminary refutation can bring the list down to a much lower number, say, about fifty or so. From this much shorter list, your task is to locate about ten or so companies that meet certain criteria, build a portfolio from them and then monitor them with the full knowledge of what makes them tick.

Once such a core portfolio is constructed, all other investment opportunities that come along are then evaluated in light of the improvements they might be able to make to the existing group of companies. When you have additional funds to invest, the most productive use of those funds is likely to be investment in companies already in the core portfolio; or in another company with an enticing valuation and in a sector not yet adequately represented. More likely than not, the addition to the core portfolio would come from an intermediate list of fifty or so companies derived from the preliminary efforts to refute and disconfirm.

Depending on your confidence in the quality of valuation and the discount of price from it, the core portfolio can form anywhere between 50 and 80 percent of the total dollar amounts allocated to the company market. The remainder could be set aside for experimentation and opportunistic investments that may come about from periodic panic about the prospects of a sound company or generally from market-wide disenchantment with particular sectors or companies.

The proportion of the portfolio that each company represents in the portfolio may again be informed by the extent of undervaluation given the strength of the underlying business. So, a single company could accounts for up to 20 percent of the core portfolio.

Core portfolios, in essence, reduce the noise in which you are always engulfed and, as such, they improve the overall quality of the investment experience. With greater knowledge of the few companies in the portfolio comes the confidence in the ability to monitor them and, therefore, less anxiety about sudden changes in their fortunes. As such, core portfolios lower the incentive to trade and to chase performance, both of which are about as good for you as are drugs to an addict. Both trading and short-term performance-chasing not only increase transactions costs that inevitably mount up, they also lead to lost opportunities by dissipating your energies and trapping capital in non-productive activities, leaving little or nothing to invest when genuine opportunities come along.

In a way, your core portfolio is to the defensive pocket as you are to a good quarterback. It relieves pressure from the outside and gives you time to find attractive opportunities. The difference is that a well-constructed core portfolio almost never collapses as defensive pockets are prone to do in the face of aggressive opponents; you have all the time that may be necessary to locate and evaluate additional investment candidates that would further strengthen the investment returns.

Certainly, investors need to be open to the possibility that the performance of any one or more companies in the core portfolio may deteriorate over time. Such deterioration is often a long time in the making and is usually visible through periodic, perhaps annual, disconfirmation analysis of companies that may be undergoing discontinuous change. With skill and diligence, in other words, it is generally possible for investors to see when a particular company begins to go in the wrong direction and take corrective measures, such as redefining the portfolio by eliminating or replacing the corrupted company.

In essence, carefully constructing a core portfolio is the common sense answer to the obfuscating math of the modern portfolio theory. It brings investing back to business analysis and valuation of individual companies. Yet, recognizing the benefits of grouping, as articulated by Markowitz about sixty years ago, core portfolios also integrate business analysis with the common sense notion to spread the bets but, first and foremost, to keep the common sense focus on making good bets.

24

Growth

————

Adopting a cautious orientation to build a core portfolio of just a few carefully-selected companies raises the obvious questions: What about growth? Would not the strong focus on defensive valuation and caution remove from consideration those growth companies that have the potential to provide extraordinary returns?

Yes and No. Operationalizing and applying the principle of negation, as we have done, encourages investors to be cautious and accept the opportunity cost of possibly missing out on fast growing companies. That is, in trying to avoid Type I error of investing in what could be a poor investment, cautious investors end up with a good number of Type II errors of not investing in what could be a good investment. Growth companies highlight this dilemma.

As discussed in chapter 9, this trade-off between the two types of errors is inevitable. As such, when seeking growth, we must make choices about how far outside our zone of defense we are willing to go.

The Hazards of Growth Investing

In our way of thinking, investors have good reasons to avoid fast-growing companies. Sure enough, growth companies usually trade at high valuations that can be easily refuted using criteria such as the future growth rate implied in prevailing prices. Expectations about aggressive future growth are often already built into the price at which such companies trade, with implied growth rates much in excess of historical growth rates; sometimes growth companies are priced high in spite of not having much of an operating history. Such stocks usually trade based not on stability of the historical track record but on rosy expectations about future prospects. A few years or even a few months of fast growth is extrapolated well into the distant future to justify lofty prices.

Similarly, earnings yields are usually very low and dividends mostly non-existent for such companies, as they typically do not generate enough free cash to justify shareholder-friendly actions. As they pursue an expanding set of opportunities, growth companies also require a great deal of capital for investment into a growing base of assets; they get such needed capital either by taking on debt or by issuing more equity that dilutes existing shareholders.

Rapidly rising prices makes growth companies highly visible and fodder for endless speculation in the media, thereby providing them the marketing exposure that other stocks don't usually get. The hype around such names then creates demand and attracts a mix of traders, gamblers, speculators, and the masses of retail investors, all afraid of missing out on what may seem like a spectacular opportunity. It is easy for growth stocks to become speculative, in other words, as rapidly rising prices attract attention and create their own demand.

Defensive valuation plays only a small role, moreover, or none at all in the pricing of high-flying growth stocks. The high prices at which they usually trade cannot be justified using any combination of reasonable assumptions in the discount model. Instead, the lack of grounding in realistic economic prospects makes growth stocks particularly suitable for speculating. Greed and unfettered optimism drive unrealistic expectations about the future and play a dominant role in how such stocks are priced.

Mixed in with the speculative stocks, however, are the stocks of genuine growth companies with sound business models and competent leadership; but it is usually quite difficult to clearly distinguish one from the other. There is little by way of short cuts that can help sort true growth stocks from the ones that only appear to be so. A great deal of uncertainty often surrounds the investment potential of fast-growing companies, and it is seldom obvious whether they will continue on their rapid growth trajectory or come to a screeching halt and plunge.

All this makes growth stocks tantalizing and a source of much excitement to many. Untethered to economic value as they might be, growth stocks can continue rising to new heights, only to come crashing down when the spell breaks. Their performance depends almost entirely on collective imaginings about the future and expectations that everybody may have about what everybody else would do in the near term; whether the herd would recommit to the stock with new vigor or stampede toward the exits.

It is little surprise, then, that growth stocks tend to attract adrenaline-seeking traders and momentum investors who buy to gain from the rising prices but also are quick to sell when the prices seem to be turning and going the other way. As such, not only do growth stocks tend to become disconnected from any underlying economic reality of the companies in question, they usually also are much more volatile than other stocks.

This kind of excitement is often too much for cautious investors to bear. They are, for the most part, neither interested in nor psychologically equipped to ride the emotional roller coaster that speculators may find appealing. As a general rule, they are disinclined to allow the performance of their core portfolio to depend on the impossible task of correctly anticipating when the herd will turn one way or the other. The constant fear of imminent price collapse more than negates any joy that may be derived from another temporary ascent to a new high.

There are many reasons why high-flying stocks come crashing down. If the expected rapid growth does not materialize or the company falters for any of the many reasons, the stock price is prone to plummet. General economic slowdown, darkening of the social mood, slowdown in the demand for the company's products, missteps by the management, or any number of other factors internal or external to the firm can easily create investor disenchantment and, as a result, mass exodus from the stock.

In spite of the many genuine growth companies that periodically come on the scene, a more common occurrence is a sudden and sharp drop in the prices of erstwhile high flyers.

Instead of providing spectacular returns, ill-chosen growth stocks can quite easily undermine or even negate the slower but steadier gains that truly valuation-driven core portfolios are usually designed to deliver.

So, growth stocks pose a dilemma for cautious investors. They offer the chance to make outsized profits but at potentially significant hazards to the otherwise well-constructed core portfolios. How, then, can you build growth in your investment program?

Solving the Growth Puzzle

Discussed below are two broad ways of inserting growth in a defense-oriented core portfolio. The first approach, *safe growth*, continues to emphasize caution and defense but with an openness to opportunities that arise periodically from temporary mispricing in the markets. Safe growth can be attained by staying true to the disconfirmation approach and looking for specific opportunities where you expect mispricing of stocks to be corrected because of the fundamental soundness of the company. Buying undervalued growth companies and buying good companies during market panics can both add a growth boost to defensive portfolios.

The second approach, *risky growth*, relaxes the quantitative refutation criteria somewhat and relies instead on deep qualitative analysis to understand the motivation and ability of managers to create and capture business opportunities. Cautious investors can pursue risky growth from a defensive perch either by investigating turnaround of good companies that previously got in trouble or by scrutinizing select companies that are leaders in emerging new sectors of the economy.

Both safe and risky approaches to growth—and two approaches within each—are discussed below.

Safe Growth: Value Mispricing

Given the danger that what seems to be a growth stock may actually be a highly speculative bet, a cautious attitude remains indispensable for growth investing.

Yet, there is the natural way to insert growth in the portfolio. Value, it turns out, has growth built into it for the simple reason that purchasing at a price sufficiently below robust estimates of intrinsic value brings with it a potential upside.

So, consider a stock that trades for $20 per share when conservative estimates suggest an intrinsic valuation of $50 and the usual tests are unable to refute it on the various criteria. Provided our analysis is correct, the price will rise over time as the market weighs the differential and corrects the mispricing. This way of obtaining growth is perhaps the closest to the spirit of bargain-hunting that undergirds the traditional emphasis on safety.

Bargain hunting provides only temporary growth, however, as the catching up of price to value removes the opportunity for further gain; price can, in fact, overshoot valuation and, in the process, makes the investment vulnerable to future losses.

As such, mispriced companies that have a historical track record of steady growth provide the next obvious upside for the portfolio. When mispriced by the market because of a temporary setback in delivering expected performance, these companies provide good opportunities for growth because the market correction would then catch the price up to a rising intrinsic economic worth.

Such would be the case, for instance, for a stock trading for $20 when conservative valuation puts it at $50 and the historical growth trend shows intrinsic valuation growing at an annual rate of, say, 12 percent. The intrinsic valuation of such a company can grow to about $100 in six years and provides, therefore, greater growth potential than that visible at the time of initial screen. The undercurrents of business growth provide continuing opportunities for steadily rising prices even after the initial mispricing has been corrected.

Clearly, the risk in doing the above is that the historical growth rates may not materialize, that the mispricing is an indication of a fundamental structural change and, therefore, a precursor to a diminishing future.

For defensively oriented growth investors who have evaluated the company using the process of disconfirmation, such companies with decline on the horizon are likely to have been already filtered out. A cautious evaluation would limit consideration to only those companies where the fundamentals of good value are still in place. Mispricing of such steadily growing companies can provide substantial opportunities for growth in the core portfolios.

Safe Growth: Panic Mispricing

Closely related to the above is purchase of healthy and steadily growing companies during a market-wide panic. Virtually every broad sell-off creates opportunities to investigate a short-list of companies with strong track record, as their prices fall for reasons that are not specific to their own operations or competitiveness.

Usually, the prices of good companies drop because of general disenchantment with the stock market or with a particular sector, and the key rationale for the selling is often that the prices are on their way down. This expectation of prices dropping puts a selling pressure on the stock, which then triggers additional selling as traders and speculators try to avoid short-term loss and capitalize on the momentum of falling prices.

Remember that intrinsic valuation of a company is driven by its long-term prospects and, specifically, by the expected permanence and growth of future cash flows. As such, strong companies have their valuation tied to deeply entrenched market positions, sound financial condition, and competent leadership, all of which together reflect the ability to continue generating healthy cash flows.

To the extent that the economic fundamentals of a company remain strong and in place, its intrinsic valuation should remain stable even though stock prices rise or fall in response to emotions of the moment or collective misperceptions in the marketplace.

Stock market dynamics may create opportunities, in other words, to invest in sound companies at attractive prices. The key to being able to do so is the ability to see that in spite of widespread fear and broad sell-off, the fundamentals of the company are still in place. A defensive orientation and the disconfirmation approach remain indispensable, therefore, in retaining the focus on the economic fundamentals and in selectively picking out companies that can add growth into a portfolio.

Risky Growth: Turnaround and Transformation

While mispricing of fundamentally sound companies can provide growth opportunities for your portfolio, sometimes good companies do get in trouble and their prices fall to reflect worsening competitive position. For the most part, you should avoid such companies because their valuations shrink to indicate dimming prospects.

Yet, depending on the reasons for their past troubles and depending on the quality of the managers leading the turnaround or transformation, some such companies offer good opportunities for adding growth to a core portfolio. When successful, transformation reinvigorates companies and their renewed growth shows up in fast-rising intrinsic economic worth.

Yet, not all companies are good candidates for successful turnaround and very few would be worth the trouble. For most companies in trouble, there are considerable risks that the downward slide of the business cannot be reversed. Consider Blockbuster Video, for instance, or any number of other companies, such as American Italian Pasta Company.

Once strong and dominant, these companies eventually succumbed to external events that undermined their competitive positions. Unable to respond quickly and adequately, these companies went under within a few years of the start of their troubles, and took down with them many investors who hung on too long in the hope that the turnaround would eventually come. It never did. The circumstances were overwhelming and managers were simply not up to it.

It is important for you to be highly selective, therefore, and to understand very specifically the basis on which the return to previous heights can be accomplished. Unless such reasons are credible, it is best to stay away from companies that are in industries undergoing secular decline or those that have a low or declining average return on invested capital.

In most cases, the basis for a successful turnaround is the achievable potential for high margins so that the profits can be plowed back to fund reinvestment in the business. Companies with strong brands or market position are, therefore, often good candidates for a turnaround.

Because of the complexity of turning around or transforming a company in trouble, defensively oriented investors ought to limit their search to companies that are deeply entrenched in stable or growing markets and have a strong competitive position even if that position has been weakened for a time. The fundamentals to look for in turnaround situations are the same as those in all core investments.

Turnarounds usually accompany a change in the top management and a sharply articulated commitment to reinvigorate the core businesses of the company. Investors need to closely monitor what the managers say, therefore, and follow their progress over at least a year and more so as to be able to clearly see if they agree with the game plan and to ensure that their renewal efforts are indeed beginning to get traction. For, large companies have complex operating structures and byzantine politics; successfully reinvigorating the business is usually a multi-year process and takes considerable leadership skills. The people recruited to lead such efforts are critically important.

Naturally, monitoring and investing in turnaround situations requires considerable analytical and conceptual skills. Quantitative skills are less helpful in such cases, as the historical record is not a good indicator of things to come. More helpful are skills at qualitative analysis, the ability to evaluate the coherence of the turnaround plan and an assessment of the leadership who is to deliver on it. Given that such analysis is difficult to do well, you should be realistic about your own motivations and skills to engage with this type of investing.

When done well, however, turnaround analysis can provide rare opportunities for strong long-term growth in core portfolios. Strong companies with decades of operating history have undergone transformations that lifted them from years of anemic performance to sustained periods of strong growth.

Companies such as General Electric (Jack Welch), Coca-Cola (Roberto Goizueta), International Business Machines (Louis Gerstner), and Apple (Steve Jobs) are some of the largest names that went through a significant positive change. In each case, the company had stagnated for a period of years, because of which a change in management started a process of rebuilding that re-installed them as highly profitable leaders in their industries. Clearly, rare though they are, such opportunities can provide a significant boost if you have the skills and patience to methodically uncover and follow companies undergoing a renewal.

As of this writing in May 2012, one large company in the throes of turnaround is Hewlett Packard. After a series of failed leaders and internal scandals that undermined its competitive position and depressed the market valuation, the company hired a high-profile executive (Margaret Whitman) in the hopes that she would restore the organization to strong competitiveness. If other successful turnarounds are any guide, this is the beginning of a multi-year process; interested investors with the right skills should follow the company to keep an eye on signs of improvement. Given the complexity of the endeavor, the results can go either way.

Risky Growth: Emerging Leaders

Perhaps the most exciting and the most challenging way to seek growth is through new companies in emerging niches or in entirely new industries. When most people think about growth investing, they have in mind the fast-growing small companies of yesteryear that have come to dominate the economic landscape today. In fact, all dominant companies in our midst now once were very small. Companies such as Wal-Mart, Home Depot and many others were once fast-growing small companies.

Wal-Mart, for instance, had revenues of about $44.3 million in 1970, its first year as a publicly traded company. It grew exceedingly fast over the next several years and reported revenues in excess of $1.2 billion by 1979 fiscal year end. During the same period, the market value of the company's equity increased more than 12-fold from $44.8 million to just under $540 million.

Similarly, Home Depot reported revenues of $22.3 million in 1980, its first year as a public company. By the end of fiscal 1990, revenues had grown to $3.8 billion and the market value of common equity had climbed to $5.1 billion. The examples are numerous, with such stalwarts today as Microsoft, Intel, and many others that continue to grow albeit at a much slower pace.

These examples tell only one side of the story, however. They ignore the fact that for every small company that later became a giant, many others fell by the wayside. The successes of a few are matched by an equal or greater number of companies that did not deliver on the promise of growth that was evident in the pace of the first few years.

Perhaps the greatest mistake people make when seeking growth is *not* paying attention to the economics and become hopeful instead because the stock price of a company has been on a tear. There were many instances of this during the heyday of the late 1990s, when the lay public got sucked into the hype of the companies that had anything to do with the Internet.

One example of *faux*-growth is e.Digital, a Canadian producer of the earliest portable digital voice recording devices. The company was founded in 1988 as 340520 B.C. Ltd, changed its name twice before being listed in 1993 and then traded between $2 and $4 per share for many years. Its share price then began a rapid decline down to about 6 cents in early 1999, at which time the shareholders approved the name change to e.Digital. Then, perhaps caught in the hype of the era, the share price of the company made its rapid ascent, rising to almost $16 per share in early 2000 and then, on January 24, to an intraday high of $24.50 per share—only to plummet back to under a dollar by late 2001. As of the May 2012, the company was trading at about 4 cents a share.

All through its rise and fall, e.Digital never reported any operating profits. Yet, investors stampeded to purchase its shares when the prices started rising fast, only to see their investment destroyed when the spell broke. There were many companies like e.Digital during the Internet bubble, before and after. The fact that such companies don't have a sustainable business does not seem to matter for those chasing fast-rising stock prices. Such investments are almost always later regretted.

Yet, the real problem for defensive investors arises not from chasing fast-rising stocks with no sustainable business model. A more common problem is misjudging and paying too much for genuine growth.

Consider Cisco Systems, for instance. The company became public in 1989 with annual revenues of $28 million and then began its rapid rise, growing revenues to $12 billion in 1999. The rapid growth attracted many investors and the stock price followed the revenue growth. In 2000, the revenues were $18 billion and the market value shot up to $467 billion, an incredible 25 times the revenue for that year.

Clearly, Cisco was a genuine growth company, but investors were paying more than a hefty premium to own its shares. Within two years, the Internet bubble had collapsed and the market value of the company's common equity had dropped sharply.

Cisco was not the only company to have taken growth investors on an unfortunate ride. During the same period, those investing in other dominant companies, such as Wal-Mart, Home Depot, Microsoft, and Intel, experienced a similar fate. They paid too much for good companies. Interestingly, as of May 2012, the market value of equity for Cisco was about $100 billion, even though the sales had grown to over $43 billion. That is, the company was selling for about 2.3 times its annual revenues.

So, yes, investors *can* get in trouble even when the companies in which they invest are excellent operators and dominant in their respective spheres of activity. Paying too much in the hopes of growing the portfolio can actually backfire when the high prices come tumbling down, destroying the painstaking gains made elsewhere.

Investing in fast-growing companies is, therefore, fraught with risk. The greater the reach, the higher the price premium over reasonable estimates of intrinsic worth, the greater are the hazards.

For every investor who is able to catch a rising stock and exit before the collapse, there are many others who get in at the top or perhaps just before and then stay too long, only to see their investments plummet or in some cases disappear altogether. That is a natural, even expected consequence of carelessly pursuing risky growth. Both turnaround situations and fast-growing companies bring with them hopes of outsized gains, yet only a few deliver.

The question remains, therefore, whether we can sort productive growth opportunities, such as Home Depot and Wal-Mart in their early years, from unproductive growth opportunities, such as the same two companies in the late 1990s, or from the likes of Enron. The short answer is that a well-calibrated skepticism can be helpful. Yet, this is a significant enough issue to require a treatise of its own and I will develop on the question of growth perhaps in another volume.

Suffice it to say that growth investing relies to a much greater extent on qualitative analysis, on judgments about the sources of value creation and the quality of the leadership in charge of executing a well-articulated strategy. Turnarounds and fast growth demand highly competent management, and the leadership of such companies need especially careful evaluation.

Along with strategy and leadership, moreover, valuation remains important for successfully investing in growth companies. Investors routinely get in trouble when they pay too much for strong and well-managed companies, optimistic and hopeful that a growing company will continue its breakneck pace indefinitely. Sure, depending on the situation, growth opportunities may justify relaxing assumptions about risk and growth in the discount flow model. But those assumptions still need to be reasonable given that real companies in a real world can only do so much. Unwisely chosen growth companies can create illusions of profits but are liable to produce significant losses. As such, growth investing creates significant challenges for investors who are inclined to be cautious by temperament.

Yet, experienced and cautious investors can accomplish growth by applying the portfolio logic of mathematical expectations to a small group of well-chosen companies, each selected using refutation analysis and each unable to be disconfirmed despite serious attempts to do so. By inserting companies with marginally higher probability of loss but with much higher potential for the upside, investors can improve significantly the long-term expected returns from their stock portfolios.

For instance, if you have an equal-weighted portfolio of five companies as in table 23.1, where each company has 10 percent probability of 20 percent loss, 40 percent probability of zero return, and 50 percent probability of +20 percent gain, the mathematical expectation for the portfolio as a whole is 40 percent. Assume for the time being that the economic performance of the companies is largely independent from those of the others in the portfolios.

Suppose that you replace one of the five companies with another, whose asymmetric returns are as follows: a higher, 30 percent, probability of 20 percent loss, 40 percent probability of no return, and 50 percent probability of much higher, +100 percent gain. In such a scenario, the mathematical expectation for returns to the portfolio as a whole rises almost two times to 76 percent. That is, investors who may have the ability to find growth companies with asymmetric returns as in the second case above can increase substantially the profit potential from their portfolios with only a marginally more increase in the probability of loss.

Identifying genuine growth opportunities can be very profitable for investors, in other words—provided, of course, they use disconfirmation analysis and portfolio logic to turn the mathematical odds strongly in their favor. In this context, investors can boost their portfolios quite significantly by identifying companies that have strong potential to continue to grow consistently and over time. Such companies obviate the need to try to catch a rising star and then following up with the virtually impossible task of correctly timing the exit.

25

The Buffett Portfolio

———

While there are many examples of core portfolios, perhaps one way to illustrate the concept is through the stock portfolio of Berkshire Hathaway—built and managed by Warren Buffett. The company's stock portfolio is presented in the annual letters to shareholders going back to 1977; the letters were obtained from the company website.

Note one thing about the data on which the following analysis is based. Ideally, we would use the data provided in the quarterly 13F-HR filings that investment companies are required to submit to the Securities and Exchange Commission (SEC). In that filing, the number of shares and market value of each stock in the portfolio is disclosed as of the end of each reporting period. Lining up these data, we can see the positions and changes from quarter to quarter and see the portfolio evolve over time. Unfortunately, these filings are available only for about ten or so years.

In the case of Berkshire Hathaway, Buffett has been unusually candid in his well-read annual letter to shareholders; he discloses not only the number of shares and market value of each significant investment as of the end of each fiscal year but, very generously, also his cost basis. He does not report the minor positions, however, so it is only possible to see how big his significant positions were relative to the full stock portfolio.

It should be kept in mind that the stock portfolio analyzed here is only one of the many ways in which Buffett puts Berkshire Hathaway's capital to work. Not covered in this analysis are other investment operations, such as in convertibles, bonds, and private company transactions. I limit this brief analysis, therefore, to the stock portfolio.

It is evident that for quite some time Berkshire Hathaway has been active in the market for corporate control, frequently buying whole companies both private and public. As Buffett has stated publicly, however, his approach to investment analysis remains about the same whether a company is private or public. Private companies are usually bought whole, whereas public companies are bought through acquisition of a portion of the outstanding common shares and, occasionally, convertible preferred shares or bonds. Sometimes, as in the case of Burlington Northern/Santa Fe and Lubrizol, Berkshire Hathaway has increased its initial minority equity stake to buy up the whole company.

The analysis here is only of the stock portfolio that is comprised almost entirely of common shares of publicly traded companies, and as reported in Buffett's letters to shareholders.

Recent Moves

In a September 13F filing made public in November of 2011, Berkshire disclosed that it had purchased just over 57 million shares of International Business Machines (IBM) at a total commitment of just over $10 billion. As such, IBM was one of thirty-three stocks at the time and it accounted for about 17 percent of the $59 billion stock portfolio. The average position at the end of the quarter was about $1.8 billion per stock.

Let us see table 25.1 for the context in which Buffett made the investment in IBM. As of the end of the quarter in June 2011, Berkshire Hathaway had a $52 billion stock portfolio with twenty-seven companies; yet, as shown in the table, just five companies accounted for nearly 76 percent or almost $40 billion of the total; the top ten companies comprised about 95 percent or nearly $50 billion of the total stock portfolio.

In essence, the portfolio was highly concentrated in the top five and ten companies. Portfolio performance was, therefore, dependent on the performance of the largest investments. Clearly, care had to be taken to limit the downside for these large positions, as errors in judgment when selecting these companies would be quite costly. The key to building such a concentrated portfolio, it can be assumed, is to avoid the errors by sparing no effort in due diligence.

Note also that the top ten companies appeared to be judiciously spread across different industries. While they were all American companies, they were in different sectors of the economy, ranging from non-alcoholic beverages to credit rating services.

Table 25.1

Company	Ticker	% Portfolio June '11	Industry
Coca Cola	KO	25.77%	Non-Alcoholic Beverages
Wells Fargo	WFC	18.93%	Money Center Bank
American Express	AXP	15.01%	Credit & Travel Services
Proctor & Gamble	PG	9.35%	Personal Products
Kraft Foods	KFT	6.71%	Packaged Foods
Johnson & Johnson	JNJ	5.16%	Health Care
ConocoPhillips	COP	4.19%	Integrated Oil
Wal-Mart Stores	WMT	3.97%	Discount Retail
US Bancorp	USB	3.37%	Regional Bank
Moody's	MCO	2.09%	Credit Ratings & Services
Top 10 as % Total Portfolio		94.56%	
Top 5 as % Total Portfolio		75.78%	
Total Portfolio $ Billion		$52.22	

As shown in table 25.2, the top four companies had been in the stock portfolio for several years, ranging from twenty years for Gillette/Proctor & Gamble to twenty-three years for Coca-Cola. The average holding period for the top ten companies was just under twelve years. There was very little turnover at the top of the portfolio.

Notably, the average holding period for the top four companies in Berkshire Hathaway's portfolio was more than twenty years: Coca-Cola (twenty-three years), Wells Fargo (twenty-one years), American Express (seventeen years), and Proctor & Gamble (twenty years). Note that Proctor & Gamble came into the portfolio after it acquired Gillette in 2005. Gillette, in turn, was in the common stock portfolio since 1991, at which time Berkshire Hathaway had been forced to convert its $600 million preferred share holdings to common shares. The preferred shares were reported to have been purchased in 1989.

Table 25.2

| Company | Ticker | Holding Period | | Initial Outlay | |
		Since	Years	$ Million	% Port*
Coca Cola	KO	1988	23	592	20%
Wells Fargo	WFC	1990	21	289	5%
American Express	AXP	1994	17	724	6%
Gillette/Proctor & Gamble	PG	1991	20	600	15%

* As Percent of Stock Portfolio in the year of initial outlay

It is clear, therefore, that the top stocks had been part of Berkshire's core portfolio for quite some time. The initial outlay in each of the four largest holdings was significant as well (see table 25.2). When Berkshire bought Coca-Cola in 1988, for instance, it committed $592 million for over 14 million shares. This represented about 20 percent of the $3 billion stock portfolio at the time. Similarly, when Berkshire converted its Gillette preferred share holdings into common share in 1991, its $600 million commitment represented 6.67 percent of the $9 billion stock portfolio.

The initial outlay in Wells Fargo (1991) was $289 million, or over 5 percent of the portfolio at the time. American Express began showing up in top ten in 1994, with the initial outlay of $723 million or about 5 percent of the stock portfolio at that time. Smaller investments than those for Coca-Cola and Gillette, both these initial outlays were also significant commitments of resources. All these investments must have required considerable due diligence, as any errors could undermine the entire portfolio operation.

It was in this historical context that Berkshire Hathaway made the large investment in IBM, making it the second largest holding in the updated stock portfolio. Clearly, IBM was a big bet.

Yet, in spite of the big bet on IBM, Berkshire's stock portfolio remained highly concentrated as before: the top five companies accounted for over 74 percent and the top ten companies accounted for 93 percent of the portfolio. The previously largest holdings in Coca-Cola, Wells Fargo, American Express, and Proctor & Gamble all maintained a strong presence in the new portfolio. Moreover, as a software and services company, IBM was a type of business not previously well-represented in the portfolio and, as such, it helped Berkshire spread its bets some more.

Berkshire appears to accomplish diversification intuitively and most likely without consideration of standard deviations and variances of the past returns. From the public comments made by Buffett, it seems that valuation and the quality of the business are usually the main drivers of the stock portfolio and any significant changes to it.[95]

Evaluating IBM

Given Berkshire Hathaway's significant commitment to IBM, let's evaluate the company by trying to refute the thesis that it was an attractive investment opportunity at the price that Buffett paid for it. See table 25.3 for the top ten companies in the Berkshire stock portfolio at the time IBM was purchased.

In his letter to shareholders for the year, Warren Buffett reported that Berkshire Hathaway owned 63,905,931 shares of IBM at the cost basis of $10.586 billion, or at the cost of approximately $170 per share.

IBM reported diluted earnings of $12.06 per share for the year ending December 2010 and the three-year average earnings were $10.32 per share. As such, the earnings yields for one and three years were 7.09 percent (EY1) and 6.07 percent (EY3), respectively.

Table 25.3

Company	Ticker	% Portfolio Sept '11	% Portfolio June '11
Coca Cola	KO	22.88%	25.77%
Intn'l Business Machines	**IBM**	**16.98%**	*
Wells Fargo	WFC	14.76%	18.93%
American Express	AXP	11.53%	15.01%
Proctor & Gamble	PG	8.21%	9.35%
Kraft Foods	KFT	5.10%	6.71%
Johnson & Johnson	JNJ	4.04%	5.16%
ConocoPhillips..	WMT	3.43%	3.97%
Wal-Mart Stores	COP	3.12%	4.19%
US Bancorp	USB	2.75%	3.37%
Moody's	MCO	1.47%	2.09%
Top 10 as % Total Portfolio		92.81%	94.56%
Top 5 as % Total Portfolio		74.36%	75.78%
Total Portfolio $ Billion		$59.05	$52.22

In order to estimate the discount rate for the company, let's look again at the yields on the long-term bonds. It so happens that, in November 2011, IBM issued a 10-year bond (cusip: 459200HA2) with a fixed coupon of 2.90 percent. Assuming that there was no significant speculation going on with these bonds, let's take the discount rate for the company as about three times this yield, or 9 percent.

Given the above information, we can compute the growth rate implied in the purchase price of $170 per share. For EY1, the annualized long-term implied growth ($g1$) is 1.78 percent and for EY3, the implied growth rate ($g3$) turned out to be 2.76 percent.

Historically, IBM had grown diluted earnings at the annualized rate of 11.43 percent since 2001 and at the annualized rate of 17.18 percent since 2006. As such, the implied growth was considerably below the earnings growth that the company had delivered in recent years.

Yet, the numbers suggest that at the purchase price of $170 per share, IBM was being priced with the expectation of future growth much lower than what the company had delivered during the past decade. This means that the market was being pessimistic about the future prospects for a company that had delivered strong growth in the recent past.

A closer look shows that even though the company grew earnings per share at a good clip, its revenue growth had been quite anemic. The company's top line grew from under $89 billion in 2001 to just under $100 billion as of the end of fiscal 2010, making for a compounded annual growth of 1.69 percent. During the same period, the company's total net income grew at the rate of annualized 7.5 percent and its book value remained essentially flat. The slow top-line growth during the preceding ten years occurred in spite of the fact that the company had been on an acquisitions spree, having spent more than $26 billion purchasing property and assets all around the world.

Further analysis shows that the company had been undergoing massive transformation since 1993, when Louis Gerstner was brought in to reinvigorate the then faltering company. He made massive changes and initiated a significant shift in the mix of businesses.[96] So, for the past several years, even as it grew the top line rather slowly, the company was expanding its margins by changing the company profile away from low-margin hardware to much higher-margin software and services. The difference in the top-line and bottom-line growth rates was, therefore, driven by such structural changes.

IBM showed high growth on a per share basis also because it bought back over $66 billion worth of its own common stock during the period, thus reducing its share count by almost 29 percent. In addition, the company gave just under $18 billion in cash dividends during those years. The company made these shareholder-friendly actions likely because they were highly profitable (strong profit margins) and generated significant amounts of free cash flows.

Additional tests showed that the company's three-year earnings yield at about 6.07 percent was comfortably higher than the yields then prevailing on the 10-year treasury or corporate bonds. The operating earnings yields and free cash flow yields were also respectable. In the same vein, the company had a long history of paying cash dividends on the common and the dividend yield then prevailing was just about 1.45 percent, and at the time growing at a 10-year average annual rate of more than 18 percent. As such, we could not refute IBM on the implied growth rate and yield tests.

The stability tests showed that IBM had delivered stable performance over the preceding decade. Margins were strong and growing, and inventory turns were stable with a slight uptick over the last several years. Furthermore, although the total debt-to-equity ratio at the end of fiscal 2010 was high at 1.24, it was so because of high leverage (about seven-to-one) the company maintained in its financing business. About two-thirds of the total debt was attributable to the financing business. The financial leverage on non-finance businesses appeared to be quite reasonable, and the interest coverage ratio was about forty-five.

In addition, the balance sheet showed almost $30 billion in cash and short/long investments. As such, the analysis indicated that the company could not be refuted on the basis of stability and strength tests.

The slow growth in the top line was still a concern, however, that required digging into the company literature to evaluate competitive positioning and future prospects. A quick qualitative analysis revealed that IBM was a strong company with a good recent history, a marquee brand, and a competent yet shareholder-friendly leadership team. The company appeared to be well positioned as a premium, high-margin player in a robust and growing global market for enterprise software and business process consulting.

The compensation policies of the company seemed appropriate as well. The compensation of the top executives was driven largely by results through the annual incentive plan, and performance equity awards. Salary accounted for 9 percent for the CEO and 14 percent for the senior vice presidents. The funding of the Annual Incentive Program, which affected about 4,800 executives in 2009 and 2010, was based on performance as measured by Net Income (60 percent), Revenue Growth (20 percent), and Cash Flow (20 percent). Equity grants to executives were based on rolling three-year earnings per share (80 percent) and cash flow (20 percent).

Further evaluation of the compensation structure revealed that the Chairman and CEO, Sam Palmisano, was by far the highest paid executive and he was rewarded largely with variable pay. All in all, the compensation structure for the top executives seemed appropriate and did not provide grounds for disconfirming the investment thesis.

A review of the pension plans revealed that they were underfunded, but within reason in relation to the company's annual free cash flows. The annual operating lease commitments were significant in relation to annual interest expense, but the adjusted fixed expenses were still comfortably much lower than the operating income and cash flows.

While it is not clear what Buffett may have seen when evaluating the company, it appears that IBM had good business fundamentals and was a strong company in growing businesses. It is also likely that Buffett and others who paid $170 per share were not able to disconfirm the positive narrative about the company: IBM was well-aligned with and appeared to be leading the charge into the secular trends of globalization and technological innovation.

Careful investors would have also made sure that there were no significant liabilities hidden from view in the thicket of their filings, and that their assets were of high quality.

Both quantitative and qualitative analyses were, in short, unable to cast doubt on the thesis that IBM was an attractive investment at the purchase price of $170 per share. Such would have been the thinking to enable large commitment of capital that Buffett made.

In sum, then, the historical record and current composition of Buffett's stock portfolio illustrates quite well the idea of core portfolios and the importance of business valuation.

Conclusion

Noise Control

In the world of investment research, there is so much information to process and interpret that anybody can easily drown in it. The numerous mandatory filings, marketing materials, third-party reports and commentaries, and an unending stream of opinions that public companies invite, all have the capacity to overwhelm the senses. The challenge for investors, therefore, is that a great deal of noise obfuscates the nuggets of data that may be critical to a keen understanding of an investment thesis. Sometimes, there are no nuggets of data at all but only a vast jumble of plausible but confusing claims and counter-claims, or no claims at all, just a noisy din.

Investors can easily dilute their efforts by chasing any number of seemingly plausible ideas or by becoming mired in meaningless detail. In spite of the best efforts, they can also misinterpret the signals and stray deeper into the information jungle with no way out. It is frighteningly easy, in short, for even experienced investors to get lost in the noise and make any number of unforced errors.

Overabundance of information is not the only problem, however; acute problems arise from our emotional and psychological vulnerabilities. Part of our biological heritage, emotions intervene in all choices we make and they predispose us to distort even the simplest and seemingly straightforward information.

So, what can we do to sort through and make meaning from the vast troves of information, when emotional and psychological factors so impede true understanding? How do we get to the nub of the problem in a world full of sights and sounds that confuse and distract, and persistent sales pitches that fuel hopes and fears and more? How, in short, do we invest sanely in the insane world of investing, and do so with such a defective computing apparatus as eons of biological evolution has delivered in us?

Impossible though investing seems, there are things that we as investors can do to improve our odds of success. Paramount for investing successfully, I have argued in this book, is a cautious temperament and a well-grounded approach that helps stabilize emotions and facilitates careful analysis. Central to our approach is posing the investor as a sense-maker in an immensely complex world of information and emotion. Let's review below the keys to our approach for investing wisely.

The first step in becoming a wise investor is to define investing as a *problem of choice* as opposed to defining it as a *problem of chance*. Putting choice at the center of investing tempers the propensity to gamble and to take unnecessary chances in the hope that luck might shine our way. We have argued that even though the markets are unpredictable and prices move randomly in the short run, gambling when investing is a fool's errand, as it invites reckless behavior that dissipates energy and capital. Instead, we have cast investing as deliberately deploying capital in sound businesses and doing so on economically favorable terms such that preservation of capital remains paramount as an objective.

The second step in learning to invest wisely is to understand that good choices do not always connect with good results in the chaotic world of investing. Because the strongest emotions of the moment drive prices in the short run, good analysis does not guarantee success and poor analysis (or no analysis at all) does not guarantee failure in the near term. That is, the chaos of the markets obfuscates the connections as may exist between thoughtful analysis and investment performance—and makes some mistakenly conclude that analysis is pointless.

What thoughtful analysis does is improve the odds of good performance over time. It anchors the thinking and helps make selections that are sound on economic fundamentals; it enables investors to put events and news in perspective and not overreact to every bit of new information that comes along. Not having good analysis to anchor the investment decisions is, in fact, the undoing of most who dabble in the markets. They become highly vulnerable to being whiplashed by the unpredictable price swings, entering the markets with optimism and hope, but then quickly abandoning their positions when the mood darkens and the prices suddenly plummet. Absence of analysis almost inevitably leads to wrong choices. Hence, thoughtful and thorough analysis is important for investing wisely.

The third step in becoming a wise investor is to understand that, in many ways, investing is a "head game" in the sense that it requires considerable judgments about when to invest and when to stay put, and to be able to see deceptions and self-deceptions that could trap the invested capital. Of course, analytical skills are critical; but success in investing comes from stabilizing the mind so that we may be able to grasp the essence of things and differentiate true opportunity from the many illusions of it. Doing so requires that investors invest first in self-reflection or in gaining knowledge about how our own minds work, how we think, how we process information, and how our moods and emotions influence the choices we make.

That is, success in investing requires that we cultivate a capacity for self-reflection, for metacognition—thinking about thinking—and for understanding how we know what we know so that we may be able to regulate our own learning process and manage information as appropriate.

The importance of this kind of self-awareness cannot be overstated. We are usually under the sway of a great many influences of which we are only dimly aware. The larger environment of hope and fear powerfully affects how we evaluate opportunities and, absent self-awareness, can easily lead us into stunningly poor choices. Rising markets create optimism, for instance, and encourage hopeful valuations; falling markets create pessimism, which usually results in fearful valuations. For most of us, this dynamic induces just the wrong kinds of reactive behaviors, where we buy high on hope and sell low on fear. As self-aware investors, on the other hand, we are likely to integrate analytical skill with mindfulness and be better prepared to play the head games of investing.

The fourth step for investing wisely is to develop an analytical strategy for controlling our emotions and biases. In particular, we have discussed at length the potentially destructive role of *confirmation bias*, or our deep-seated inclination to seek data that agree with our priors and to interpret the data such that they support our thesis. As an antidote to the confirmation bias, we have formalized the *principle of negation* and turned investing into a negative art. That is, we have sought to improve the quality of our choices by being skeptical about our investment thesis and cautious about our own perceptions.

Instead of trying to *prove* why our investment thesis has merit and potentially succumbing to confirmation bias, our approach is to doubt the validity of the thesis and to develop a formal method with which to try to *disconfirm* or *refute* it. This analytical strategy has the dual advantage of controlling our biases and helping us manage the overabundance of information that invades our senses. In actively seeking information that may refute our thesis, we at once control our urge to confirm and limit the range of information we need in order to do good investment analysis.

The principle of negation and the derivative framework for refutation provide investors the conceptual apparatus with which to sort through the noise and hone in on signals that are directly relevant for developing and testing our investment thesis. Together, they help us cut our way through the noise so that we may be able to make good investment choices.

Using the principle of negation, moreover, we have framed the specific analytical techniques with which to assess the safety and attractiveness of investments under consideration. Recognizing the hazards that lurk in the markets, our attitude has been one of caution and defense. Playing intelligent defense has been our *modus operandi*, even though it is clear that such an approach to investing does sometimes lead to loss of opportunity. Such lost opportunities, or Type II errors, we have taken as the acceptable and necessary costs of investing wisely.

The cautious approach to investment analysis is particularly important because of our view that measures of objective risk are misleading, and investors should rely instead on subjectively evaluating the many uncertainties that surround an investment thesis. Such subjective evaluations can easily succumb to confirmation bias, however, so investors need to be especially cautious when doing so. Sequential and gradual updating of the thesis in light of new information is also an important part of good analysis. Investors should retain a skeptical orientation that seeks to refute and disconfirm.

Finally, integral to our approach of investing wisely is to construct robust portfolios. No matter how thorough the analysis of companies and stocks, we understand that every investment thesis suffers from unknowns and unknow-ables, and factors that can neither be controlled nor anticipated by the investor. That is, even the best analysis can accomplish only so much, and irreducible uncertainties remain at the end of even the most thorough due diligence.

Investors can mitigate the adverse effects of such irreducible uncertainties by constructing diversified portfolios. Grouping carefully selected stocks in a well-conceived portfolio is, therefore, the final step in investing wisely. Port-folio-level thinking remains important, in other words, for investing wisely. As Markowitz had noted back in the 1950s, investors should think of their stock investment program not in terms of individual stocks but in terms of all the stocks they own. That is, investors should think of the stock portfolio as a unit and evaluate individual selections in the context of the other stocks they may already own. Grouping companies that are uncorrelated or partially correlated on economic fundamentals can markedly reduce the adverse effects of the irreducible uncertainties and unknown risks.

Yet, too many companies in the portfolio can once again make noise and information overload a problem for investors. Avoiding this problem of noise is paramount, as it detracts from deeply understanding each individual company in the portfolio and makes the investor vulnerable to grave errors. The final key to investing wisely is, therefore, to form portfolios with only a handful of core holdings, each carefully selected using the techniques of refu-tation and disconfirmation as discussed in this book.

Analysis and Intuition

Note that while diligence and analysis are both important, wise investors also allow their sixth sense, or intuition, to play an important role in stock selection and portfolio formation.

Overemphasizing hard analysis creates the hazard that we get lost in the data and lose the forest for the trees. Data and analysis, when taken to the extreme, can be such that a larger sense of things can go missing.

The process of making good investment decisions requires more than simply the analysis; it also requires discernment, or a keen sense of the larger and deeper meanings that the data are capable of creating. It requires silence of the mind, quiet listening, and taking your time, allowing the various aspects of the understanding to settle in so that you can think holistically about the situation at hand.

For investors contemplating committing significant capital to a particular investment, perhaps the greatest enemy is the sense of urgency, and the best friend is the lack of pressure to make decisions quickly. Time allows us to calm the internal urges so that critical information can come into focus, so that we can see the interconnections and get true insights into a situation. Time allows for intuition to work, for the subconscious to grasp the meaning of it all and give its verdict. This acting slowly, with intuition given the space to assimilate the key notes lost in the jumble of information, is crucial for investing wisely.

Slowing down the decision-making process also allows you to ask such meta-analytic questions as: What is truly happening with this company? What are they really trying to accomplish? What larger trends appear to be emerging and how might they affect the operating performance of the company? How are they leveraging, or suffering from, the evolving technologies and consumption patterns?

Answers to such questions, even when incomplete as they are likely to be, encourage you to look around outside the data and outside your own analysis to get a sense of the bigger picture, and perhaps better understand the consequences of your decisions. Incorporating the larger context into your thinking and weaving a careful narrative is critically important to making good investment choices.

Another important component of making good choices is for investors to be aware of and to resist the rigidity that can sometimes set in when using decision frameworks. The refutation framework we have developed in this book is just that. It is a means for thoroughly evaluating an investment thesis; it not an end unto itself. It is not a panacea.

In fact, rigidity can easily set in our ways of thinking, as the need to confirm what we already believe is deeply ingrained in our human psyche. As such, we should be aware that even our well thought-out frameworks can get us in trouble because their fundamental logic can be corrupted in order to justify preconceived notions.

Sure, the refutation framework is grounded in more than two thousand years of progressively insightful Western thought about how we humans reason. Yet, as investors, we are still left to sort out the much harder part of maintaining mental flexibility without becoming unhinged from the facts at hand. We still need to ask the right questions and properly set up the investment thesis that needs to be refuted and disconfirmed.

Investors should strive, therefore, to consider the refutation/disconfirmation framework as resilient but malleable, and subject to modification in light of experiences. Not only should we see the data in terms of the framework, in other words, but we should also put the framework itself to test with the data. This dialectic between the frame and the data, the back and forth between the two, is the essential way in which we can make sense of the world with a truly open mind. Over time, this symbiotic relationship between the frame and the facts, of one informing the other in an endless cycle, strengthens intuition and helps truly grasp the essence of the matter at hand.

Investor Temperament

We should note that refutation and disconfirmation, although encouraging analysis and emphasizing caution, are really about reinforcing or acquiring and cultivating the correct temperament for investing cautiously and wisely, with a medium-to-long-term investment horizon.

Diligence, stability of emotions, independence of thought, caution, and patience are the hallmarks of such a temperament as is necessary for investing wisely. Absent these traits, it is difficult to apply the approach to investing that we have discussed in this book. Without these, any manner of mishaps or perturbations in the larger environment can throw the investor off his game, inducing blind imitation or reckless gambling—and quickly undo years of painstaking work that may have gone into building one or more core portfolios. Hence, cultivating the correct temperament is essential for learning to be a wise investor.

Certainly, the traits mentioned above are a tall order for us mortals. Given our many emotional and psychological vulnerabilities, we all fall short on one or the other most of the time, and especially when engaged in as complex an endeavor as investing. For most of us, the ideal temperament and the supporting traits are something to strive for, not only so that we may become better investors but so that we become better people who make good choices, including investment choices.

Acknowledgements

———

A long time in the making, this book could not have been written without the help of my students, colleagues, friends, and family.

Foremost, I thank the many students whom I have had the privilege to teach during the past dozen or so years. Their excellent questions helped refine and strengthen the reasons that we need to recast investing as a problem of choice, and especially as an issue that requires business judgment; their enthusiasm for the subject matter propelled my own desire to gather these thoughts systematically and in writing.

I have been fortunate to be part of a rich scholarly environment that my department colleagues have built and sustained over the years. The intellectual diversity and openness of those around me at the Isenberg School were the key ingredients that enabled me to pursue ideas wherever they led me—including the wide range of disciplines outside the area of scholarship that I call my intellectual home.

Larry Zacharias and Bob Nakosteen, in particular, have deeply influenced my thinking through the endless and enjoyable conversations over many years. Larry was instrumental in my shifting the emphasis from falsification to disconfirmation; Bob was especially helpful in turning me to the role that subjective probability plays in investing choices. I thank Ben Branch for his comments on my approach to diversification; Pam Trafford for reading the sections on off-balance-sheet liabilities; and Tom O'Brien for being a wonderful and supportive colleague that he is.

I would like to thank Ali de Groot for her guidance and excellent professional support in my journey to build this book. Without her sharp eye and frequent words of encouragement, this book would have stayed in a draft form. I am grateful to Dana Johnson for her expertise on the Serbian conflict and for one last look at this manuscript before I shipped it to the printers. I thank Brian Charette for catching another set of errors after the first print. I thank my friend Surojeet Ghatak for the photo on the back cover.

Content issues aside, this project has benefitted immensely from the love and support of my family, far and near. I could not have pulled it off without the good-natured prodding of those dearest to me. Mary, Helen, and Monika have been part of this process every step of the way; they are, without doubt, the co-producers of this book. The moral support of my mother (Savita), brother (Alok), and sister (Anshu) were crucial for me to continue working on this project and seeing it to completion. [97]

Notes

1. See Buffett (1984), a now-famous speech at the Columbia University School of Business in honor of the 50th anniversary of the publication of Security Analysis by Benjamin Graham and David Dodd.

2. See, for instance, Price & Kelly (2004).

3. My friend Larry Zacharias tells me that Adolf Berle, one of Berle-and-Means duo who wrote the 1932 classic on corporate governance, argued as far back as in 1952 that shareholders were little more than gamblers and, therefore, their interests ought to be subordinated to those of employees and customers.

4. See Markowitz (1952) and Markowitz (1999). The second paper is a retrospective on the modern portfolio theory.

5. See Smith (1924).

6. In his dissertation, Markowitz specifically notes chapter IX (on mathematical expectations) of a popular text. See Uspensky (1937).

7. See Bayes & Price (1763). The essay was read to the Royal Society of London by Richard Price but only after he updated the raw manuscript he had found among Bayes' papers. Bayes had died in 1761.

8. See Savage (1954).

9. Interestingly, Markowitz wrote the Foreword to a recent book by Jimmy Savage's son, Sam Savage. See Savage (2009).

10. A few years later, Friedman was to write an immensely popular book,

Capitalism and Freedom (See Friedman, 1962). The book encapsulated his belief that political freedom was inseparable from economic freedom. Free markets play an important role in this ideology and market efficiency is an important part of that argument. Perhaps, Markowitz had Friedman's blessings to make the fundamental assumption of market efficiency when building the modern portfolio theory. Efficiency was an important piece of the puzzle.

11 Uspensky did cover subjective probability in Chapter IV on Bayes' Theorem. Yet, consistent with the low esteem in which statisticians of the period held Bayes, he devoted only that one chapter to it in the book and ended it with "criticism of underlying assumptions."

12 Bob Nakosteen reminds me that, although subjective judgments are all too common in real life, the math required for applying the Bayes' rule on subjective probability and updating is incredibly cumbersome and complex—especially when compared with the relatively much easier math that Markowitz ended up using. As a graduate student who had found and defined a topic for his thesis and obtained the blessing of his advisors, therefore, Markowitz had strong incentives to pursue the path of least resistance. He could have come back to subjectivity later on, but he never did. Rest is history.

13 The math becomes more complex when the returns are correlated.

14 Capital Asset Pricing Model (CAPM).

15 Recognizing the limitations of normal distribution in defining risk, researchers have considered other tools such as the fat tails, skewed distributions, power law and, lately, jump models where stock prices are expected to jump as they quite frequently do. Yet, the focus remains on mathematical risk.

16 Perhaps influenced by Savage, Markowitz had in fact counseled that risk be assessed using statistical analysis as well as judgments based on security analysis. But he focused on the former and never showed how to incorporate subjective assessments of risk into his model; those who followed him essentially ignored the importance of carefully making judgments about business risks.

17 Ben Branch reminds me that objections to the idea of fully rational economic agent have been longstanding. Already by the late 1890s,

economists such as Thorsten Veblen and those aligned with the Austrian school were questioning the assumption that the historical, social, and institutional contexts did not figure prominently in economic choices. See Branch (2008).

18 See Mandelbrot (2004).

19 See Taleb (2007).

20 A series of papers by professors Brad Barber and Terrence Odean lead to this conclusion. See, for instance, Barber & Odean (2000).

21 Just before sending this book to the press, I came upon an article on this point. In that *New York Times Magazine* article, Nate Silver argued that defense does indeed win championships. He showed that, in forty of the ninety-two Super Bowls in which best ranked defensive and offensive teams played, the defensive teams won the Super Bowl nearly 80 percent of the time—including three games in which both competitors were strong defensive teams. See Silver (2013). Interestingly though, even the offense in football relies a great deal on the ability of the offensive line to protect (defend) the quarterback or open channels for the running back. And, of course, good defense in football is always very aggressive as it tries to prevent completion of plays. In this sense, defense always wins!

22 See Lefèvre (1923).

23 See Graham & Dodd (1934). See also Graham (1959).

24 See Fisher (1959).

25 See Soros (1987).

26 See Buffett & Cunningham (2008).

27 See Malkiel (2012).

28 The correct term for this is mathematical expectations, which require estimating weighted probabilities of gains and losses. Both gamblers and investors desire positive mathematical expectations, but they differ greatly in what they consider are good odds and how they structure their expectations.

29 Important to note that venture capitalists fall somewhere between gamblers and investors. Like gamblers, they seek very high payoff opportunities and

know that the odds of success of any one of their well-selected invest-ments are rather low. Yet, like investors, they are obsessed with trying to understand the factors shaping the underlying odds. The difference is that, unlike investors in the stock market, venture capitalists try to shape the odds by their own due diligence and involvement in decision making in the companies in which they invest. Moreover, they manage the odds by taking a disciplined approach to portfolio logic and the mathematical expectations inherent in that logic. In this sense, venture capitalists are both gamblers *and* investors.

30 For a very good review article on this topic, see Nickerson (1998). I have learned a great deal, and borrowed liberally, from this article.

31 See, for example, Meijers (2001).

32 I have drawn these and several other examples in this chapter from Nickerson, an excellent article that very competently reviews the extant thinking on confirmation bias.

33 See Ferrell (2005). Again, see also Nickerson (1998).

34 See, for example, Croskerry (2003).

35 See, for example, Hastie (1994).

36 See Coval, Hirshleifer, & Teoh (2005). Professor Hirshleifer has built an extensive body of work on herding and other imperfections in the finan-cial markets. Several of his papers are very good reads.

37 See Park, Konana, Gu, Kumar, & Raghunathan (2010).

38 See Mackay (1841). The quote is from the Preface of Mackay's book.

39 For an entertaining and highly instructive but very short book on finan-cial manias, see Galbraith (1994). In a similar vein, see also Chancellor (1999).

40 VIX, or Chicago Board Options Exchange Market Volatility Index, is a measure of the expected volatility over the next thirty day period. As such, it measures how much the market expects the stocks to fluctuate, or the uncertainty that the traders face.

41 See Norris (2008).

42 Serbians consider the original Battle of Kosovo a highly significant event in their history. Many good writings are available on this subject; for our purposes here, a very good read is Zirojevic (2000). The author contends that facts about the battle remain elusive but the legend of Kosovo was established at a very early date, with religion at its center and Prince Lazar as its main character. The author also reports of an early eighteenth century annihilation of converts to Islam as a direct consequence of the legend and its implication that divisions among the peoples, and fears of traitors amongst their midst, were the main reasons for the defeat at the Battle of Kosovo. Ironically, such fears can become self-fulfilling prophesies.

43 I thank Dana Johnson for her many insightful comments, based on first-hand experience as a peace activist in Serbia, on Serb nationalism and the ethnic conflict in the former Yugoslavia.

44 See page 18 and page 98 in Verdery (1999).

45 See Bokanowski, T., Fiorini, L. G., & Lewkowicz, S. (2009).

46 These ideas were later captured by Sigmund Freud in his book, *Civilization and Its Discontents* (1930).

47 See Le Bon (1897). All quotes are from the digital copy obtained from the Electronic Text Center at the University of Virginia. The publisher of the digital book is The Macmillan Company, New York.

48 See Bendersky (2007).

49 See Bernays (1928). All quotes from the third printing (1930).

50 A full complement of Rushkoff's very interesting work is available on his website rushkoff.com.

51 See Lowenstein (1996). The author has built an impressive body of work on the role of emotion and psychology in economic decisions.

52 See Anderson (2007), Consumer Fraud in the United States.

53 See Federal Trade Commission (2009). See also Consumer Fraud Research Group (2006).

54 Again, see Loewenstein (1996).

55 See Browning & Dugan (2002).

56 For a historical treatise on doubt, see Hecht (2004). According to her, all great thinkers have been doubters.

57 See Aristotle (2012).

58 From Book 1, On Sophistical Refutations.

59 See Bacon's *New Organon*. All quotes from 1963 English translation by Spedding, Ellis, and Heath.

60 Section L in *New Organon*.

61 See Popper (1953). "Conjectures and Refutations" was first given as a lecture in 1953 in Cambridge, England and then published as "Philosophy of Science: a Personal Report" in *British Philosophy in Mid-Century*, ed. C. A. Mace, 1957. Source obtained from Wikipedia.

62 Émile Durkheim, the French sociologist, once wrote that social phenomenon such as values and norms arise from interactions between individuals—but then also act as social constrains. As such, he argued, they were social facts and could be studied as such.

63 See Hershliefer & Teoh (2003). The two seminal papers on herd behavior among investors are Banerjee (1992) and Bikhchandani, Hirshliefer & Welch (1992). This literature suggests that herding is "rational" because it often makes sense for people to follow others or, technically, to value their own private information about a stock less than the information available elsewhere.

64 Again, see Malkiel (2012).

65 Again, see Park, Konana, Gu, Kumar, & Raghunathan (2012).

66 In certain cases, estimates of worth may also be made using alternate methodologies such as liquidation or break-up value or valuation when controlling interest is at stake.

67 All financial information in this book is obtained from or derived from public sources such as the 10-K filings and proxy statements, as well as public websites. The author cannot guarantee the accuracy of the source data.

68 Free Cash Flow (FCF) = Operating Cash Flow (OCF) – Capital Expenditures (CapEx). So, FCF increases if CapEx is reduced. This reduction in CapEx may be legitimate but it can also be a way to miscast FCF.

69 See Knight (1921).

70 Another important concept is that of ambiguity, where the same facts inspire many different, sometimes conflicting interpretations or no clear interpretations at all. In ambiguous situations, investors would not even know what to make of a particular event or piece of information. Such ambiguity is very common in investing but I will not elaborate on it in these pages and fold it, instead, in the broader concept of uncertainty. Suffice it to say that investors need to work through ambiguous situations until their mind slowly settles on a plausible interpretation that is supported by logic, data, and doubt.

71 See Mandelbrot & Hudson (2004).

72 There appears to be no credible theory that guides empirical choices regarding the time window to be used for computing β or the index against which to measure it. Researchers also know that β itself is unstable, as it has been shown to change over time.

73 For an early synthesis of technical ideas related to subjective risk, see Savage (1954). Also, see Jeffrey (2004).

74 Here I refer to Bayes' rule, of course, about systematically updating beliefs, a logic for reasoning in a world where objectivity and precision are unattainable. For a history of the Bayes' rule, see McGrayne (2011).

75 Downgrade is only a problem if the bondholder sells prior to maturity. So long as the company does not default, holding on to maturity preserves the coupons as they remain unchanged. A downgrade may increase the chances that the future coupons might not be paid. There may be other unknowns, such as bond recall, but they are not of concern here. I thank Ben Branch for this point.

76 The discount model is discussed in the next chapter. Suffice it to know at this stage that it is the standard formulation for estimating intrinsic economic worth. The formulation is: Intrinsic Value = Expected Future Cash Flows / (Discount Rate − Expected Growth).

77 According to Graham's purported formula, Intrinsic Value 1 (V1) = Earnings Per Share (EPS) x (8.5 + 2 x expected EPS growth rate).

78 Intrinsic Value 2 (V2) = V1 x· (4.4/AAA) Corporate Bond Yield.

79 An alternate formulation for the implied growth rate can be derived using the price-to-book (PB) and return on equity (ROE): g = (PB · r −ROE)/ (PB + ROE). Once again, it is necessary to assume the discount rate for estimating the growth rate implied in prevailing prices.

80 This is captured by the well-known β, which captures the degree to which the returns to shareholders of a company vary with the returns from investing in an index such as the Standard & Poor's 500 Index.

81 The idea of using a multiple of the bond yield is owed in part to Williams (1938), especially his suggestion to estimate the discount rate by starting with the risk free rate and then adding on a risk or equity premium based on overall judgment about the company. High uncertainty about future prospects would call for high multiples.

82 The choice of these three factors is inspired by Benjamin Graham (1949: 103) when he notes that, "The investor should demand, in addition, a satisfactory ratio of earnings to price, a sufficiently strong financial position, and the prospect that its earnings will at least be maintained over the years."

83 The three largest and most well-known rating agencies in the United States are Moody's, Standard & Poor's, and Fitch.

84 For a full list of SEC Forms, see 1) http://www.sec.gov/info/edgar/forms/ edgform.pdf and 2) http://www.sec.gov/about/forms/secformsalpha.htm. (Both last checked February 22, 2013).

85 To put this in context, the number of people on Wal-Mart's payroll is larger than the number of state and local government workers in the state of California (1.85 million as last checked end of 2010).

86 The discussion below is based on the current accounting rules for reporting leases. New rules, likely to take effect in 2013, will require companies to report all their leases on the balance sheet. Meant to stop significant off-balance-sheet financing, these rules will put significant debt on the balance sheets of some companies. I thank Pam Trafford for pointing this out. For details about the expected changes, see http://www.fasb.org/jsp/FASB/ FASBContent_C/ProjectUpdatePage&cid=900000011123#objective. (Last checked February 22, 2013).

87 http://www.bloomberg.com/apps/news?pid=newsarchive&sid=aUrAVZt2gZZk. (Last checked February 22, 2013).

88 http://ftalphaville.ft.com/blog/2008/10/02/16576/sigma-collapse-marks-end-of-siv-era/. (Last checked February 22, 2013. Login required).

89 See Valukas (2010). Chapter 11 Case No. 08-13555 (JMP).

90 For a detailed discussion and empirical evidence supporting this statement, see Sharma, Branch, Chawla, and Qiu (2013).

91 As of the end of September 2012, the owner of South Bay, Douglas Dey, had pleaded guilty to the charge that he made the corrupt payments. Finazzo maintained his innocence but was found guilty n sixteen charges by a jury in a Brooklyn federal court. He faced up to 20 years in prison on each of the fourteen fraud counts. See http://www.bloomberg.com/news/2013-04-25/ex-aeropostale-executive-found-guilty-in-vendor-deal.html. (Last checked May 20, 2013).

92 As of this writing, repurchasing shares seems to be a tradition largely in American and some European companies. Chinese (e.g., SNP, PTR), Indian (e.g., INFY, TTM), and Brazilian companies (e.g., PBR) do not seem to have a tradition of buying back their own shares.

93 Technically, two events are independent when $p(B)=p(B|A)$ and $p(A)=p(A|B)$. That is, events A and B are independent when the conditional probability of one given the other is unchanged from the probability of it happening on its own.

94 Note that theoretically the covariance needs to be between the expected future returns of the two stocks. In practice, however, the data for future expected returns are rarely credible and, for the long future, not available at all. As such, the easily-available past returns are typically used to compute variances and co-variances.

95 Again, see Buffett & Cunningham (2008).

96 See Gerstner (2002).

97

Bibliography

Anderson, K. B. (2007). *Consumer fraud in the United States: The second FTC survey.* Staff Report of the Bureaus of Economics and Consumer Protection, Federal Trade Commission.

Aristotle. (2012). *On sophistical refutations.* Trans. W.A. Pickard [Web Edition eBook]. Adelaide, Australia: University of Adelaide.

Bacon, F. (1863). *The new organon or true directions concerning the interpretation of nature* [1620]. Trans.James Spedding, Robert Leslie Ellis and Douglas Denon Heath.

Banerjee, A. V. (1992). A simple model of herd behavior. *The Quarterly Journal of Economics, 107*(3), 797-817.

Barber, B. M., & Odean, T. (2000). Trading is hazardous to your wealth: The common stock investment performance of individual investors. *The Journal of Finance, 55*(2), 773-806.

Bayes, M., & Price, M. (1763). An essay towards solving a problem in the doctrine of chances. by the late Rev. Mr. Bayes, F. R. S. communicated by Mr. Price, in a letter to John Canton, A. M. F. R. S. *Philosophical Transactions (1683-1775), 53*, 370-418.

Bendersky, J. W. (2007). "Panic": The impact of Le Bon's crowd psychology on US military thought. *Journal of the History of the Behavioral Sciences, 43*(3), 257-283.

Berkery, D. (2008). *Raising venture capital for the serious entrepreneur.* New York: McGraw-Hill.

Bernays, E. L. (1928). *Propaganda*. New York: H. Liveright.

Bikhchandani, S., Hirshleifer, D., & Welch, I. (1992). A theory of fads, fashion, custom, and cultural change as informational cascades. *Journal of Political Economy*, 992-1026.

Bokanowski, T., Fiorini, L. G., & Lewkowicz, S. (2009). *On Freud's 'mourning and melancholia.'* London: Karnac Books.

Branch, B. 2008. Institutional Economics and Behavioral Finance. *Working Paper, Isenberg School of Management, University of Massachusetts at Amherst.*

Browning, E., & Dugan, I. (2002). Lying low: With main street on the sidelines, market rally stalls. *Wall Street Journal*, A1, A8.

Buffett, W. E. (1984). The superinvestors of Graham-and-Doddsville. *Hermes: The Columbia Business School Magazine*, May, 17: 4-15

Buffett, W. E., & Cunningham, L. A. (2008). *The essays of Warren Buffett: Lessons for Corporate America*. New York: L. Cunningham.

Chancellor, E. (1999). *Devil take the hindmost: A history of financial speculation*. New York: Farrar, Straus, Giroux.

Consumer Fraud Research Group. (2006). *Investor fraud study final report*. Washington, DC: NASD Investor Education Foundation.

Coval, J., Hirshleifer, D., & Teoh, S. H. (2005). Self-deception and deception in capital markets. *Deception in Markets: An Economic Analysis. Basingstoke: Palgrave Macmillan*, 113-130.

Croskerry, P. (2003). The importance of cognitive errors in diagnosis and strategies to minimize them. *Academic Medicine, 78*(8), 775.

Farrell, J. (2005). *The day without yesterday: Lemaître, Einstein, and the birth of modern cosmology*. New York: Thunder's Mouth Press.

Federal Trade Commission. 2009. A Staff Report on the Federal Trade Commission's Fraud Forum. Washington, DC: Federal trade Commission.

Fisher, P. A. (1958). *Common stocks and uncommon profits*. New York: Harper.

Freud, S. (1930). *Civilization and its discontents.* London: L. & Virginia Woolf at the Hogarth press [etc.].

Friedman, M. (1962). *Capitalism and freedom.* Chicago: University of Chicago Press.

Galbraith, J. K. (1993). *A short history of financial euphoria.* New York: Whittle Books in association with Viking.

Gerstner, L. V. (2002). *Who says elephants can't dance? Inside IBM's historic turnaround.* New York, NY: HarperBusiness.

Graham, B. (1949). *The intelligent investor: a book of practical counsel.* New York: Harper.

Graham, B., & Dodd, D. L. (1934). *Security analysis.* San Francisco: Whittlesey House, McGraw-Hill

Hastie, R. (1993). *Inside the juror: The psychology of juror decision making.* Cambridge, England; New York: Cambridge University Press.

Hecht, J. M., (2003). *Doubt: A history: The great doubters and their legacy of innovation, from Socrates and Jesus to Thomas Jefferson and Emily Dickinson.* San Francisco: HarperSanFrancisco.

Hirshleifer, D., & Hong Teoh, S. (2003). Herd behaviour and cascading in capital markets: A review and synthesis. *European Financial Management, 9*(1), 25-66.

Jeffrey, R. C. (2004). *Subjective probability: The real thing.* Cambridge: Cambridge University Press.

Knight, F. H. (1921). *Risk, uncertainty and profit.* Boston: Houghton Mifflin.

Le Bon, G. (1897). *The crowd, a study of the popular mind.* New York: Macmillan.

Lefevre, E. (1923). *Reminiscences of a stock operator.* New York: Doran.

Loewenstein, G. (1996). Out of control: Visceral influences on behavior. *Organizational Behavior and Human Decision Processes, 65*(3), 272-292.

Mackay, C. (1841). *Memoirs of extraordinary popular delusions and the madness of crowds*. New York: Harmony

Malkiel, B. G. (2012). *A random walk down Wall Street: The time-tested strategy for successful investing*. New York: W.W. Norton.

Mandelbrot, B. B., & Hudson, R. L. (2004). *The (mis)behavior of markets: A fractal view of risk, ruin, and reward*. New York: Basic Books.

Markowitz, H. (1952). Portfolio selection. *The Journal of Finance, 7*(1), 77-91.

Markowitz, H. M. (1999). The early history of portfolio theory: 1600-1960. *Financial Analysts Journal, 55*(4), 5-16.

McGrayne, S. B. (2011). *The theory that would not die: How Bayes' rule cracked the enigma code, hunted down Russian submarines, & emerged triumphant from two centuries of controversy*. New Haven, CT: Yale University Press.

Meijers, A. (2001). *Explaining beliefs: Lynne rudder baker and her critics*. Stanford, CA: CSLI Publications.

Nickerson, R. S. (1998). Confirmation bias: A ubiquitous phenomenon in many guises. *Review of General Psychology, 2*(2), 175-220.

Norris, F. (2008). United Panic. *The New York Times Online*, Economix Blog, October 24.

Park, J. H., Konana, P., Gu, B., Kumar, A., & Raghunathan, R. (2010). Confirmation bias, overconfidence, and investment performance: Evidence from stock message boards. *McCombs Research Paper Series* No. IROM-07-10.

Price, J., Kelly E. (2004). Warren Buffett: Investment Genius or Statistical Anomaly? In H. Pan, D. Sornette, and K. Kortanek (Eds.), *Intelligent Finance: A convergence of mathematical finance with technical and fundamental analysis*. Proceedings of the first international workshop on intelligent finance, University of Ballarat, Australia. url: http://svc160.wic022v.server-web.com/articles/news/conference/iwif.pdf (Last checked, February 22, 2013)

Popper, K. R. (1963). *Conjectures and refutations: The growth of scientific knowledge*. Routledge & K. Paul.

Savage, L. J. (1954). *The foundations of statistics*. New York: Wiley.

Savage, S. L. (2009). *The flaw of averages: Why we underestimate risk in the face of uncertainty.* New York: Wiley.

Sharma, A., Branch, B., Chawla, C., Qiu, L. (2013). Explaining Market-to-Book: The relative impact of firm performance, growth, and risk. *Business Quest.*

Silver, N. (2013). Nate Silver Picks the Super Bowl! *The New York Times Magazine*, January 30.

Smith, E. L. (1924). *Common stocks as long term investments.* New York: Macmillan.

Soros, G. (1987). *The alchemy of finance: Reading the mind of the market.* New York: Simon and Schuster.

Taleb, N. (2007). *The Black Swan: The impact of the highly improbable.* New York: Random House.

Thaler, R. H., & Shefrin, H. M. (1981). An economic theory of self-control. *The Journal of Political Economy*, 392-406.

Uspensky, J. V. (1937). *Introduction to mathematical probability.* New York; London: McGraw-Hill.

Valukas, A. R. (2010). Lehman Brothers Holdings Inc. Chapter 11 proceedings Examiner's report. *US Bankruptcy Court Southern District of New York, Jenner and Block LLP.*

Verdery, K. (1999). *The political lives of dead bodies: Reburial and postsocialist change.* New York: Columbia University Press.

Williams, J. B. (1938). *The theory of investment value.* Cambridge, Mass.: Harvard University Press.

Zirojevic, O. (2000). Kosovo in the collective memory. In N. Popov (Ed.), *The Road to War in Serbia: Trauma and Catharsis* (pp. 189-211). Budapest, Hungary: Central European University Press.

Index

Aristotle 27, 28, 30, 74, 75, 77, 79, 83, 85

Bacon, Francis, 3, 15, 77–82, 84, 85, 90

Barber, Brad M., 59, 60

Bayes, Thomas, xix

Bernays, Edward L., 39–42, 46

Buffett, Warren E., ix, xxxi, 297, 298, 301, 305

Descartes 70, 71, 75, 76, 77, 79, 84, 93

Fisher, Philip A., ix, xxxi

Freud, Sigmund, 39, 41, 46, 83

Graham, Benjamin, ix, xviii, xx, xxiv, xxv, xxvii, xxxi, 89–91, 112, 113, 143, 144, 266

Gorgias 26, 27, 42, 71, 78

Lakoff, George, P., 50

Le Bon, Gustave 35–41, 46, 51, 57

Lintner, John V., xxi

Livermore, Jesse L., xxxi

Loewenstein, George F., 52, 59

Luntz, Frank I., 50

Mackay, Charles, 7, 13

Markowitz, Harry M., x, xviii–xxiii, xxv, 262—267, 270, 272, 283, 311

Odean, Terrance, 59, 60

Packard, Vance, 43–47, 49, 50

Plato 26–30, 42, 71, 73, 74, 79, 85

Popper, Karl R., 82–86, 91, 165

Rushkoff, Douglas, 49

Savage, Leonard J., xix–xx, xxvii

Sharpe, William, F., xxi

Soros, George, xxxi

Williams, John B., xviii–xx, xxvii, 111